CLINICIAN'S TOOLKIT FOR CHILDREN'S BEHAVIORAL HEALTH

CLINICIAN'S TOOLKIT FOR CHILDREN'S BEHAVIORAL HEALTH

Edited by

MICHELE KNOX

Department of Psychiatry,
University of Toledo College of Medicine and Life Sciences,
Toledo, OH, United States

ELSEVIER

ACADEMIC PRESS

An imprint of Elsevier

Academic Press is an imprint of Elsevier
125 London Wall, London EC2Y 5AS, United Kingdom
525 B Street, Suite 1650, San Diego, CA 92101, United States
50 Hampshire Street, 5th Floor, Cambridge, MA 02139, United States
The Boulevard, Langford Lane, Kidlington, Oxford OX5 1GB, United Kingdom

Notices

Knowledge and best practice in this field are constantly changing. As new research and experience broaden our understanding, changes in research methods, professional practices, or medical treatment may become necessary.

Practitioners and researchers must always rely on their own experience and knowledge in evaluating and using any information, methods, compounds, or experiments described herein. In using such information or methods they should be mindful of their own safety and the safety of others, including parties for whom they have a professional responsibility.

To the fullest extent of the law, neither the Publisher nor the authors, contributors, or editors, assume any liability for any injury and/or damage to persons or property as a matter of products liability, negligence or otherwise, or from any use or operation of any methods, products, instructions, or ideas contained in the material herein.

British Library Cataloguing-in-Publication Data
A catalogue record for this book is available from the British Library

Library of Congress Cataloging-in-Publication Data
A catalog record for this book is available from the Library of Congress

ISBN: 978-0-12-816024-4

For Information on all Academic Press publications
visit our website at https://www.elsevier.com/books-and-journals

Publisher: Nikki Levy
Acquisition Editor: Nikki Levy
Editorial Project Manager: Barbara Makinster
Production Project Manager: Bharatwaj Varatharajan
Cover Designer: Matthew Limbert

Typeset by MPS Limited, Chennai, India

Contents

List of contributors

Aubrey L. Borgen Department of Psychology, Central Michigan University, Mount Pleasant, MI, United States

Kimberly Burkhart Pediatrics & Psychiatry, Rainbow Babies and Children's Hospital, Case Western Reserve University, Cleveland, OH, United States

Carrie Cuffman Department of Pediatrics, Division of Developmental-Behavioral Pediatrics & Psychology, Rainbow Babies and Children's Hospital, Cleveland, OH, United States

Sarah E. Domoff Department of Psychology, Central Michigan University, Mount Pleasant, MI, United States

Morgan Dynes Departments of Psychiatry and Pediatrics, The University of Toledo College of Medicine and Life Sciences, Toledo, OH, United States

Elizabeth C. Halloran Lucas County Juvenile Court, Toledo, OH, United States

Kimberly Hunter Department of Psychiatry, University of Toledo College of Medicine and Life Sciences, Toledo, OH, United States

Luke Johnson Clinical Therapist, Mercy Health Toledo Trauma Recovery Center, Toledo, OH, United States

Robert D. Keder Developmental & Behavioral Pediatrics, Connecticut Children's Medical Center, University of Connecticut School of Medicine, Farmington, CT, United States

Michele Knox Department of Psychiatry, University of Toledo College of Medicine and Life Sciences, Toledo, OH, United States

J. Ann Lentini Doc Ann Counseling, Hendersonville, NC, United States

Chelsea Robinson Department of Health Sciences, Central Michigan University, Mount Pleasant, MI, United States

Amy Russell Russell Consulting Specialists, LLC, Vancouver, WA, United States

Catherine Scherer Department of Pediatrics, Division of Developmental-Behavioral Pediatrics & Psychology, Rainbow Babies and Children's Hospital, Cleveland, OH, United States

Yazhini Srivathsal Banner Medical Group/University of Arizona College Of Medicine Phoenix, Phoenix, AZ, United States

Preface

Research suggests that just over 20% of youth experience a serious mental health problem at some point in their lives (National Alliance on Mental Illness, 2019). In fact, roughly half of all mental disorders begin early, by the age of 14 years (Kessler et al., 2007). Such mental health problems may be preventable or minimized with early intervention efforts. The evidence clearly has demonstrated that parents and caregivers are key players in much of the groundwork in the prevention and early intervention. When parents and caregivers are provided support and guidance in effective, nurturing parenting and discipline, the likelihood of child and adolescent behavioral and emotional problems, child maltreatment and youth violence significantly diminish. However, the current health system places little emphasis on the prevention and early intervention. Such efforts have been impeded by the fact that historically, there has been virtually no system of reimbursement for professionals providing preventive health care. Furthermore, despite the demonstrated need for education, support, and guidance for parents, there is no accessible system in place for parents to receive such help and information.

When opportunities for prevention are missed, mental health intervention by qualified providers is imperative to prevent long-term suffering and related costs. However, findings from large, population-based studies indicate that only 20% of the youths who need mental health treatment actually get it (American Academy of Child and Adolescent Psychiatry, 2013). Young people of color, those who live in families with limited financial resources, and those with disabilities have particularly limited access to services that would identify, prevent or treat mental health problems. Poor access is linked to the scarcity of qualified child and adolescent mental healthcare professionals in the US. The Annapolis Coalition on the Behavioral Health Workforce described a "workforce crisis in behavioral health," citing the lack of such providers to deliver care, especially in rural America (Hoge et al., 2007, p. 2). Child and adolescent psychiatry, for example, has long been recognized as a shortage subspecialty field. Even in large metropolitan areas, many youths will never be able to access psychiatry services. Nonetheless, the demand for services in child and adolescent psychiatry was expected to increase by 100% between the years 1995 and 2020 (Kim, 2003). Although efforts to bring healthcare providers, psychiatrists, and psychologists together into integrated work settings are underway, the workforce shortages will make this plan impossible in many areas of the United States.

In part due to these shortages, primary care clinicians are principal sources of prevention and care for children and adolescents "who are at risk or who are already" suffering from mental health issues. For example, research suggests that behavioral, emotional, or educational issues are brought up by families in one-fourth to one-half of pediatric visits (Cooper, Valleley, Polaha, Begeny, & Evans, 2006). Unfortunately, many healthcare clinicians often do not have the resources to address these needs and frequently report that they lack the time and training to effectively address them and are not reimbursed for these services. Consequently, families often are left without needed support. For example, in one study, 75% of the parents reported not receiving any guidance from healthcare professionals on discipline, 66% did not receive guidance on toilet training, and 59% on sleep (Schuster, Duan, Regalado, & Klein, 2000). Further, research has suggested that more than 94% of the parents have significant unmet needs for guidance or screening by pediatric service providers (Bethell, Reuland, Halfon, & Schor, 2004).

Although reimbursement for behavioral health prevention and intervention historically has been almost nonexistent for healthcare clinicians, methods of healthcare coding, billing, and reimbursement are changing to address these needs. The American Academy of Pediatrics has responded to this situation and is now training its members in how to code and bill for prevention, counseling, risk reduction, and behavior change interventions. The American Psychological Association has recommended the development of a primary mental healthcare system to rectify the inadequate access to child and adolescent mental health services, emphasizing the need for reimbursement of clinicians for prevention and early intervention services. Moreover, there is now greater recognition on the policy level of the high societal costs of untreated behavioral health conditions. Public and private systems are recognizing that consumers with behavioral health conditions are often the costliest enrollees to cover. In keeping, treatment of behavioral health conditions has become a greater priority for clinicians and policymakers, and Medicaid and insurance organizations increasingly are basing reimbursement on the combination of health and mental health outcomes. State-based systems are being redesigned in order to improve health outcomes and decrease costs. In these new systems, innovative approaches to health care, such as evidence-based methods to promote healthy lifestyles, are incentivized. Healthcare providers are now expected to move well beyond the biomedical model to address behavioral, emotional, and developmental needs.

Such changes in systems of care and reimbursement are finally removing obstacles to the effective provision of preventive care. At long last, third-party payors are newly willing to cover prevention and intervention provided by healthcare clinicians (see Chapter 9: Physical punishment and child maltreatment, for details). Promotion of healthy lifestyles and prevention of mental health disorders are being prioritized. Thus the time is right for mental health and related professionals to find innovative ways to share their expertise on behavioral, emotional, and educational issues with other professionals who treat children. One critical objective should be to help such providers to identify and use efficient methods of prevention and intervention that work within the context of the standard office visit. This book has the goal of preventing suffering, adverse emotional and behavioral outcomes, as well as their associated costs, by providing needed support, education and guidance to clinicians as well as the parents and caregivers of the children and adolescents they treat.

This book provides an update on the evidence base on issues commonly brought up by families to physicians, nurses, physician assistants, child psychologists, psychiatrists, counselors, social workers, and other professionals. It also provides evidence-based advice about how to effectively and efficiently address these topics in the context of a brief office visit. Graduate students and professionals in a wide variety of fields will find the content useful and relevant to their practice. Each chapter summarizes the most recent evidence base on normal and atypical development, mental health and health outcomes, treatment parameters, best practices, and how to most effectively address issues with families. Handouts for clinicians and families are provided to promote the dissemination and use of the information.

A few notes on the vocabulary used in the book are worth noting. Throughout the book, the term "parents" is used instead of "parents and caregivers" for simplification, but readers are advised to understand this to mean any primary caregiver of a youth. Furthermore, the term "clinicians" is used throughout to indicate any professional in the role of advising families with children on behavioral health issues. Some chapters, such as Chapter 6, Helping children succeed in school: a guide to special education services, may be useful to parents, so clinicians may want to recommend the entire book to parents. Lastly, if more information is needed on the topics addressed, readers are advised to visit websites such as Pediatrics for Parents (https://pedsforparents.com/), National Institute of Child Health and Human Development (https://www.nichd.nih.gov/health/topics), and Zero to Three (https://www.zerotothree.org/) that provide a wealth of information on a variety of children's behavioral health topics.

Michele Knox

References

American Academy of Child and Adolescent Psychiatry. (2013). Child and adolescent psychiatry workforce crisis: Solutions to improve early intervention and access to care. Retrieved March 6, 2019 from <https://www.aacap.org/App_Themes/AACAP/docs/Advocacy/policy_resources/cap_workforce_crisis_201305.pdf>.

Bethell, C., Reuland, C. H. P., Halfon, N., & Schor, E. L. (2004). Measuring the quality of preventive and developmental services for young children: National estimates and patterns of clinicians' performance. *Pediatrics, 113*(Supplement 5), 1973–1983.

Cooper, S., Valleley, R. J., Polaha, J., Begeny, J., & Evans, J. H. (2006). Running out of time: Physician management of behavioral health concerns in rural pediatric primary care. *Pediatrics, 118*(1), e132–e138.

Hoge, M. A., Morris, J. A., Daniels, A. S., Stuart, G. W., Huey, L. Y., & Adams, N. (2007). *An action plan for behavioral health workforce development*. Cincinnati, OH: Annapolis Coalition on the Behavioral Health Workforce.

Kessler, R. C., Amminger, G. P., Aguilar-Gaxiola, S., Alonso, J., Lee, S., & Ustun, T. B. (2007). Age of onset of mental disorders: A review of recent literature. *Current Opinion in Psychiatry, 20*(4), 359.

Kim, W. J. (2003). Child and adolescent psychiatry workforce: A critical shortage and national challenge. *Academic Psychiatry, 27*(4), 277–282.

National Alliance on Mental Illness. (2019). Mental health by the numbers. Retrieved March 6, 2019 from <https://www.nami.org/learn-more/mental-health-by-the-numbers>.

Schuster, M. A., Duan, N., Regalado, M., & Klein, D. J. (2000). Anticipatory guidance: What information do parents receive? What information do they want? *Archives of Pediatrics & Adolescent Medicine, 154*(12), 1191–1198.

CHAPTER

1

Parents and caregivers: creating a strong foundation for engagement

Morgan Dynes

Departments of Psychiatry and Pediatrics, The University of Toledo College of Medicine and Life Sciences, Toledo, OH, United States

Why is engagement important?

Parenthood is talked about as one of the most rewarding journeys one can embark on in life and is regarded as a highly important role across cultures. However, parenting youth of all ages can be stressful, and challenges can present at any turn. Many families experience emotional problems, behavioral challenges, and disruptions in development while raising their children and adolescents. An estimated 20%–40% of youth have a psychiatric disorder (Costello, Copeland, & Angold, 2011) and may need mental health services. Other findings suggest that between 24% and 50% of pediatric office visits involve a behavioral, emotional, or educational concern (Cassidy & Jellinek, 1998; Cooper, Valleley, Polaha, Begeny, & Evans, 2006), making pediatricians increasingly responsible for identifying and addressing these issues (NIHCM Foundation, 2009). However, the majority of pediatric providers do not receive specialized training in identifying or treating behavioral health disorders (Leaf et al., 2004; Williams, Klinepeter, Palmes, Pulley, & Foy, 2004). Untreated childhood behavior problems have been shown to predict the development of unfavorable adolescent outcomes, such as early rejection by prosocial peers, academic difficulties, school dropout, out-of-home placement, criminal involvement, substance use, and teen pregnancy

Clinician's Toolkit for Children's Behavioral Health
DOI: https://doi.org/10.1016/B978-0-12-816024-4.00001-2

(Broidy et al., 2003; Webster-Stratton & Reid, 2003). Similarly, internalizing problems in childhood, such as depression or anxiety disorders, can contribute to long-term impairments or even suicide (Copeland, Angold, Shanahan, & Costello, 2014; Copeland, Goldston, & Costello, 2017; Fergusson, Horwood, Ridder, & Beautrais, 2005).

While childhood mental health disorders exert a cost at the individual, family, and societal levels, several promising evidence-based treatments exist. For example, parent-management training is a theoretically sound, empirically well-founded, and efficacious method for the treatment and prevention of externalizing behavior problems (e.g., oppositionality, defiance, and disruptive behavior) in children (Dretzke et al., 2009; Eyberg, Nelson, & Boggs, 2008; Webster-Stratton, Reid, & Beauchaine, 2011). Cognitive-behavioral therapies (CBT) are efficacious treatments for childhood internalizing disorders. In addition to individual treatment of the child directly, CBT for youths often includes education and engagement of parents in order to facilitate positive treatment outcomes for the child (O'Neil, Brodman, Cohen, Edmunds, & Kendall, 2012; Wood, Piacentini, Southam-Gerow, Chu, & Sigman, 2006).

While the efficacy of parent-focused interventions across treatment modalities has been well documented, obstacles to treatment delivery and engagement may reduce the effective dissemination of these interventions in real-world practice settings. For example, Merikangas et al. (2010) demonstrated with national survey data that half of youth in need of treatment do not even start services. Further, half of the youth who initially engage in mental health services discontinue treatment prematurely (Nock & Ferriter, 2005; Pellerin, Costa, Weems, & Dalton, 2010; Becker, Boustani, Gellatly, & Chorpita, 2017). McKay, Pennington, Lynn, and McCadam (2001) found a third of families did not attend their requested appointments for mental health treatment, and families that were enrolled in services missed almost half of their scheduled appointments.

How does the engagement process work?

Who notices a child is suffering and decides to get her help? Who enrolls the child in treatment? Who gets the child to appointments? Who helps him to use the skills he learns in treatment? Who...? The answer is almost always "parents." For these reasons, effective service delivery of any treatment for youths depends on successful parent engagement and retention (National Institute for Health and Clinical Excellence, 2006, 2009; Nock & Ferriter, 2005; U.S. Department of Health and Human Services, 2001, 2003). There are various ways in which researchers have gone about defining the parent engagement process.

Becker et al. (2017) summarized 40 years of engagement research and propose that engagement represents an individual's multidimensional commitment to services and includes cognitive, social, and behavioral dimensions. Cognitive dimensions include a parent's attitudes, beliefs, and expectations about themselves, their children, and the services or treatment they are seeking. Some examples of these cognitive dimensions include a parent's overall attitudes toward mental health services and possible preconceived ideas about treatment providers; past experiences with providers; their understanding of their role in treatment and how it would address their child's needs; a parent's confidence in their efficacy as a parent; a parent's beliefs about their child and their child's problems, a parent's locus of control, and the parent's readiness for change (Lindsey et al., 2014; Lindsey, Chambers, Pohle, Beall, & Lucksted, 2013). Behavioral dimensions of engagement include treatment enrollment, appointment attendance, participation in session, and completion of homework or assigned intervention activities outside of session (Lindsey et al., 2014; Nock & Ferriter, 2005). A parent's transportation, financial resources and insurance status, and availability of childcare should also be considered when thinking about behavioral dimensions of engagement. Social dimensions (e.g., quality of the therapeutic alliance) also are included by some researchers in their understanding of the engagement process (Staudt, 2007). A strong therapeutic alliance could be seen as a result of a successfully navigated engagement process, during which cognitive and behavioral dimensions are assessed and addressed with respect.

It should be noted that these aforementioned dimensions of engagement can operate as *barriers* or *promoters* of the engagement process. For example, if a parent has positive attitudes toward treatment, believes in their own and their child's abilities to participate in treatment, has a strong therapeutic alliance with child's provider, and makes efforts to try the suggestions of the provider inside and outside of session, the parent is likely to be positively engaged in their child's services. For example, Joe brings his 8-year-old son into your pediatric practice for diarrhea that seems to relate to stress. Joe's son has been your patient since birth. He had the same problem as a child and it was successfully treated. Joe recalls his mother being patient as they helped him manage his stress better, and you notice Joe take a few quick notes on his phone to remember your suggestions.

However, if the parent does not feel comfortable with the provider, is unsure if the child will benefit from treatment, is not sure of his or her role in the child's care, and has unreliable transportation, then this parent will struggle to be meaningfully engaged in services. For example, Kendra is a 55-year-old African-American woman who has custody of her 6-year-old granddaughter. Kendra brings her granddaughter to a licensed mental health counselor, Allison, at their local community mental health center to get help for her granddaughter's behavior problems at school and sleep issues at home. Allison is White, in her early 20s, and makes very little eye contact. Kendra is nervous and uncertain when first meeting Allison, because she is reflecting on how she tried to take her granddaughter to another young White counselor in a neighboring town. Kendra was never asked to participate in any of her granddaughter's appointments and was only given a 2-minute summary of the session activities by her previous counselor in the waiting room at the end of the appointment. Her granddaughter's behavior and sleep issues were not improving, and Kendra was growing more concerned that something has happened to her granddaughter when not in her care. Despite her negative experiences with mental health services, Kendra feels at a loss of how to help her granddaughter on her own, so she decides to try another community mental health center, in hopes of a better experience.

Becker and Chorpita (2016, as cited in Becker et al., 2017) created an organizing framework where they propose five domains of engagement, using the relationship, expectancy, attendance, clarity, and homework (REACH) acronym. These domains can be seen as engagement "outcomes" that practitioners are hoping to positively influence by effectively addressing and navigating the aforementioned cognitive and behavioral dimensions of engagement.

- *Relationship*—Therapeutic alliance between clinician and parent or patient (Shirk, Karver, & Brown, 2011)
- *Expectancy*—Parents' attitudes and beliefs about their children, themselves, and treatment services (Nock & Kazdin, 2001)
- *Attendance*—Presence at treatment sessions (Nock & Ferriter, 2005)
- *Clarity*—Understanding the treatment approach or parent's role in treatment (Shuman & Shapiro, 2002)
- *Homework*—Multiple adherence and participation dimensions such as completion of homework or in-session participation (Nock & Ferriter, 2005).

Engagement is also a dynamic process that occurs across time in services and is transactional in which service providers play a primary role. Across studies (Becker et al., 2017; Eames et al., 2010; Ingoldsby, 2010; Koerting et al., 2013; Lindsey et al., 2014), researchers have identified multiple behaviors of service providers that may *enhance* the parent engagement process:

- Using effective assessment skills
- Assessing parents' *practical* (e.g., transportation and childcare) and *perceptual* (e.g., stigma about disorders and services, negative

experiences with prior treatment, and beliefs about illness and acceptable treatments) barriers to treatment
- Psychoeducation about treatment, presenting problems, or service delivery
- Addressing parents' perceptions about services
- Discussing with parents their beliefs about their children and themselves as parents
- Building positive parent–therapist alliances based on trust and mutual respect
- Evaluating parents' stages of change and motivation

Best practices for navigating the engagement process

Researchers across disciplines have been working to clarify how providers can facilitate and navigate the parent engagement process, in order to provide parent-focused, evidence-based interventions that will positively impact children in need. For example, Becker et al. (2017) identified 30 practice elements in their comprehensive review of the engagement literature. The five practice elements most frequently included in effective engagement interventions were *Assessment, Psychoeducation, Accessibility promotion, Barriers to treatment,* and *Goal setting.* Table 1.1 connects the practice elements with the respective REACH domain outcomes that they facilitate and provides examples of how these practice elements could be used in a usual care setting. An additional factor to consider when trying to navigate the engagement process is a family's cultural background. Researchers suggest that ethnic minorities underutilize mental health services due to differential beliefs about the causes of mental health problems (Hoberman, 1992; Ruiz, 1995; U.S. Department of Health and Human Services, 2001). Further, differences between the way the parent and the service provider view the source of the child's problems may impede treatment progress and compliance (Foulks, Persons, & Merkel, 1986). Therefore it is important to adapt program content or delivery to address specific characteristics of the culture of families being served (McDonald, Coover, Sandler, Thao, & Shalhoub, 2012; McDonald, FitzRoy, Fuchs, Fooken, & Klasen, 2012). Please find examples across the five practice elements in Table 1.1 of how to assess components of a family's cultural, ethnic, and religious background in order to facilitate a collaborative relationship with parents that fosters engagement, while honoring important aspects of their culture (Ecklund & Johnson, 2007).

While researchers have identified multiple practice elements that may *enhance* the parent engagement process, there are also provider-related factors and behaviors that can *hinder* the engagement process. In other words, as providers are trying to implement the practice elements

TABLE 1.1 Parent engagement practice elements: practice applications

Practice element	Practical application/resource
Assessment	Gathering information about parents' and clients' strengths and needs by conducting interviews, using questionnaires, and through observation. Assessing parents' expectations for treatment, their beliefs about their children and their children's problems, their confidence in their abilities as parents, and their readiness for change is likely to further facilitate the engagement process *Case example* A 10-year-old boy, Matthew, and his mother, Kristen, show up to their first appointment with you for individual counseling because he has become increasingly irritable and defiant, and his grades are dropping in school. While asking all of your usual new client questions, you make sure to understand Kristen's beliefs about Matthew's problems, and what she has already tried to address her concerns about Matthew. You ask Matthew and his mother to play a game together to observe Matthew and his mother's interactions and have Kristen complete the Parent Expectancies for Therapy Scale (PETS) and the Parent Motivation Inventory (PMI) at the end of your first appointment. You ask Kristin if she is willing to come to the next appointment without Matthew, so you can create a timeline with her for Matthew's life and get a better understanding of what life has been like for her living with Matthew. During this appointment, you plan to build rapport with Kristen, ask questions about her confidence as a parent and assess her readiness to be an agent of change for Matthew. You plan to review her responses on the questionnaires she completed, and give her your observations from the play interactions from the first session. You will highlight strengths in their relationship and interactions, but also make connections between Kristen's concerns and Matthew's behavior during the initial session *Parent beliefs about child problems* • "How do you make sense of these problems that he is having? Where do you think they come from?" • "What past and current events have caused or contributed to these problems?" • "To what degree do you believe that your child can change or improve?" • "Who will have the biggest impact on your child's improvement?" *Parent past efforts to alter child's problems and parent confidence* • "What have you tried to do in the past to change these problems your child is having?" • "What have you done that has worked, and for how long did/has it worked?" • "What have you tried that has not worked? Why do you think it did not work?" • "How confident do you feel in your ability to help change your child's behavior?"

(*Continued*)

TABLE 1.1 (Continued)

Practice element	Practical application/resource
Assessment (Continued)	*Parent readiness to be an agent of change in child treatment* • "What are the pros and cons, for you and your child, of simply accepting this problem(s) as an unchangeable part of your child?" • "What are the pros and cons, for you and your child, of viewing this problem as something that can change, and taking an active role as a parent in changing it?" • "What are the pros and cons, for you and your child, of your child displaying a desirable behavior instead?" • "What are the pros and cons, for you and your child, of you taking an active role to encourage desirable child behavior?" *Cultural factors* • "How does your family understand what is going on? Your religious supports? Your cultural group supports? What have your supports suggested you do? What does the school staff say about what is going on? What do you think about their ideas?" • "Do the problems occur at X (place of worship, school, community)? How do they handle it?" • (If the problem is different in different settings) "Are there cultural factors that can explain why it is different in setting X?" • "Do you think there is racial or cultural prejudice at work? Do you think racism is a factor in what is going on? Do you think X is biased (teacher, coach, person with whom behavior is a problem)? Tell me about that" • "Who helps you? What activities/groups make it better? Do your cultural and kinship networks provide help? Do they make it easier or more difficult?" • If the family is acculturating, how do parents feel about the child becoming "Americanized"? If the family is multicultural and the child is identifying with a culture different from the parents' primary identification, how do the parents feel about the child identifying with Y culture? • "How has your family experienced oppression?—Isms? Prejudice? Bias? How has it affected the child? How aware is the child of it? How does the child understand it?" *Relevant measures* • PETS (Kazdin & Holland, 1991) • Expectations of therapy outcome scale (Bonner & Everett, 1986) • PMI (Nock & Photos, 2006)
Psychoeducation	Providing information to the family about how to understand the presenting problems, the chosen treatment approach, how treatment relates to presenting problems, and specific aspects of service delivery (e.g., session content/frequency, roles of the provider and youth in treatment, and expectations for attendance) "We have talked about your concerns around your son's aggressive behavior today, and using parent–child interaction therapy to address those issues. I mentioned that many researchers have

(Continued)

TABLE 1.1 (Continued)

Practice element	Practical application/resource
	tested PCIT with parents whose kids have problems just like your son, and they learned that PCIT helped improve their relationship and follow directions better. Does that seem like a good fit to you?"
Barriers to treatment	Eliciting and addressing practical and perceived barriers that might interfere with treatment (e.g., transportation, scheduling, previous experiences with services, stigma around medical/mental health treatment) *Case example* When a parent called for an appointment, your staff member asks what language the family speaks at home and they report they speak mostly English, but also some Spanish. Your staff offers an interpreter for the appointment, but the parent declines. The patient, a 15-year-old girl, Grace, her mother, and her father attend their first counseling appointment with you after Grace was released from staying three nights in the local youth inpatient unit after having suicidal thoughts while at school. Grace explained that her parents were both born in Mexico, and moved to the United States as adults, before having her and her younger brother. While assessing Grace's understanding of her symptoms and doing a risk assessment, her parents are silent. You then ask Grace's parents if they would mind if you had Grace wait in the waiting room for the remainder of the session. With Grace's parents alone, you ask about what this entire experience has been like for them: Grace saying she wants to die, having school staff involved in their family's personal matters, and taking Grace to the hospital. You assess what the parents liked and did not like about these experiences. You assess the parents' culture and spiritual beliefs and explore what role culture, spirituality or religion plays in their lives. You ask about ways that the family has resolved issues in the past, and how helpful those approaches have been. You listen intently, validate their experiences and concerns, and only ask questions to further your understanding of their beliefs and experience with previous systems (i.e., school and hospital). You assure parents that there are many ways to help Grace feel better. You explain that your job is to help create a plan with all of them that honors what is important to their family and what their family already does well. You also explain that while you know some things that have helped other teenagers like Grace, in the end only Grace and her family are "experts" on what will be best for them. *Beliefs about treatment and past experiences with providers* • "Have you ever heard of X treatment before? Did you have any thoughts/ideas about it before today?" • "People have different ideas and feelings about taking medication. How do you feel about it?" • "Some people find it difficult to speak to a stranger about such personal matters, and some people feel more comfortable solving problems within their family and spiritual community. Before today, what were your thoughts on seeing a counselor?"

(Continued)

TABLE 1.1 (Continued)

Practice element	Practical application/resource
Barriers to treatment (Continued)	• "How was your experience with your last pediatrician? What did you like? What are you hoping we can do differently?" *Practical barriers* • "Is transportation a source of stress for you?" "Our staff have resources to help make transportation easier if you are interested" • "Would it be helpful for us to have an interpreter attend the appointment?" • "Do you need help in understanding your coverage for these services?" • "Are there matters in your life currently that may make it difficult to make and keep our appointments?" • "Scheduling and keeping appointments can be stressful for everyone. Is there something we can do to make it easier for you? Are you signed up for our text/phone call/email reminder system?" *Relevant measure* • BTPS (Kazdin, Holland, & Breton, 1991)
Goal setting	Explicitly selecting a therapeutic goal for the purpose of making a plan to achieve that goal. Collaboratively determining and agreeing on the tasks or interventions that will be used to reach those goals *Case example* An 8-year-old girl, Paige, and her father, Jim, show up for their first appointment with you. At the beginning of your appointment with Paige and Jim, you turn to Paige and ask, "Do you know what made your father decide to bring you here today?" Paige is quiet and looks at the ground. You assure Paige that is it okay to not be sure why she is here, and that we will figure it out together. You turn to Jim and have him describe his concerns, and he tells you about Paige's dropping grades and difficulties going to bed and staying asleep. After gathering some standard new client information from Jim, you spend some time alone with Paige. You explain that your job is to help kids with their feelings, help kids and families solve different problems they may have, and help families get along better. You ask Paige the Miracle Question (de Shazer, 1988), in order to get a better idea about what she may see as problems in her life. You say, "Imagine tonight, while you slept, a miracle happened. When you woke up, things in your life were better, just the way you want them to be! What would be some of the things you would notice if your life had gotten better?" Paige says, "When I woke up, I wouldn't be so scared to go to school. I would have more friends at school, and I wouldn't be scared to talk to other girls in my class. There's a new girl in our class, I think everyone thinks she's cool, but she's mean to me." You ask Paige if you can share with her father her answer to the Miracle Question, and she nods. You bring Paige's father back into the session and ask, "If therapy were to be really helpful for Paige, how would her life look different?" Jim says, "She would be able to talk to me and

(Continued)

TABLE 1.1 (Continued)

Practice element	Practical application/resource
Goal setting (Continued)	her mother about how she is feeling and what is bothering her. She just started doing poorly in school and not turning in her homework, and we don't know why." You educate Paige and her father on the importance of having a "treatment plan" for their therapy, and this plan will include 1–2 goals. You explain that these goals are the "destination" for treatment, where you want your therapy to take you. You go on to explain that, for each goal, you will work together to identify what new skills we are going to learn to reach that goal. You emphasize that Paige's concerns about making friends at school—and her parents' concerns about her communication and schoolwork—can all be on your treatment plan. *Follow-up questions to the Miracle Question* (de Shazer, 1988) • "When you got out of bed the next morning, what would be different?" • "As you went on throughout your day, what would be different?" • "What would be clues to you that the miracle worked?" • "How would you be feeling differently?" • "How would you be thinking differently?" • "What would you be doing that would be different?" • "What would be different about the people or things around you?"
Accessibility Promotion	Using strategies to make services convenient and accessible such as on-site child-care, taxi vouchers, bus tokens, supporting families in accessing transportation *Case example* Dr. Smith is a primary care pediatrician who works in a group practice in a medium-size suburb that sits directly next to a medium-size metropolitan city and is also surrounded by rural and semirural communities. Dr. Smith has trained her medical assistants and front-desk staff to review with families the transportation assistance offered by their state-funded insurance programs. She also provides a land-line phone in a small sectioned-off corner of her waiting room, where step-by-step instructions are placed on how to contact their insurance company and set up transportation assistance. Low-cost child-care services that use sliding fee scales are also advertised in this area.

BTPS, Barriers to Treatment Participation Scale; *PETS*, Parent Expectancies for Therapy Scale; *PMI*, Parent Motivation Inventory.

outlined in Table 1.1, they are bound to encounter "bumps in the road" as they navigate parents' responses to these engagement efforts. Parent disengagement, nonadherence, or resistance (e.g., poor attendance, refusals to participate in discussions and activities, incomplete homework assignments; Wilson, Wildman, Ciesla, Smith, & Dempster, 2015) have been associated with negative practitioner attitudes and behaviors toward parents (Wilson et al., 2015). Specifically, barriers to the parent engagement process can occur because of how clinicians think about and respond to the parent and their behaviors (Patterson & Chamberlain, 1994; Patterson & Forgatch, 1985).

Barriers to the parent engagement process can occur because of how clinicians think about and respond to the parent and their behaviors (Patterson & Chamberlain, 1994; Patterson & Forgatch, 1985).

If the clinician perceives that a parent is not participating in treatment, and externalizes the blame to the parent (i.e., sees the parent as "resistant" to treatment), the clinician may have negative emotional reactions toward this parent, and disengage from trying to include them in their child's treatment. The ways in which clinicians understand or view a parent's behaviors, particularly any behaviors that seem "resistant"—and a clinician's emotional reactions to their understanding of that parent behavior—can change a clinician's communication with a parent, decrease their empathy for that parent, or decrease their interest in a parent's progress in treatment (see Figs. 1.1 and 1.2 for examples).

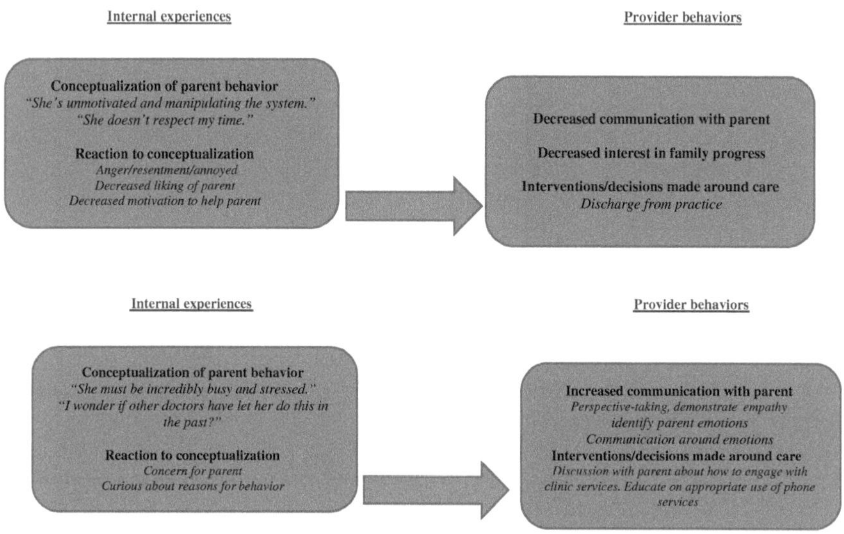

FIGURE 1.1 A mother has canceled and no-showed multiple appointments for her 4-year-old son.
She continues to call your office to ask for advice about her son's aggressive behavior and sleep problems, and request changes be made to his medication.

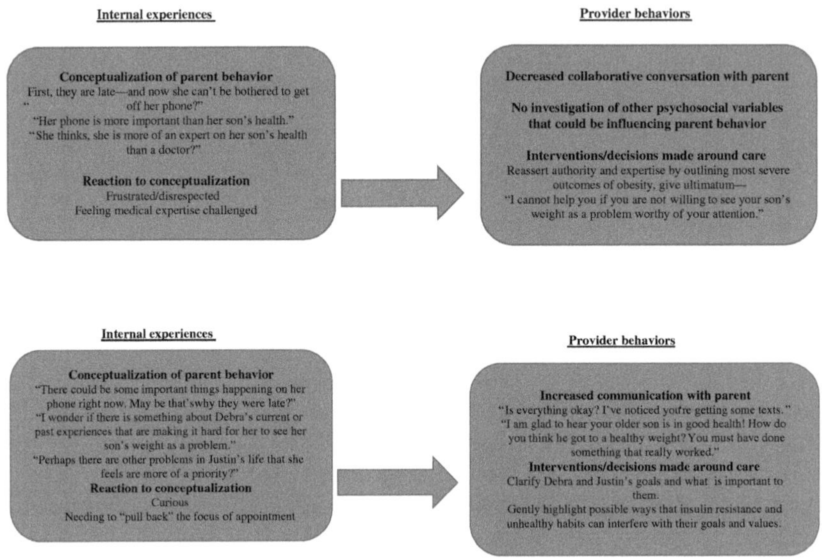

FIGURE 1.2 Debra and her 12-year-old son, Justin, show up 15 min late to your pediatric clinic for a follow-up visit to have his weight checked. Six months ago at his well-care visit, his BMI was in the overweight range, and his labs showed preliminary signs of insulin resistance. While meeting with Debra and her son, you discover that he has not lost any weight. Justin struggled to explain the reasons for this lack of progress. You notice Debra has been on her cell phone during the entire appointment, texting and not looking at you or her son. You ask for her thoughts as to why her son has not been able to lose any weight, and she says, "Honestly, I don't think he needs to lose weight. That's just baby fat, and his older brother weighed the same when he was his age, and he is fine now."

In such cases, practitioner experiences and behaviors could be a focal point for intervention in addressing engagement-related issues. Practical suggestions could entail viewing a conflict or disagreement between parent and provider, or family disengagement, as "red flags." These red flags could be seen as opportunities to check-in with how the engagement process is going. Red flags will likely fall under one or more of the five REACH engagement outcomes. The examples below highlight situations where there was disruption in one of the REACH outcomes, and how the practice elements mentioned in Table 1.1 can be used to improve engagement in that outcome area:

Your 14-year-old patient Jessica has no-showed for her last two therapy appointments in a row (*Attendance*, see aforementioned REACH acronym). You call her mother, who brought Jessica to her last four appointments, and ask if everything is okay, and if she is still interested in receiving therapy services for her daughter. Jessica's mother first mentions in a matter-of-fact tone, "We have had car trouble." You empathize with this stressor and mention that you would be happy to help them look into transportation assistance (*Barriers to Treatment*, Table 1.1). Then, you ask if there are any other reasons that have made Jessica not want to come to therapy. Her mother then says, "Actually, I am glad you called because it has offended me that you have not asked me to come to meet with you and Jessica for any of the sessions, and I'm her mother after all. I have the right to know what you are talking to her about!" You realize that you must not have thoroughly assessed this mother's expectations for treatment and her understanding of her role in therapy (*Assessment*, Table 1.1), or provided enough education around what to expect from individual therapy for her teenage daughter. You thank Jessica's mother for being honest with you and go on to explain how important she truly is in Jessica's treatment. You also explain that for teens Jessica's age, it is important for you to meet with her alone for several sessions in order to build a positive, trusting relationship with Jessica—so she can feel comfortable sharing her thoughts and feelings honestly in therapy. You add that, as a teen, Jessica is going through a phase of development where it is important for her to feel independent and like her own person. You make a plan to meet with Jessica's mother alone for your next session, so you can plan more together on how she will be involved in Jessica's care (*Psychoeducation*, Table 1.1).

A father and his 8-year-old son have shown up for their second follow-up appointment in a row for their child's bed-wetting issues, without getting any of the lab work completed that you request, or without seeing the pediatric urologist and gastroenterologist you referred them to (*Homework*: Adherence to referrals/recommendations in between appointments, REACH). You review the lab and specialist referrals that you ordered with the father and ask what is getting in the way of him following through with these recommendations for his son. He explains, "Look, I know you told us to get those tests and go see those people—but I went to a urologist when I was a kid for the same problem, and he was rude to me and my mom and did not help us at all. And I really don't understand how this person is supposed to help my son stop wetting the bed. I like talking with you, so why can't you just help us fix this?" You realize that in your last visit with this family, you may not have had enough time to go over in detail the treatment plan, the sequence of treatment events, and how the specialist referrals all fit together to address his son's bed wetting problems. You see now that this father had some negative experiences with a urologist in his past, so you ask him more about this experience (*Perceived Barriers to Treatment*, Table 1.1), in order to be able to address his anticipated concerns about his son's urologist visit. You also provide education on each lab test, how the urologist and GI specialist will work together to determine the possible driving forces behind his son's issues, and your role as the pediatrician in this treatment process (*Psychoeducation and Goal setting*, Table 1.1).

These points in service delivery mentioned above could also prompt providers to reflect on what they are thinking about the parent and the parent's behavior, and their emotional reactions to this parent in treatment. This provider "check-in" can also include determining if their thoughts and feelings have influenced their behavior toward this parent during appointments. The results of this provider self-assessment could suggest the need for a clinician to conceptualize a parent's behavior from multiple perspectives before moving forward with an intervention or decision about the family's care. It should be noted that in a national study of child and family mental health providers, therapist internal barriers to engaging parents were experienced by the majority of participants (Dynes, Tompsett, & Domoff, 2018).

While this study was small and cross-sectional, these findings suggest that it may be common for providers to experience negative attitudes and reactions to parent behaviors. In other research conducted with primary care providers (Phelan et al., 2015), there was considerable evidence that negative attitudes toward patients influence person-perceptions, judgment, interpersonal behavior, and decision-making—and that these attitudes may impact the care they provide. Researchers have suggested broad strategies that can be implemented on the organizational/clinic level, and provider level, to improve provider attitudes toward patients with obesity (Phelan et al., 2015). These strategies can be applied in a similar fashion to clinicians working with youth and families more broadly. These strategies can help identify and manage providers' attitudes, interpretations, and emotional reactions to parent resistance and disengagement. They include the following:

- Perspective-taking exercises to increase provider empathy and help providers identify and manage attitudes and interpretations of situations they experience when interacting with parents (Batson et al., 2003).
- Group practice meetings can include small portions of time to recognize, explore, and counteract negative interpretation and attitudes toward parent behaviors—with a focus on identifying the reasons behind patient's behavior versus judgment on surface-level observations. These meetings may include evaluation and modification of break room culture, including issues such as how staff talk about patients when they are not around.
- Dedicated education and practice for emotion regulation techniques that help promote calm and measured responding by providers in the workplace.
- Emotion regulation tools, such as meditation or deep breathing, may help providers overcome these negative emotions and improve compassion (Lillis & Hayes, 2007; Kemeny et al., 2012).
- Workplace culture and associated practices, informal or structured, which hold staff accountable for perspective-taking and alter perceived norms around patient resistance/disengagement.
- Mission statements that reflect values around patient engagement and that prioritize respect and concern for parents as well as youths.

Conclusion

This chapter was intended to "set the stage" and provide suggestions for how to create a strong foundation of engagement with families, in order to improve the implementation of evidence-based interventions when working with youth and families. Providers need to feel prepared for how to navigate parent engagement because youth typically cannot receive treatment without the help and support of their parents. In many cases, parents are the focus of intervention when the child is struggling with behavior problems, or when a pediatrician has concerns about a child's development. Providers can effectively assess parents' practical and perceptual barriers to treatment, educate them thoroughly about treatment, and build a positive parent–provider alliance in order to promote parent engagement.

Alternatively, how clinicians think about and respond to the parent and their behaviors can hinder the parent engagement process. Providers should view a conflict or disagreement between parent and provider, or family disengagement, as an opportunity to check-in with how the engagement process is going. Effective ways to address these ruptures in the parent engagement process include regular individual and group reflection on how clinicians think about and respond to the parent and their behaviors, self-care techniques, and policies and mission statements that prioritize respect and concern for parents and the challenges they face when trying to participate in their child's care.

References

Batson, C. D., Lishner, D. A., Carpenter, A., Dulin, L., Harjusola-Webb, S., Stocks, E. L., & Sampat, B. (2003). "... As you would have them do unto you": Does imagining yourself in the other's place stimulate moral action? *Personality and Social Psychology Bulletin*, *29*(9), 1190–1201. Available from https://doi.org/10.1177/0146167203254600.

Becker, K., Boustani, M., Gellatly, R., & Chorpita, B. (2017). Forty years of engagement research in children's mental health services: Multidimensional measurement and practice elements. *Journal of Clinical Child & Adolescent Psychology*, *47*(1), 1–23. Available from https://doi.org/10.1080/15374416.2017.1326121.

Becker, K. D., & Chorpita, B. (2016). Enhancing the design of engagement interventions to enhance the public health impact of mental health treatments for youth. In: K. Becker (Chair), *Extending the reach and impact of science on clinical care for youth and families: Looking for new models for the old challenges*. Symposium conducted at the NIMH conference on mental health services research: Harnessing science to strengthen the public health impact, Bethesda, MD.

Bonner, B. L., & Everett, F. L. (1986). Influence of client preparation and problem severity on attitudes and expectations in child psychotherapy. *Professional Psychology: Research and Practice*, *17*(3), 223–229. Available from https://doi.org/10.1037/0735-7028.17.3.223.

Broidy, L. M., Nagin, D. S., Tremblay, R. E., Bates, J. E., Brame, B., Dodge, K. A., & Vitaro, F. (2003). Developmental trajectories of childhood disruptive behaviors and adolescent delinquency: A six-site, cross-national study. *Developmental Psychology*, *39*(2), 222–245.

Cassidy, L., & Jellinek, M. (1998). Approaches to recognition and management of childhood psychiatric disorders in pediatric primary care. *Pediatric Clinics of North America*, *45*, 1037–1052. Available from https://doi.org/10.1016/S0031-3955(05)70061-4.

Cooper, S., Valleley, R. J., Polaha, J., Begeny, J., & Evans, J. H. (2006). Running out of time: Physician management of behavioral health concerns in rural pediatric primary care. *Pediatrics, 118*(1), e132–e138, PubMed PMID: 16818528.

Copeland, W. E., Angold, A., Shanahan, L., & Costello, E. J. (2014). Longitudinal patterns of anxiety from childhood to adulthood: the Great Smoky Mountains Study. *Journal of the American Academy of Child and Adolescent Psychiatry, 53*(1), 21–33. Available from https://doi.org/10.1016/j.jaac.2013.09.017.

Copeland, W. E., Goldston, D. B., & Costello, E. J. (2017). Adult associations of childhood suicidal thoughts and behaviors: A prospective, longitudinal analysis. *Journal of the American Academy of Child and Adolescent Psychiatry, 56*(11), 958–965.e4. Available from https://doi.org/10.1016/j.jaac.2017.08.015.

Costello, J., Copeland, W., & Angold, A. (2011). Trends in psychopathology across adolescent years: What changes when children become adolescents, and when adolescents become adults? *Journal of Child Psychology and Psychiatry, 52*(10), 1015–1025. Available from https://doi.org/10.1111/j.14697610.2011.02446.x.

de Shazer, S. (1988). *Clues: Investigating solutions in brief therapy*. New York: W. W. Norton & Co.

Dretzke, J., Davenport, C., Frew, E., Barlow, J., Stewart-Brown, S., Bayliss, S., & Hyde, C. (2009). The clinical effectiveness of different parenting programmes for children with conduct problems: A systematic review of randomised controlled trials. *Child and Adolescent Psychiatry and Mental Health, 3*(1), 7. Available from https://doi.org/10.1186/1753-2000-3-7.

Dynes, M. E., Tompsett, C. J., & Domoff, S. E. (2018). Development and validation of the Therapist Barriers to Engaging Parents (TBEP) measure. *Community Mental Health Journal, 54*(7), 967–977.

Eames, C., Daley, D., Hutchings, J., Whitaker, C. J., Bywater, T., Jones, K., & Hughes, J. C. (2010). The impact of group leaders' behaviour on parents acquisition of key parenting skills during parent training. *Behaviour Research and Therapy, 48*, 1221–1226. Available from https://doi.org/10.1016/j.brat.2010.07.011.

Ecklund, K., & Johnson, W. B. (2007). Toward cultural competence in child intake assessments. *Professional Psychology: Research and Practice, 38*(4), 356. Available from https://doi.org/10.1037/0735-7028.38.4.356.

Eyberg, S. M., Nelson, M. M., & Boggs, S. R. (2008). Evidence-based psychosocial treatment for children and adolescents with disruptive behavior. *Journal of Clinical Child and Adolescent Psychology, 37*, 215–237. Available from https://doi.org/10.1080/15374410701820117.

Fergusson, D. M., Horwood, L. J., Ridder, E. M., & Beautrais, A. L. (2005). Suicidal behaviour in adolescence and subsequent mental health outcomes in young adulthood. *Psychological Medicine, 35*, 983–993.

Foulks, E. F., Persons, J. B., & Merkel, R. L. (1986). The effect of patients' beliefs about their illnesses on compliance in psychotherapy. *The American Journal of Psychiatry, 143*(3), 340–344. Available from http://dx.doi.org/10.1176/ajp.143.3.340.

Hoberman, H. M. (1992). Ethnic minority status and adolescent mental health services utilization. *The Journal of Mental Health Administration, 19*(3), 246–267.

Ingoldsby, E. M. (2010). Review of interventions to improve family engagement and retention in parent and child mental health programs. *Journal of Child and Family Studies, 19* (5), 629–645. Available from https://doi.org/10.1007/s10826-009-9350-2.

Kazdin, A. E., & Holland, L. (1991). *Parent Expectancies for Therapy Scale*. New Haven, CT: Yale University, Child Conduct Clinic.

Kazdin, A. E., Holland, L., & Breton, S. (1991). *Barriers to participation in treatment scale—Parent and therapist versions*. New Haven, CT: Yale University.

Kemeny, M. E., Foltz, C., Cavanagh, J. F., Cullen, M., Giese-Davis, J., Jennings, P., & Ekman, P. (2012). Contemplative/emotion training reduces negative emotional behavior and promotes prosocial responses. *Emotion, 12*(2), 338–350. Available from https://doi.org/10.1037/a0026118.

Koerting, J., Smith, E., Knowles, M. M., Latter, S., Elsey, H., McCann, D. C., & Sonuga-Barke, E. J. (2013). Barriers to, and facilitators of, parenting programmes for childhood behaviour problems: A qualitative synthesis of studies of parents' and professionals' perceptions. *European Child & Adolescent Psychiatry, 22*(11), 653–670. Available from https://doi.org/10.1007/s00787-013-0401-2.

Leaf, P. J., Owens, P. L., Leventhal, J. M., Forsyth, B. W. C., Vaden-Kiernan, M., Epstein, L. D., & Horwitz, S. M. (2004). Pediatricians' training and identification and management of psychosocial problems. *Clinical Pediatrics, 43*(4), 355–365. Available from https://doi.org/10.1177/000992280404300407.

Lillis, J., & Hayes, S. C. (2007). Applying acceptance, mindfulness, and values to the reduction of prejudice: A pilot study. *Behavior Modification, 31*(4), 389–411. Available from https://doi.org/10.1177/0145445506298413.

Lindsey, M. A., Brandt, N. E., Becker, K. D., Lee, B. R., Barth, R. P., Daleiden, E. L., & Chorpita, B. F. (2014). Identifying the common elements of treatment engagement interventions in children's mental health services. *Clinical Child and Family Psychology Review, 17*(3), 283–298. Available from https://doi.org/10.1007/s10567-013-0163-x.

Lindsey, M. A., Chambers, K., Pohle, C., Beall, P., & Lucksted, A. (2013). Understanding the behavioral determinants of mental health service use by urban, under-resourced Black youth: Adolescent and caregiver perspectives. *Journal of Child and Family Studies, 22*(1), 107–121. Available from https://doi.org/10.1007/s10826-012-9668-z.

McDonald, L., Coover, G., Sandler, J., Thao, T., & Shalhoub, H. (2012). Cultural adaptation of an evidence-based parenting program with elders from South East Asia in the US: Co-producing Families and Schools Together–FAST. *Journal of Children's Services, 7*(2), 113–127. Available from https://doi.org/10.152/aeap.210.224.273.

McDonald, L., FitzRoy, S., Fuchs, I., Fooken, I., & Klasen, H. (2012). Strategies for high retention rates of low-income families in FAST (Families and Schools Together): An evidence-based parenting program in the USA, UK, Holland and Germany. *European Journal of Developmental Psychology, 9*(1), 75–88. Available from https://doi.org/10.1080/17405629.2011.632134.

McKay, M. M., Pennington, J., Lynn, C. J., & McCadam, K. (2001). Understanding urban child mental health service use: Two studies of child, family, and environmental correlates. *Journal of Behavioral Health Services and Research, 28*, 475–483. Available from https://doi.org/10.1007/BF02287777.

Merikangas, K. R., He, J. P., Brody, D., Fisher, P. W., Bourdon, K., & Koretz, D. S. (2010). Prevalence and treatment of mental disorders among US children in the 2001-2004 NHANES. *Pediatrics, 125*(1), 75–81. Available from https://doi.org/10.1542/peds.2008-2598.

National Institute for Health and Clinical Excellence & Social Care Institute for Excellence. Parent-training/education programmes in the management of children with conduct disorders. NICE Technology Appraisal 102 July 2006.

National Institute for Health and Clinical Excellence. (2009). Attention deficit hyperactivity disorder (ADHD): The NICE guideline on diagnosis and management of ADHD in children, young people and adults. In National clinical practice guideline number 72.

NIHCM Foundation. Executive summary, strategies to support the integration of mental health into pediatric primary care. In NIHCM foundation, issue paper, 8/2009. <https://www.nihcm.org/pdf/PediatricMH-FINAL.pdf>.

Nock, M. K., & Ferriter, C. (2005). Parent management of attendance and adherence in child and adolescent therapy: A conceptual and empirical review. *Clinical Child and Family Psychology Review, 8*, 149–166. Available from https://doi.org/10.1007/s10567-005-4753-0.

Nock, M. K., & Kazdin, A. E. (2001). Parent expectancies for child therapy: Assessment and relation to participation in treatment. *Journal of Child and Family Studies, 10*, 155–180. Available from https://doi.org/10.1023/A:1016699424731.

Nock, M. K., & Photos, V. (2006). Parent motivation to participate in treatment: Assessment and prediction of subsequent participation. *Journal of Child and Family Studies, 15*, 345–358. Available from https://doi.org/10.1007/s10826-006-9022-4.

O'Neil, K. A., Brodman, D. M., Cohen, J. S., Edmunds, J. M., & Kendall, P. C. (2012). Childhood anxiety disorders: The Coping Cat Program. In E. Szigethy, J. R. Weisz, R. L. Findling, E. Szigethy, J. R. Weisz, & R. L. Findling (Eds.), *Cognitive-behavior therapy for children and adolescents* (pp. 227–261). Arlington, VA: American Psychiatric Publishing, Inc. Available from https://doi.org/10.1176/appi.books.9781615370955.es07.

Patterson, G. R., & Chamberlain, P. (1994). A functional analysis of resistance during parent training therapy. *Clinical Psychology: Science and Practice, 1*, 53–70. Available from https://doi.org/10.1111/j.1468-2850.1994.tb00006.x.

Patterson, G. R., & Forgatch, M. S. (1985). Therapist behavior as a determinant for client noncompliance: A paradox for the behavior modifier. *Journal of Consulting and Clinical Psychology, 53*, 846–851. Available from https://doi.org/10.1037/0022-006X.53.6.846.

Pellerin, K. A., Costa, N. M., Weems, C. F., & Dalton, R. F. (2010). An examination of treatment completers and non-completers at a child and adolescent community mental health clinic. *Community Mental Health Journal, 46*(3), 273–281. Available from https://doi.org/10.1007/s10597-009-9285-5.

Phelan, S. M., Burgess, D. J., Yeazel, M. W., Hellerstedt, W. L., Griffin, J. M., & van Ryn, M. (2015). Impact of weight bias and stigma on quality of care and outcomes for patients with obesity. *Obesity Reviews: An Official Journal of the International Association for the Study of Obesity, 16*(4), 319–326. Available from https://doi.org/10.1111/obr.12266.

Ruiz, P. (1995). Assessing, diagnosing and treating culturally diverse individuals: A Hispanic perspective. *Psychiatric Quarterly, 66*(4), 329–341. Available from https://doi.org/10.1007/BF02238753.

Shirk, S. R., Karver, M. S., & Brown, R. (2011). The alliance in child and adolescent psychotherapy. *Psychotherapy, 48*(1), 17–24. Available from https://doi.org/10.1037/a0022181.

Shuman, A. L., & Shapiro, J. P. (2002). The effects of preparing parents for child psychotherapy on accuracy of expectations and treatment attendance. *Community Mental Health Journal, 38*(1), 3–16. Available from https://doi.org/10.1023/A:1013908629870.

Staudt, M. (2007). Treatment engagement with caregivers of at-risk children: Gaps in research and conceptualization. *Journal of Child and Family Studies, 16*, 183–196. Available from https://doi.org/10.1007/s10826-006-9077-2.

U.S. Department of Health and Human Services. (2001). *Mental health: Culture, race, and ethnicity—A supplement to mental health: A report of the surgeon general*. Rockville, MD: U.S. Department of Health and Human Services.

U.S. Department of Health and Human Services. (2003). *Achieving the promise: Transforming mental health care in America*. Rockville, MD: U.S. Department of Health and Human Services, Final Report.

Webster-Stratton, C., & Reid, M. J. (2003). Treating conduct problems and strengthening social and emotional competence in young children: The Dina Dinosaur treatment program. *Journal of Emotional and Behavioral Disorders, 11*(3), 130–143. Available from https://doi.org/10.1177/10634266030110030101.

Webster-Stratton, C. H., Reid, M. J., & Beauchaine, T. (2011). Combining parent and child training for young children with ADHD. *Journal of Clinical Child & Adolescent Psychology, 40*(2), 191–203. Available from https://doi.org/10.1080/15374416.2011.546044.

Williams, J., Klinepeter, K., Palmes, G., Pulley, A., & Foy, J. M. (2004). Diagnosis and treatment of behavioral health disorders in pediatric practice. *Pediatrics, 114*(3), 601–606.

Wilson, S. M., Wildman, B. G., Ciesla, J., Smith, A. W., & Dempster, R. (2015). Factor structure of the Obstacles to Engagement Scale: Problems, solutions, and hypotheses. *Journal of Child and Family Studies, 24*(4), 891–898. Available from https://doi.org/10.1007/s10826-014-9899-2.

Wood, J. J., Piacentini, J. C., Southam-Gerow, M., Chu, B. C., & Sigman, M. (2006). Family cognitive behavioral therapy for child anxiety disorders. *Journal of the American Academy of Child & Adolescent Psychiatry, 45*(3), 314–321. Available from https://doi.org/10.1097/01.chi.0000196425.88341.b0.

CHAPTER

2

Positive approaches to parenting and discipline: evidence-based, century old ideas still not used enough

Elizabeth C. Halloran

Lucas County Juvenile Court, Toledo, OH, United States

Introduction

Parenting is critically important to children's well-being. Indeed children's survival depends on how parents protect, care for, and teach them. Parents' interactions with children literally shape and grow their brains. In fact, neuroscientists now know, "parenting is the social phenomenon most profoundly affecting brain development of the young" (Feldman, 2015, p. 387). Children's brains are not fully developed at birth, and many aspects of brain development are shaped throughout the child's life. Naturally, parents feel the responsibility of helping their children thrive, and this enormous task can make parenting stressful. Parenting can be taxing in every way—physically, emotionally, financially, cognitively, and spiritually. It is no wonder there are hundreds of parenting books at our fingertips; not only is it taxing but also anxiety provoking at the same time. Adding to the stress is that many parents are overwhelmed by conflicting advice and the lack of an agreed-upon approach to childrearing. How do we know if we are doing the right thing as parents? How do we best teach them our values? How do we avoid the judgments from extended family and others about our children's behavior? How parents should respond to their children's

Clinician's Toolkit for Children's Behavioral Health
DOI: https://doi.org/10.1016/B978-0-12-816024-4.00002-4

misbehavior has been discussed and debated for ages with no real end in sight. Some of these questions, however, do have answers or at least a guiding framework for parents, supported by decades of research.

Nearly 100 years ago, Adler (1930) noted the importance of *belonging* as a motivator. The misbehavior of children was seen as resulting from children having mistaken ideas about how to have a sense of belonging. The positive discipline approach (Nelsen, 2006) is based on Adler's work and focuses parents on ensuring children have a sense of connection. Decades of research support the idea that a sense of belonging, having attachments, and having perceived social support are all important to children's well-being. They aid in the development of resiliency and protect children from the negative impact of stressors (Gfroerer, Nelsen, & Kern, 2013).

Similarly, over 50 years ago, Ginott (1965) focused on the communication between parents and children in order to generate mutual respect within the family. Ginott (1965) recommended: (1) parents showing understanding and respect for children's feelings, (2) parents helping children channel feelings appropriately and limiting destructive behaviors, and (3) parents fostering responsibility in children by allowing children to make choices and have appropriate levels of autonomy.

Not long after Ginott published his work, Baumrind (1971) described the effects of three different parenting styles: permissive, authoritative, and authoritarian. Much research has supported the use of a more authoritative style for positive child outcomes including independence, self-assuredness, social skills, and creativity (Arnett, 2012). The authoritative style combines high levels of parental responsiveness to the child's needs with clear, high expectations and demands of the child. Whereas permissive parents may be warm and responsive toward their children, they do not have high expectations or enforce rules. Authoritarian parents are strict but may be overly controlling and inflexible as well as lacking in warmth toward their children. The authoritative parents seem to balance the two roles of enforcing rules as well as being responsive and warm. They supportively listen to their children and allow for negotiation as needed while still setting clear limits and high expectations.

Research on the impact of parents on children shows parental influence to be greatly complicated. There are multiple interactions and moderator effects influencing the relationship such as genetics, child characteristics, and peer influences (Collins, Maccoby, Steinberg, Hetherington, & Bornstein, 2000). These complex interactions include, for example, prosocial children *eliciting* positive parent–child interactions rather than such interactions simply being driven by the parent (Pastorelli et al., 2016). Furthermore, teasing apart child versus parental effects of the relationship between parenting and externalizing behavior is often difficult (Boeldt et al., 2012). While the reality of parenting is far more complicated than parents simply molding their children, there is much overlap in the recommendations of parenting experts. Parents can set their children up for the best possible outcome despite there being no guarantees. The complex interactions of dispositional tendencies of the child, parenting, family, peers, neighborhood, schools, culture, and random events are real, but parents can make the most of the moments they have with their children. While every child is unique and affects the parent–child relationship differently, parents are often in a position to contribute to the child's growth in positive ways.

This chapter will discuss the common factors of positive approaches to parenting and the outcomes associated with them. The goal of this chapter is to increase providers' awareness of the benefits of positive approaches to parenting with the hope that such approaches can be promoted. Physicians, nurses, social workers, therapists, counselors, and other care providers are all in positions to influence parenting and thereby contribute to the development of healthier and more resilient children. While not difficult to understand, positive approaches can be very difficult to enact. The chapter, therefore, will address obstacles to using these methods and possible reasons parents still hesitate to use positive strategies over punitive ones despite decades of research establishing their effectiveness.

Aspects of positive parenting

General concepts

What is positive parenting? Positive parenting is not just one thing. It incorporates certain behaviors as well as a mindset. It rests on a developmental understanding of the child. It requires good judgment in that parents must decide to respond to certain behaviors and resist responding to other behaviors. Positive parenting demands patience and kindness. It uses creativity at times and persistence at other times. Parents using positive approaches are often described as warm, nurturing, affectionate, responsive, attentive, accepting, respectful, supportive, nonjudgmental, sensitive, empathic, consistent but not rigid, encouraging of autonomy, able to take the child's perspective, able to reflect feelings, and able to communicate effectively. Positive parenting includes preventing problems, providing guided choices, setting clear expectations, using positive reinforcement and rewards, helping children learn from mistakes, allowing for natural consequences, using time out, setting limits, taking an active role in the child's life, and stimulating children in healthy ways. It is neither harsh nor permissive. It builds the parent–child relationship and trust in the parent.

Often the goal of parent training is to increase parental skills and knowledge about children as well as to increase positive interactions with children. While negative consequences can be a part of effective discipline, parent training is often focused on skill building using positive approaches. A positive approach can be delivered even while putting a child in time-out or taking away a privilege. The literature on parenting clearly supports the effectiveness of parent training programs that teach skills for managing child behavior (Grusec, Danyliuk, Kil, & O'Neill, 2017; Kaminski, Valle, Filene, & Boyle, 2008; Sanders, Kirby, Tellegen, & Day, 2014). Below are some descriptions and examples of positive parenting approaches:

- Being aware of the child's level of hunger or fatigue before going to the store or running errands.
- Tolerating the messes made by children when they are playing and being creative. (I personally took great solace from the sign in the primate area of the zoo that read, "It's not messy, it's enrichment.")
- Sitting still even when you have a long list of things to do because the child would benefit from your undivided attention.
- Responding to the child's anger and frustration with none of your own.
- Focusing more on what the child does well rather than mistakes.
- Accepting that children do not have all the coping skills of adults and often act their age.
- Expecting the child to have certain age-appropriate responsibilities and tolerating them not liking you (*really* not liking you *at all* as an adolescent) because of those expectations or because of limits you set on their freedoms.
- Saying "no" to things the child wants and calmly dealing with the negative emotions that may follow.

While it is impossible to enact a positive approach to parenting 100% of the time, attempting to parent in this way is the goal. Parents are human too and will struggle at times to remain calm and use these positive approaches. However, the more knowledge and skills parents have, the more likely they will choose a parenting strategy that not only works in that situation but sets up success in the future.

Understanding normal development

One way the parent–child relationship is built is by the parent seeking to understand the reasons behind a child's behavior without assuming those reasons are negative. When a parent assumes the child has some devious intent or begins to label the child with negative descriptors (lazy, stubborn, and mean), opportunities for learning, growth, and supportive relationships are cut off. Behavior is usually very understandable when (1) developmental issues are kept in mind and (2) detailed information is obtained about the events, thoughts, and feelings leading up to the situation. A common example of this is believing the child is "lying" to parents when really children do not understand things the way adults do and fill in the gaps in their knowledge with things that do make sense to them. Of course, their perceptions and recollections are different than those of adults, but that does not mean they are telling lies. While children often deny they did the things that make their parents angry, this also does not mean they are untrustworthy liars. Children are very attached to parents and fear disappointing them. Understanding the reasons children might deny behaviors helps parents address behaviors. The goal is to help children take responsibility for their actions, not to lead them to thinking of themselves as a liar. Saying to a child, "I know you did this and are probably afraid to tell me because you are worried I'll be upset," has a different effect on the child than "You are such a liar! I'm sick and tired of you always lying to my face!"

A different example of parents being in a better position to parent by having some understanding of the child is when a child does not get off a video game immediately upon the parent asking. Sometimes if the parent really knew how the video game worked, it would be less of a personal affront that the child was not minding the parent immediately. Sometimes the child wants to finish a level and will lose their "work" if the game is stopped. Acknowledging that people generally do not like to be interrupted in the middle of something and told to immediately switch to a new task can help a parent understand the child's point of view. Parents who are patient and empathic with these issues can prevent conflict while still setting limits.

Understanding atypical development

Understanding the typical challenges that children face helps parents support children and builds the parent–child relationship. In addition to understanding normal development, parents should also be guided in understanding their children's identified struggles. Disorders, such as attention-deficit/hyperactivity disorder, autism spectrum disorder, learning disabilities, and mood disorders, can significantly interfere with children's abilities to manage their own behavior and emotions. Positive approaches to parenting keep avenues open by targeting obstacles interfering with children making better choices. When barriers can be overcome, children develop skills. The more skills developed, the less likely the special needs child is to be pigeonholed with negative qualities.

Building skills

Parents help children build skills. Vygotsky, a developmental psychologist from the early 1900s, noted that the key to children's learning is challenging them at the right level (the zone of proximal development) and providing the help they need to succeed ("scaffolding"; Arnett, 2012, p. 190). While Vygotsky focused on cognitive development, the same principles seem relevant to other aspects of development. It is important not to overwhelm children but persistently challenge them to do better socially, emotionally, and behaviorally. Thus positive approaches to parenting are in no way lax or permissive. They require enormous attention to the child's skill sets as well as supervision of the child's behavior in order to determine when to provide needed assistance and when to allow the child to struggle on her own.

In order to promote growth and skill building, effective parents praise a child's *effort* more than the outcome of the behavior. The research by Dweck (2006) shows that praising effort contributes to continued work toward a goal. Furthermore, Faber and Mazlish (2002) recommend using praise that is very specific and descriptive without value judgments. Instead of saying "good job" a parent should describe the behavior. For example, "I see you drew a yellow circle and a purple squiggle, and a red mark on this paper," or "I see you picked up the toys off the floor and put them away," or "I noticed you were ready when the ball was passed to you because you were paying attention during the game," or "I noticed that when your friend was over, you asked him what he wanted to play and did what he wanted first." These specific ways of giving feedback and reinforcement can be very effective in promoting a variety of positive behaviors.

Acceptance of feelings/collaboration

In addition to the understanding, support, and skill building described above, the parent–child relationship is also enhanced when parents help children sort out their thoughts and feelings without judgment or fear of punishment. Children need to learn how thoughts and feelings are related to the behavioral choices they make. Parents are in a unique position to help their children identify and differentiate amongst various feeling states and learn from their experiences, both positive and negative. For example, allowing children to have sad, anxious, or angry feelings and guiding them to express those feelings appropriately can result in adaptive coping.

A collaborative, problem-solving approach builds the parent–child relationship more than power assertion (e.g., coercion, using physical or psychological force) on the part of the parent. Power assertion techniques come with risks (see Knox, 2020) and are not recommended.

Showing respect

The parent–child relationship is also strengthened by showing respect. Adults who want children to respect them are encouraged to model that respect toward their children. For example, saying "Thank you," to children for doing tasks models behavior and provides positive reinforcement for the behavior. People, including children, are generally more responsive and open with others who have regard for their thoughts and feelings and treat them well. Here is an example of a parent being unnecessarily disrespectful to a child:

> During dinner at a restaurant, a 6 year old child misheard the waiter say "corn bread" instead of "warm bread." The child asked why the family was getting corn bread, and the parent scoffed at him in a demeaning way for mishearing.

This parent is communicating that the child's thoughts or questions are a nuisance of some sort. While any parent can be overly stressed and have less than ideal interactions with children on a given day, if this is an ongoing dynamic, it is problematic. Over time such interactions could promote feelings of inferiority, shame, and/or embarrassment in the child. Such negative feelings tend to be acted out by children with negative behaviors. Parents' respectful acceptance of children making mistakes builds the relationship and keeps dialog open. It is important to forgive the child for lacking skills or knowledge. An enormous amount of learning is taking place in them, but perfection will never be reached (as we adults are so very aware of for ourselves).

Prevention of problems

Parents using a positive approach to discipline attempt to prevent problematic situations as much as possible. Ensuring children get adequate sleep, providing healthy nutrition, and finding ways for children to burn off their energy through positive activities are essential. Prevention also means having structure at home with clear limits and expectations. Having a fairly organized approach to life helps tremendously and includes planning ahead, having routines, and following through on tasks. Positive parenting is strength based, and parents are encouraged to focus on the behaviors they *like* much more than those they view as negative or problematic. The behaviors given the most attention are the ones parents will see increase over time. Having expectations based on realistic appraisals of the child's level is crucial to having a strength based and developmentally appropriate approach to parenting. This is where a parent's understanding of the child's abilities is necessary. When the parent knows what the child is and is not capable of doing, the parent is able to challenge the child appropriately. For example, while some children are capable of remembering to bring home the things they need from school, other children need help with this.

Child behavior management strategies

When children are acting up, a first-tier parenting strategy would be to describe what the child is doing and reflect the possible feelings behind the behavior. This often leads to calming down and problem solving. Giving the child a prosocial choice and guiding the child may be all that's needed once the child is calmer. If reflecting feelings, describing behaviors, and providing gentle guidance are not enough, a system of positive reinforcement may be beneficial.

Token or point systems could be considered a second-tier strategy. Such systems allowing children to earn rewards for positive behaviors can be used to replace a recurring maladaptive behavior with an adaptive one. Working on one or two target behaviors at a time sets everybody up for success rather than failure. For example, helping a child to share toys with a younger sibling can involve noting the times the child shares, giving immediate positive verbal feedback, and assigning points. With a certain number of points the child earns a larger reward at the end of the activity or the day depending on the child's abilities and developmental level. The reward should be the child's choice from a menu of rewards the parent feels is appropriate. It is important to have a variety of possible small rewards including special time with a parent. Possibilities include small toys, special snacks, or special trips to the park or children's museum. For an older child, rewards can include time on their electronic devices as well as having friends over. Older children sometimes have to work on the completion of homework and being respectful to parents. Again points can be earned on a daily basis for such positive behaviors and then cashed in at a later date. Even if using a point system for rewards, reflecting feelings is helpful. For example, the feelings of not wanting to do homework can easily be acknowledged and validated while expecting the student to get the homework done and earn a reward (e.g., screen or playtime).

One common behavior many parents complain about is the child leaving the wet towel on the floor. The parent should carefully monitor the behavior, to consistently and quickly notice the towel on the floor or the rack. If the towel is on the rack verbal praise or a simple "thank you" can be given. If the towel is on the floor, the parent may give a reminder. If the child hangs it up with just one quick reminder, points can be earned. When the child masters doing this with a reminder, the parent can tell the child that she now will earn points for hanging it up without the reminder. Reminders should be a simple description of the problem, such as "I see a wet towel on the floor." It is important to resist the temptation to add negative comments such as "How many times do I have to tell you ...." If the wet towel on the floor becomes an emotionally charged situation, it becomes much more difficult to resolve.

If the child is unable or unwilling to stop an unacceptable behavior following the above positive strategies, then the third-tier strategy would be to deliver a mild negative consequence such as time out or removal of privileges. The proper use of time out is described by Dadds and Tully (2019) and includes explaining it to the child before use, using it in a predictable fashion for behaviors the child can actually control, remaining calm while using it, and making sure the use of time out does not involve any threat to the attachment relationship between the parent and the child. Time out from reinforcement is only effective if there are reinforcing and rewarding aspects of the child's life. Lack of attention from a parent is only useful if the child regularly receives positive attention from a parent. Thus time out must be used in the context of a warm and positive parent–child relationship. During time out, parents should avoid engaging verbally and nonverbally with the child. Time outs should be done in a place without reinforcers, namely away from fun, engaging or reinforcing people, objects, screens, etc. Time outs should be as brief as possible while still making the point that the behavior is unacceptable. The suggestion for a minute for every year of a child's age is often recommended meaning a 3-year old gets 3 minutes, etc. However, Dadds and Tully (2019) recommend ending time out when the child has calmed down rather than using an arbitrary time period. Ideally the procedure helps teach self-regulation and alternative positive behaviors. If time out is not effective, it is likely that caregivers are not using it properly. In that case a review of how time out fits in with the overall discipline strategy and parent–child relationship would be in order.

Removal of privileges is another negative consequence that is useful in the parenting toolbox. However, this tool should be used judiciously. Privilege removal needs to be planned in advance, that is, children should be told if the target behavior occurs, a specific privilege will be removed for a certain amount of time. Included in this plan should be a very clear description of when and how the child can then earn it back with good behavior. This plan should be well understood by the child prior to use of the technique, rather than introduced in the heat of the moment once negative behavior has occurred. It is easy to come up with less than ideal ways of removing privileges when angry (e.g., grounding the child "for life"). Parents should avoid giving consequences that wind up punishing themselves (canceling a night over at a grandmother's house that would relieve the parents of childcare, canceling dinner plans for the family). Parents should not threaten consequences that would be too hard to carry out without the child developing significant resentment (e.g., not taking a 6-year-old trick or treating, missing a best friend's birthday party). The purpose of discipline is to teach children how to behave better, not leave them with lasting memories of significant disappointment and anger.

Hitting is an example of a behavior that might warrant time out or removal of privileges. Time out for hitting could include the parent calmly doing the following:

- Removal of a child to a time out chair facing a wall.
- 5-minute time out for a 5-year old.
- No interaction during time out.
- If a child is cooperative going to time out, release the child at 3 minutes or as soon as able to calmly process the situation (e.g., discussion of feelings, what led up to behavior, and other ways of handling difficult feelings and situations).
- If child is uncooperative going to time out, release the child at 6–7 minutes. Process the situation when both parent and child are calm.

Removal of privileges for ongoing hitting could include the following:

- Calm discussion of ongoing problem of hitting.
- Acceptance and discussion of angry feelings with parental validation of angry feelings while communicating that hitting is unacceptable even when angry.
- Clear understanding that from now on, the child will lose electronics for an hour or for the day (parent decides ahead of time) if the child hits.
- Privilege (e.g., electronics) will be returned at the end of the time only if no hitting has occurred during that time.

Parent behavior management strategies

Because it is important for the consequences to fit the child's behavior, parents need to be able to think through how best to teach a child a lesson. Handout 1 provides reminders and tips to guide parents through this process. It is important to stay calm during parenting in order to think about the situation in different ways. Clearly, the behavior strategies described thus far require planning and forethought as well as a good judgment about how best to respond. It is a lot to ask of parents. Because all parents lose their temper from time to time and say things they do not mean, it is also recommended to own this when it happens. Apologies from parents to children for things said or done do all of the following: (1) model appropriate behavior, (2) communicate that parents are human and make mistakes too, and (3) show the child the care and concern that the parent feels.

Keeping the long-term goal in mind during parenting and not being overreactive to every misstep is also fundamental to this approach. Children internalize values over time, seem to question them (if not completely lose them) during the teenage years, and then often return to the ways they have been taught. It is important for parents to understand that their job is to *influence* behavior rather than *control* it. Children have to take responsibility for their behavior. If parents are attempting to control children's behavior, they do not get a chance to be responsible for themselves. Even in the most anxiety-provoking situations such as a child not eating following a choking incident, it is the child who must decide to swallow food again. Parents have powerful strategies of being able to guide, model, incentivize, and teach behavior reflecting the values they hope children will internalize. However, none of these reflect absolute control, and there is no guarantee children will follow the parent's lead. Parents can do their part in fostering the success of the child but cannot prevent all failures. Learning from mistakes requires the child taking responsibility for the failure. Acceptance of who the child is, instead of who the parent wanted the child to be, is vital to this process.

When children are young, they are generally eager to please and seem malleable. However, even when young, they assert themselves. Using strategies other than power assertion has a payoff in the long run, particularly during the teenage years. Teens often respond to power assertion with their own assertion of power. It is developmentally normal for adolescent youths to assert themselves more intensely despite continued immaturity. Thus the common occurrence of slammed doors, disrespectful tone of voice, and outright telling parents how "crazy," "stupid," or "mean" they are. Parents understandably do not like these undiplomatic attempts at independence and may choose to implement planned negative consequences as described above. However, some parents may react with power assertion rather than planned consequences or collaborative problem solving. Power assertion is particularly risky during the teenage years as teens are much more likely to react to parental force with their own use of force which ultimately can lead to domestic violence between parent and youth. Parents managing their own behavior can help children of all ages thrive.

Evidence in support of positive approaches to parenting

So what's the evidence that these positive, collaborative approaches to parenting are beneficial? To some, they sound like they would generate spoiled kids who cannot handle the reality of life. Life can be harsh, so kids should be raised to know that and get used to it, right? Parents cannot always be pandering to kids; bosses are not going to coddle them the way today's parents do. While such questions are understandable, the research would suggest that children raised with positive parenting strategies are in the best position to handle the general stresses and responsibilities of being an adult. Examples of research findings from each area of child development: physiological/health, cognitive, socioemotional, and behavioral are examined next. This is not meant to be an exhaustive review but rather to give a flavor of the type of research findings related to positive parenting and child development.

Health

Research has identified multiple health benefits of positive approaches to parenting. For example, maternal nurturing behavior offsets the negative consequences of low socioeconomic status (SES) on risk factors for diabetes, heart disease, and stroke (Miller et al., 2011). Low SES is associated with a higher prevalence of metabolic syndrome in adulthood. However, maternal nurturance (as measured in part by time, attention, and understanding) proved to be a protective factor against metabolic syndrome among adults from low SES backgrounds. Similarly, Chen, Brody, and Miller (2017) summarize findings with regard to high maternal responsiveness and parental support mitigating the effects of stress on adolescent allostatic load and adolescent telomere length, respectively.

Gottman and Declaire (1997) found that children have better physical health when their parents are good "emotional coaches." These parents guide their children in dealing with naturally occurring emotions by recognizing the emotion, validating it, helping the child verbalize the feelings, and setting limits on behaviors while exploring ways of dealing with problems. Looking at vagal tone from physiological data, these children are more able to self-soothe and recover more quickly from stress compared to children without "emotion-coaching" parents.

Children are able to remain calmer when adults reflect their feelings back to them. Putting a name to feelings calms the amygdala and activates the prefrontal region in the brain to help slow emotional responses and feel better (Lieberman et al., 2007).

Cognitive development

With regard to cognitive development, Neville et al. (2013) cite research showing that parenting impacts stress levels and learning in children. The researchers developed a parent training intervention to increase selective attention, a core capacity involved in learning. In addition to exercises in selective attention, a parent training group addressed family stress regulation, contingency-based discipline, parental responsiveness, and language use. It was modified from the Linking the Interests of Families and Teachers program (Eddy, Reid, & Fetrow, 2000) which is developmentally sensitive, collaborative, and strength based. Neville et al. (2013) found that children from Head Start whose parents participated in the parent training group had the most improvements in selective attention, language, and IQ. Furthermore, the researchers reported gains in children's social skills and decreases in problem behaviors.

Armor (2017) identifies parental nurturing as an important factor in improving a child's IQ and academic achievement. He estimates small but significant gains in children's IQ and achievement when parents provide emotional support. Such gains are estimated to be most salient in children who have parents who are average in their teaching skills. In other words, most parents are the most effective in teaching children when teaching is combined with emotional support for the task of learning.

It is possible that the improved academic gains are due to emotional support calming the stress level of the child, and thus decreasing the amount of cortisol in the system. Cortisol is the hormone released under stress. Some stress is necessary for learning something new. However, too much cortisol can damage neurons in the hippocampus, a brain structure involved in learning and memory. Children who experience repeated stress and trauma have been shown to have changes in the hippocampus (Perry, 2001).

Social–emotional/behavioral development

Data from Gottman and Declaire (1997) suggest that children of parents who do a lot of "emotion-coaching" score higher academically have fewer behavior problems and get along better with friends than children whose parents do not provide such guidance. More recently, Waller et al. (2015) report longitudinal data to show that higher levels of positive behavior support from parents at age 2 were related to better outcomes in children at age 7. Specifically (1) increased effortful control, (2) higher academic skills, (3) better social competence, and (4) decreased problem behaviors were noted. Positive behavior support is described as parents providing structure proactively, being warm, being sensitive to children's emotions, and providing rewards for positive child behaviors.

Outcomes for specific parenting interventions such as the Positive Parenting Program (Triple P) also support the idea that positive parenting is effective (Bodenmann, Cina, Ledermann, & Sanders, 2008; Nowak & Heinrichs, 2008; Sanders et al., 2014). Triple P teaches parents strategies for developing their child's competence and managing their behavior. Furthermore, parents are taught to plan routine activities, set goals, and observe both their child's and their own behaviors. Nowak and Heinrichs' (2008) metaanalysis of Triple P shows improvements in (1) parenting skills, (2) child problem behavior, and (3) parental well-being. The meta-analysis by Sanders et al. (2014) shows short- and long-term positive effects on (1) child social, emotional, and behavioral outcomes; (2) parenting practices; (3) parenting satisfaction and efficacy; and (4) parental adjustment. These results demonstrate that parents who avoid aversive interactions with children and replace those interactions with supportive, positive interactions experience better child and parent outcomes.

The power of positive approaches to parenting in promoting the desired social, emotional, and behavioral outcomes in children is well-supported. Biglan, Flay, Embry, and Sandler (2012) argue, "if we want to prevent multiple problems and increase the prevalence of young people who develop successfully, we must increase the prevalence of nurturing environments" (p. 258). These researchers discuss how a nurturing environment is a common factor in the *prevention* of problems that often cooccur: academic failure, crime, mental illness, drug addiction, risky sexual behavior, and other societal problems. They review the evidence that nurturing environments at home and school do the following: (1) minimize aversive events and the impact of toxic conditions, (2) augment prosocial skills important to living productively and having caring relationships, (3) reduce opportunities for problem behavior, and (4) promote psychological flexibility which includes awareness of one's thoughts and feelings. The benefits of these four areas in preventing mental, emotional, and behavioral problems strongly support their thesis that nurturing environments are critical for human well-being.

Evidence with special populations

What about children who are more challenging? What about kids with attention deficit hyperactivity disorder (ADHD), oppositional defiant disorder, depression, or anxiety? What about children with significant family stress like conflict and divorce? What about children prone to aggression or delinquency? Do they need more "serious" discipline? It turns out that at-risk children can benefit significantly from positive parenting approaches. Examples from children with internalizing and externalizing disorders are discussed below after a brief discussion of examples of other at-risk youth.

Children in families with high levels of parental conflict are considered at-risk. However, the quality of the parent–child relationship is a better predictor of children's outcomes than the interparental conflict, as long as the conflict is not so severe that it becomes violent (Nielson, 2017). Furthermore, Gottman and Declaire (1997) found that parents who were good at emotional coaching protected their children from the negative sequelae of conflict, separation, and divorce.

Physiologically, early puberty is a risk factor for aggressive behavior. However, Chen and Raine (2018) showed that parenting style impacted the relationship between early puberty and aggression. Harsh parenting was associated with aggressive behavior in early maturing individuals as compared to on-time or late-maturing individuals. However, positive parenting of early maturing individuals was negatively associated with aggressive behavior. In other words, the more positive the parenting, the less likely the early maturing youths were to be aggressive despite the risk associated with early maturity.

Similarly, temperamental fearlessness in children poses some risk for the development of callous-unemotional behaviors (Waller et al., 2016). Waller et al. (2016) found that adoptive parents high in positive parenting provided a protective factor for fearless children. The fearless children with parents high in positive parenting had no additional risk of callous-unemotional behaviors. This was in contrast to those fearless children whose adoptive parents were low in positive parenting. Those children showed a much higher correlation between fearlessness and callous-unemotional behaviors. Thus the risk of the development of callous-unemotional behaviors in fearless children is mitigated by positive parenting techniques.

Internalizing disorders

Other children with vulnerabilities include those with mental health diagnoses. Youths with anxiety and depression benefit from positive parenting. The Anxiety and Depression Association of America (n.d.) recommends the following tips for parenting a child with anxiety: pay attention to your child's feelings, stay calm, praise small accomplishments, do not punish mistakes, be flexible, have appropriate expectations, and plan for difficult situations. Parenting a child with a mood disorder like depression is complicated as the child may act up easily due to irritability but may also be quick to feel worthless and deserving of whatever punishment is meted out. Anxious children can be difficult to parent given the lengths they will go to avoid whatever it is they fear. This often looks like extremely defiant behavior but comes from anxiety. In either of these cases, parents using a gentle and more understanding approach may be the most effective and beneficial. This does not mean that children with internalizing disorders are routinely excused from chores, school, or family events. Understanding the behavior gives parents more tools and strategies to promote more adaptive behavior. Picking which issues to work on and supporting the youth during the process are key aspects of a positive approach to parenting children with internalizing disorders, as the example below illustrates.

> A child with significant social anxiety refused to go to school out of overwhelming anxiety more than out of defiance to parents. While the goal was to return the child to school, the child had to be challenged at the right level so that the anxiety was manageable and confidence was built. It took several steps to help the child back to school. One of those steps involved really understanding from the child's point of view the difficulty in attending school. This understanding was used to facilitate visualizing overcoming the specific hurdles with the child and then collaboratively making a plan for the child to return to school. The pacing of the return to school was faster than the youth preferred but slower than the parent wanted. This youth was not in school at all in the Spring when the debilitating anxiety began. The youth had a large summer packet of work over the Summer and sought treatment. The youth attended 2 classes at school in the Fall with additional on-line classes, and subsequently attended 4 classes at school in the Spring with additional classes taken on-line. This was the pace that allowed for success for this youth. Forcing the anxious youth back in to school without preparation and practice of skills might have resulted in the youth going to school and having a full blown panic attack. This would have only added to the youth's social embarrassment, resistance going to school, and oppositional behaviors.

Researchers reviewing positive parenting and its association with anxiety and depression in African-American children have found a buffering effect of parenting practices (Washington et al., 2017). Parental support, parental encouragement, and positive parental role models were associated with lower levels of anxiety and depression in the studies reviewed. Similarly, in an ethnically diverse sample, Graham and Weems (2014) found that positive parenting including praise and compliments moderated the association between parent and child anxiety sensitivity. Children of parents high in positive parenting had less anxiety sensitivity than children of parents low in positive parenting.

Externalizing disorders

Much has been written about the importance of parenting with regard to managing the behavior of children with the externalizing disorders. Barkley's (2013) recommendations for parenting a child with ADHD are in line with positive parenting approaches. He suggests, for example, providing brief, simple, clear commands one step at a time; giving immediate, frequent, positive praise and reinforcement for good behaviors; using powerful incentives; using time out for misbehavior; planning ahead for problems; understanding ADHD as a disability; providing external supports (especially for motivation and time management); and not taking the child's behavior personally. All of these fit with a positive approach to parenting—pay attention to the child, challenge the child at the right level, use rewards more than punishment, understand the world through the child's point of view, accept the child for who he is while guiding him to his potential. And, stay calm.

One study examined outcomes of an eight-session behavioral parent training class for parents who presented to outpatient treatment for difficulties associated with raising a child with ADHD (Loren et al., 2015). This intervention focused on parent–child interactions, child compliance, increasing positive child behaviors, and strategies like time out to reduce problem behaviors. Results indicated significant improvements in the parent–child interactions, reduced overall impairment in the child, and reduced negative impact of ADHD on the family.

Greene's (2014) "Collaborative and Proactive Solutions" program draws on principles of staying calm to think clearly in order to get to collaborative problem solving. His first step of collaborative problem solving is for the parent to be empathic with the child and to be a "surrogate frontal lobe" as needed for the child. Furthermore, he recommends being very clear about which problem behaviors need to be addressed and which can be let go. In this program, parents are taught to solve problems using a collaborative approach with their child and taught to abandon the use of imposing adult will on children. The results of research on Collaborative and Proactive Solutions show that it is effective in addressing oppositional and defiant behaviors. Both a collaborative approach and a Barkley-based behavioral management approach result in equivalent decreases in problem child behaviors (Ollendick et al., 2016).

Parent–Child Interaction Therapy, developed by Eyberg (1988) for oppositional and defiant children, is similarly encouraging of parents to be very attentive to children and describe the positives in the child's behavior. Through guided parent/child play interactions, parents learn to use PRIDE skills (Praise, Reflect, Imitate, Describe, and Enjoyment) that are designed to enhance the parent–child relationship and promote positive child behaviors. The results of research on this program indicate improved child behavior with reductions in the frequency and intensity of problem behavior (Cooley, Veldorale-Griffin, Petren, & Mullis, 2014)

The ACT Raising Safe Kids program (Silva, 2011) is an interactive, nine-session program that addresses child development, roots and consequences of violence; anger management for adults; anger management for children; social problem solving; positive discipline; and media violence. The program helps parents to master nonviolent discipline techniques, such as positive reinforcement for compliant and prosocial behavior, use of developmentally appropriate consequences, and consistent limit-setting. Research on ACT has demonstrated reduced harsh, coercive, and punitive parenting, and increased parental nurturing and positive parenting practices (Howe et al., 2017; Portwood, Lambert, Abrams, & Nelson, 2011). Children whose parents participated in ACT have been shown to have fewer behavioral problems including less bullying behavior (Burkhart, Knox, & Brockmyer, 2013; Knox & Burkhart, 2014).

In addition to children with various disorders and problematic behaviors, there is also a support for more positive approaches for youth involved in the justice system and youth prone to psychopathy. Juvenile justice has undergone a reformation due to the negative outcomes associated with punitive approaches. Locking young people up with other troubled youths contributes to a higher, not lower, risk of delinquency (PEW Charitable Trusts, 2015). Stephen Bishop, a senior associate with the Annie E Casey Foundation's Juvenile Justice Strategy Group summarizes the positive approach to juvenile justice nicely, "All kids need to be held accountable, but it does not need to be in a punitive way" (Personal communication, July 2018). The Balanced and Restorative Justice Model (Office of Juvenile Justice and Delinquency Prevention, 1998) focuses on true accountability rather than punishment and following rules. True accountability involves acknowledging one's role in harming another, repairing the harm as much as possible, and learning not to cause harm in the future. Such a program was implemented in Oakland, California using a community conferencing model. This model allows for juvenile offenders to make amends with their victims. During the conference, youths are asked to be completely candid about what they have done. A plan for restitution is then made that the victim agrees is fair. Initial data show that juveniles involved in this program have an 11.8% rate of recidivism versus a rate of 31.4% for matched controls (Kelly, 2015).

Experts working in Juvenile Justice have learned that focusing on the deficits of troubled teens does not lead to the desired outcomes. The development of a strength-based approach, called Positive Youth Justice (PYJ), shows far more promise. Relationship building is a crucial aspect of

PYJ which helps youth increase feelings of attachment and belonging in a community. PYJ also works to increase the youths' skills by engaging in prosocial activities and demonstrating competencies. Outcomes include high rates of prosocial relationships, low rates of recidivism, and high levels of graduation and employment (Butts, Bazemore, & Meroe, 2010).

Lastly, a relevant case study supporting the impact of positive parenting:

> Neuroscientist James Fallon became suspicious of his brain scan due to it being similar to those of psychopaths. Furthermore, genetic testing supported the idea that while a productive member of society, he is prone to psychopathy and violence. Dr. Fallon came to the conclusion that he is indeed a psychopath but what he calls a "pro-social psychopath." He argues that the love he received from his parents protected him. He was given an especially large amount of attention due to a series of miscarriages preceding his birth. Dr. Fallon believes this attention and the parental affection he received were crucial to him becoming a nonviolent, although "obnoxiously competitive," successful person (Stromberg, 2013).

Obstacles to positive parenting and recommendations to overcome them

Now that positive parenting approaches have been described and shown to be supported by research, let us turn to why it is so hard to implement them at times. With all the evidence in support of positive parenting approaches why are they not part of the public lexicon, well-known and practiced widely? Why is it hard for people to embrace the ideas of (1) nurturance over harshness and (2) learning from mistakes over punishment? There are multiple obstacles to using positive approaches: remaining calm, time, energy, executive functioning skills of prioritizing and planning, verbal skills, emotion regulation, empathy, developmental understanding of the child, and feeling effective as a parent. These barriers are discussed next with some ideas of how to overcome them.

Remaining calm

The role of stress likely impacts parenting as demonstrated by a report from the Office of the Minister for Children and Youth Affairs (2009) that found that parents report being a "bit more likely" to use physical punishment when they are worried or scared about the child, when the child behaved aggressively, or if the parent has had a hard day. These are all situations in which stress would be high. Remaining calm or making a point to calm down before disciplining is particularly important. In fact, the biology of stress is incompatible with the biology of self-control because "nothing drains willpower faster than stress" (McGonigal, 2012, p. 51). When humans are stressed, the fight-or-flight response directs people to act instinctively with immediate, short-term goals in mind. However, effective parenting requires keeping the bigger picture in mind. When parents purposefully manage their stress and calm themselves in order to remain in control while disciplining, their physiology changes. The physiological system activated when people engage in any sort of effortful self-regulation (e.g., acting thoughtfully or carefully) has been named the "Pause and Plan" system (Segerstrom, Boggero, & Evans, 2016). The Pause and Plan system lowers heart rate along with increasing heart rate variability. These physiological changes are associated with increased self-control. Thus parental efforts make a difference at a physiological level, and these physiological changes help make a difference at a behavioral level. Parents taking deep breaths, counting to 10, or naming their internal struggle (e.g., "I want to scream at him but that won't help") involve purposeful effort and thus likely activate the Pause and Plan system. It is vital that parents remain in control as actions toward youth that show the adult to be out of control are particularly problematic. Such behaviors can escalate the conflict, leading to harsh parenting, and even abuse. Furthermore, youth see through the hypocrisy of adults who do not self-regulate while asking youth do so at all times (Ford, Chapman, Connor, & Cruise, 2012).

Time

One obstacle to using positive parenting approaches is having limited time. It takes time to lay the foundation for success. For example, walking through a chore with a child many times before the child does it on her own takes time but can be well worth it. When there is misbehavior, it takes time to describe and reflect feelings, to calm down and think about possible responses, and to implement the consequence a parent has decided is appropriate. Sometimes there is not enough time to intervene before Johnny has hit Susie about 20 more times. A brief intervention in this case would be for the parent to physically stop the aggression by separating the kids or taking away any objects used for aggression. A parent can say something like "You're angry but hitting is not okay." A brief time-out may be given. Then later when there is more time and everyone is calm, several things can be done: (1) reflect the anger that led to the hitting, (2) discuss how the child can notice internal sensations associated with anger (e.g., feeling hot, muscles tensing, fists clenching) before any explosive behavior, (3) discuss thoughts that occurred before during and after the incident, (4) explore other ways to express anger, (5) practice asking for help when angry feelings are noticed; (6) find appropriate amends for having hit, and (7) decide on appropriate consequences for future hitting. Such a conversation would clearly take time and would likely be more productive if participants did not feel rushed.

Prioritizing, planning, and being proactive

Being *pro*active versus *re*active to children requires energy, thoughtfulness, and planning. It is important for parents to be careful with how their energy is expended and make sure to leave some for themselves and their children. Parents thinking carefully about how the family will spend time and energy and saying "no" to things that really are not a priority for the family is highly recommended. There is a lot of societal pressure to go, go, go and do, do, do but stopping to think about how a particular event fits in with the family's time, energy, and resources is part of family management. Time and energy are limited and must be used judiciously. Being clear about priorities is a way of teaching parental values to children. Making sure enough planning occurs to make time for priorities models time management skills as well as communicates values.

Verbal and emotion regulation skills

From a young age, being able to understand and express one's feelings helps a person regulate emotions, especially anger (Roben, Cole, & Armstrong, 2013). For the less naturally verbal parent, tasks of verbalizing feeling states can be challenging. Parents can learn the skills of identifying and expressing feeling states for themselves as well as their children. Ordway, Webb, Sadler, and Slade (2014) emphasize the importance of providers helping parents to recognize their own and their child's separate emotional states in order for parents to be able to properly communicate about those emotional states. When emotional states are not recognized there is a potential for miscommunication between parents and children which may result in emotional dysregulation. Ordway et al. (2014) advocate for helping parents take a "reflective stance" of curiosity and wonder about their child's behavior. Parents thinking out loud about a child's behavior can improve their own ability to regulate themselves. As with learning any skill, continued practice is essential. Parents who slow down enough to verbalize thoughts and feelings as they occur in real time are also modeling verbal and emotional regulation skills for children. Making such an effort will likely engage the Pause and Plan system described above. Parents who model, reflect, identify, and manage emotions are likely to have improved communication and relationships with their children. As the parent training literature reviewed above has shown, enhanced relationships often result in improved outcomes for parents and children.

Empathy and listening

While those who are less verbal might feel at a disadvantage, the power of listening should not be underestimated. Lippold, Duncan, Coatsworth, Nix, and Greenberg (2015) found that "mindful parenting" [characterized by (1) present-centered, nonjudgmental awareness, (2) nonreactivity, and (3) compassion] was associated with improved parent–child communication with adolescents. Youths were more likely to disclose information to parents who were rated higher in listening with full attention, having emotional awareness, being self-regulated, and displaying acceptance and compassion. These behaviors often translate to youths feeling supported. Unfortunately, local data and follow-up focus groups with high school youth in one metropolitan area in the United States (Lucas County Community Health Assessment, 2017, p. 138) reveal that youth often do not feel support from the adults in their lives. Youth perceive adults as telling them what to do, being punitive, or judging them rather than listening to them and trying to understand the issues they face. This dynamic was especially true for discussing difficult topics such as substance use and relationships. A parent who can listen in order to understand is a huge asset to a child; furthermore, listening can wind up saving time and energy. The following is an example of the importance of staying calm and keeping the conversation going in order to have the youth's point of view.

> A teenager planned to go with friends to a Hawaiian themed dance at school in February. He wanted to wear summer clothes and no coat when it was about 20 degrees outside. The parent immediately said "no" to that idea. The youth got mad and began arguing. The argument got disrespectful enough that the youth was barred from going to the dance at all, much to his disappointment. In an appointment with the teen and his mother, the healthcare provider asked the teen to tell about the incident, giving him, for the first time, a platform to verbalize his thought process as follows: He would have been dropped off at the dance. He would need to be outside in the cold for about 30 seconds getting into the car and another 30 seconds from the car to inside the school. Inside the school it would be hot with everybody dancing. He knew the coats would be strewn across a classroom floor and that people would not hesitate to walk all over them when dropping off and picking up their own coats. He did not want his coat to get trampled on. He did not think he needed his coat as he would be hot while at the dance, and he would be exposed to the cold for only two very short periods. This was the first time the youth's thought process had been explained to the mother who stated that, had she known all this, she would have readily allowed him to go to the dance without a coat.

While the youth bears responsibility for not being able to express all this without becoming disrespectful toward his mother, teens are not known for their diplomatic skills. Parents who ask about the youth's thinking are in a better position to make parenting decisions. Furthermore, keeping in mind the developmental needs of teens to be with their friends in prosocial activities is important so that parents do not take this privilege away too frequently. Resentment between teen and parent can build to unhealthy levels when this consequence is overused.

Developmental understanding

Children are like young scientists trying to understand a world that does not always make sense to them. This leads to common child behaviors that can be embarrassing (e.g., publicly asking why that person is so small and without legs). Helping children understand their world can be a challenge to parents who only see problem behavior and do not understand why a child is acting that way. Here is an example from a 7-year old at the beach which includes seemingly odd behavior from the child in a public place.

> A mother repeatedly observed her daughter rinse her body off with the showers at the beach, dry herself off with a towel, and then go lie down in the sand only to become very upset and repeat the process over starting with rinsing her body off in the shower, drying herself off and lying in the sand again. This behavior made no sense to the mother who saw her daughter become increasingly upset and crying as she continued with the behavior. She knew her daughter was prone to emotional upset and was getting increasingly nervous about how the grandparents would be reacting to such a scene. Trying to remain calm and genuinely curious about what the daughter was trying to accomplish, the mother probed what the child was doing, simply saying "You keep washing sand off but keep getting more on you." It turned out that the daughter was testing to make sure her skin was dry by lying in the sand after she dried off. She thought she was doing a poor job of drying herself off because every time she lay down, sand stuck to her. She kept trying to do a better job of drying herself off but kept failing. With this information, it was relatively easy to let the daughter know that sand will stick to bodies even when the body is as dry as possible. Being reassured that this is normal helped the daughter get dressed and leave the beach like everybody else, with a little sand still uncomfortably stuck to her despite her best efforts.

This situation righted itself, but the parent, embarrassed by the child's frantic behavior, could have easily gone down a punitive route. Being impatient or frustrated by the child's behavior may have escalated the situation with the child ultimately feeling like even more of a failure. Saying things such as "What is wrong with you?" or "Cut it out!" do not help build trust in the parent–child relationship and can shut down communication. Seeking to understand what is going through a child's head can provide key information that is indispensable to parenting effectively.

In addition to understanding the specifics of the child in a situation, it is important to have a general understanding about appropriate expectations at different ages. Children are often behaving in ways associated with their age, not because they have a personal vendetta against their parents. Infants often cry, 2-year olds frequently say "no" and tantrum; 3–4-year olds like to do things on their own even when it takes a very long time (e.g., button their own sweater); 9-year olds like to feel a sense of mastery and may cheat to win; and teens want independence but are still learning social grace. There are many resources about typical development at various ages that are worth becoming familiar with as a parent. The Centers for Disease Control and Prevention (n.d.) and the American Psychological Association (n.d.) have information about milestones and typical development, especially of younger children.

Feeling ineffective

Another significant obstacle to positive parenting is feeling helpless and desperate for some sign that parenting strategies are working. In the Irish study previously mentioned (Office of the Minister for Children and Youth Affairs, 2009), the researchers also found that parents report being a "bit more likely" to use physical punishment when the child continues misbehaving or when the parent feels he has lost control of the child. Parents can feel ineffective for a variety of reasons—the child is generally more difficult to parent, the child is having a bad day and not responsive to parenting, the parenting strategy was not the best match for that child at that time, the parent's anxieties are coming across too much, or the child will have to hear and experience this life lesson multiple times before complying. It is important not to trade feeling helpless for becoming punitive toward the child just to prove that something is being done. While that may help the parent feel better temporarily, it does not necessarily help the child learn and grow. It is not always easy to see the rewards of parenting efforts in terms of the child making progress. While parents must accept that they do not have complete control of the outcome, it does not mean their efforts are going to waste. Sometimes the child backslides despite the best efforts of parents. Unfortunately, there are no guarantees about how a child will thrive as an adult; too many factors impact development. But keeping in mind that research suggests children do best over time with positive parenting can help calm parents' fears of being ineffective.

Public embarrassment and societal pressure

Below is an example of a 3-year old running errands with his mother and grandmother after 8:00 p.m. The difference between a positive approach and a less positive approach will be highlighted as others in the store were drawn into the scene.

> The 3 year old was crying and screaming loudly while sitting in the cart being pushed by his grandmother. To the mother's credit, she said nothing negative towards the child and just tried to finish her tasks. The grandmother was charged with handling the youngster. She tried several different approaches none of which worked completely. At one point, she got him laughing by distracting him, but he soon resumed the crying and screaming. The grandmother then noticed a stranger observing and used it as a strategy of shame, saying, "That lady is looking at you." She also threatened spanking but did not carry it out.

While the grandmother had multiple strategies, there was no attempt to validate the child's feelings. There was no acknowledgment such as, "You want something and no one is giving you what you want," or "You are screaming very loudly because you are sad and mad. Let me guess what you want." She could have started a silly guessing game and had the youngster tell her she was wrong about her guesses about what he wanted. She could have reflected feelings and added distraction saying, "You want out. You want to go home. What would be fun to do when you get home?" None of this would mean that the parent would take the child out of the cart and abandon the shopping. It simply would have been acknowledgment of a bad situation and focusing on a better future. Sometimes giving the child what he wants in fantasy is enough (Faber & Mazlish, 2002). For example, imagine this youngster was crying because he really wanted the huge stuffed animal that he had seen. While still being clear no stuffed animal would be bought, a discussion of where he would put it in the house, what he would name it, and who he would share it with could all be discussed. In this way a parent can give a child the fantasy of having things that generally cannot be had. While there is no guarantee the above strategies would have consoled the child enough to have him stop screaming, they would have been preferable to what occurred next.

> During the checkout, the cashier seemingly tried to console the child to no good effect. Suddenly, the cashier loudly exclaimed, "You're mean!" to the 3 year old. She then turned to the mother and said, "Does he really think he'll get his way?!" in an incredulous tone of voice. Another worker was walking by and stated in a nonjudgmental tone of voice, "My 2 year old does the same thing." The mother replied, "He's 3," to which the easy going worker said, "Well, even as an adult, don't we all wish we could scream like that sometimes."

The difference between the accepting adult worker and the cashier is striking. The one understands that sometimes kids and adults just need to express their negative emotions and it does not mean much other than, "This stinks." The other draws a conclusion about the personality of a 3-year old and speaks to him with significant disrespect. If a child is repeatedly told he is mean or that she has some other negative quality, over time this identity could be internalized, and the child may act mean in keeping with his new identity and the expectation of others. If the child learns that his feelings are valid and understandable, he is more likely to learn to cope with negative emotions over time. Positive parenting is not about just stopping the crying with rewards and incentives; sometimes kids need to cry. When kids are upset, avoiding punitive strategies while reflecting feelings at the moment can be an effective strategy to help the child self-regulate.

Struggles between youth and parents can be very public, and one contributor to parental stress is parental fear of making mistakes and feeling judged by society. Such fears can have an impact on the ability to be positive toward children while disciplining. There is a fair amount of societal judgment of parents whose kids are acting up. Parents are expected to *do* something to stop disruptive behavior. The pressure to do something can lead to punitive approaches. Positive parenting involves the prevention of negative interactions in public by avoiding shopping when people are tired, hungry, or otherwise stressed out. Furthermore, when errands need to be run despite everyone being tired and hungry, preparing the child for this being difficult may payoff. Using collaborative problem solving to brainstorm *before* going into the store about how they will get through the store without a meltdown might be worth the 5 minutes it would take. Of course, this situation might not have needed anything other than adults accepting that children need to cry and scream sometimes when they do not get their way, but that does not make them "mean."

Summary

This chapter has focused on a positive approach to parenting in the hopes that understanding what it is, why it is recommended, and what gets in the way could help parents use it more often. The ideas have been around for some time, and research supports the power of positive parenting and nurturing environments in the prevention of negative outcomes for children. Children do better physiologically, cognitively, socially, emotionally, and behaviorally when parents use positive strategies of child management. Positive parenting is recommended for the general population as well as for parents of children with more specific needs, including internalizing and externalizing disorders. High-risk children have been shown to specifically benefit from positive parenting, although it may be more difficult for parents to maintain a positive approach with behaviorally difficult children. Parents are advised to take time to understand their children and their levels of development when making parenting decisions. Barriers to implementing positive approaches include parents' difficulty remaining calm, having the time and energy to use positive parenting strategies, not being proactive or planning ahead, not having the necessary verbal skills especially with regard to reflecting feelings, not being able to see things from the child's point of view, and feeling ineffective and/or judged. Professionals, friends, and family members can share information and guide parents in learning skills and providing support for positive approaches knowing that these strategies lead to better outcomes for parents as well as children. The stress of parenting is high, but the rewards can be even greater, especially when parents subscribe to these positive approaches and the parent–child relationship is enhanced.

Frequently asked questions

1. *Does positive parenting mean your kids should never feel bad?*

   There is no getting around having negative emotions in life. Part of positive parenting is reflecting the child's emotions in order to learn how to cope with them. It is not about trying to take away the negative feelings just because they are unpleasant. Allowing children to struggle and grow is clearly part of positive parenting. The first part of problem solving is identifying the problem, and feelings are often the first clue that a problem exists. Ignoring feelings often means a delay in problem solving. Positive parenting addresses negative feelings head-on and uses them to inform parents on how to proceed.
2. *If I react negatively to my child, am I a bad parent?*

   It is important for parents to forgive themselves for being human as well as forgiving their children. Children's behaviors can be very frustrating at times, and there is nothing wrong with having a genuine reaction to children as long as it is not out of control or purposefully hurtful. The reason positive approaches need to be taught and promoted is not only because they often *do* work but because they are so hard to implement. It is easy to threaten and punish, it is harder to be understanding and remain calm while setting limits.
3. *My son hasn't changed his behavior at all with these techniques. He keeps hitting and thinks our discipline of teaching and reasoning with him is a joke.*

While it is unclear why this son is continuing to hit others despite the values his parents are teaching him, the child clearly needs additional consequences. Reflecting the child's possible feelings of anger, frustration, or sibling jealousy when hitting is still recommended. In addition, setting limits on behavior is completely in the realm of positive parenting. What consequences should be applied really depends on the child's age and interests and parents' understanding of the reason for hitting. Is he 3 and hitting to get a toy? Is he 8 and hitting a younger brother due to sibling rivalry issues? Is he a 10 and hitting peers at school out of academic frustration? When the parent and child are calm, the parent can ask the child to explain what he is trying to communicate with hitting. The parent can give him alternative behaviors to do instead of hitting (e.g., "Use your words," listen to music or draw to calm down, go outside and run around with a ball). The parent can reward him for a certain number of hours or days without hitting. Parents can systematically and consistently reward nonhitting behavior. If none of those have worked, taking away privileges (use of toys, TV, videogames, or cell phone) might help. Other ideas for teaching parental values and promoting a more prosocial identity could include picking up litter together, volunteering at an animal shelter, helping with chores, or some other activity that allows the child to contribute to society in a constructive manner rather than with aggressive behavior. These activities need not be construed as punishment but as helping the child learn empathy for others.

4. *What do I do when my child absolutely refuses to do what I have calmly and politely asked, after I have given options and offered any help she might need?*

   Not understanding why the child is refusing to cooperate makes it difficult to know how to proceed. The parent needs to ask the child what's going on and be willing to listen without judgment before collaborating about how to get the task done. If the child cannot verbalize the reasons behind her refusal, the parent should first determine that the task is developmentally appropriate and within the skill set of the child. If it is, then asking if the child has an alternative idea for the situation might lead to a solution. Also, sometimes parents can help children verbalize their thoughts and feelings by guessing about the affect in the child and guessing what the problem might be. The parent considering whether this is just a bad day for the child and that it does not mean a whole lot more than the child not feeling well may be appropriate. Also, consideration of whether this behavior is more of a pattern that needs to be addressed is recommended. Figuring out the patterns to defiant behavior can help parents target the best approach to solving the behavior problems.

The main idea for this issue is to seek to understand what is going on with the child. This parent could easily summarize to her child exactly the problem: "I have asked nicely, I have given choices, I have offered help. I am frustrated. You have refused to cooperate and refused to give me a reason for your lack of cooperation or an alternative idea." If the child continued being uncooperative, the parent could add, "I am going to (deliver age-appropriate mild negative consequence) in the hopes that you understand how important cooperation is in this family."

5. *What about kids having to do things like chores? There is no parenting technique to make your kid want to do boring tasks instead of playing and having fun.*

This is absolutely true! So how do we teach children to do boring things? Threaten them with consequences for not doing it? Allow them not to do it? Let them be dishonest and say they did it when they did not? Or take the time and energy to walk them through the chore even if they have proven they can do it on their own previously. With some tasks, a preventative strategy is to turn off all TV, gaming, and computer screens so as not to distract a child from doing necessary routines. Validating their feelings and agreeing that most people would prefer not to have to do boring tasks helps the child feel understood. Parents should model coping with doing unpleasant things that need to be done, for example verbalizing, "The dishes need to be done, so I am going to do them before I get too tired even though I would love to watch TV right now." It may also be important not to assume that resistance to a chore is due to its boring nature. For example, there could be other reasons a child does not want to brush teeth (e.g., the child had a canker sore unknown to the parent or some other dental pain that needs to be addressed). Talk about the reasons the child does not want to do a task and talk about why it is important to do it anyway. Do this at the appropriate developmental level so that it makes sense to the child. Praise the child's efforts to do something she did not feel like doing. Give privileges or other reinforcers each time the chore is done. Plan fun things to do as a family to balance out the inevitable chores of life.

Handout 1. Quick check for positive parenting: ask yourself...

1. Do I see mistakes as opportunities to learn?
2. Do I calm myself down before problem solving with my child?
3. Do I respond to my child with kindness and firmness at the same time?
4. When my child misbehaves, do I understand the belief behind the misbehavior?
5. Do I feel comfortable problem solving with my child?
6. Do I have family meetings with my child?
7. Does how I respond to my child (my parenting style) influence how my child responds?

Source: Adapted from Carroll, P., & Hamilton, W. K. (2016). Positive discipline parenting scale: Reliability and validity of a measure. *The Journal of Individual Psychology, 72*(1), 60–74. Available from https://doi.org/10.1353/jip.2016.0002 (Carroll & Hamilton, 2016). Copyright © 2016 by the University of Texas Press.

Dealing with problem behaviors

1. Identify the problem behavior.
2. Identify the positive behaviors that are the opposite of the problem behavior.
3. Give specific praise every time you see your child doing the opposite behavior.
4. Provide small rewards for opposite behaviors.
5. Stick with these efforts over time.

Example:

1. Name-calling is identified as a problem behavior.
2. Saying nice things, giving compliments, staying quiet when angry, expressing feelings appropriately are all opposite behaviors to name-calling.
3. Each time the child does any of the opposite behaviors, the adult notices and says something like, "I can see what a good friend/sibling you can be because you didn't use any mean words even though it was clear you were very mad." Or, "Other kids are lucky to have you as a friend since you tell them such nice things like I heard you say...." Or, "You were angry and you said so in a way that people could listen and help, that's not easy."
4. Reward the opposite behaviors with small rewards (e.g., "Let's invite a friend to go to the park with us since you have been showing how good a friend you are by....").

5. Even if initially the child is not perfect at changing the problem behavior, notice and praise the efforts being made and the small successes. Over time and with practice, the child will get much better at the desired behaviors and decrease problem behaviors.

Parent resources

Typical development:
www.cdc.gov/ncbddd/actearly/milestones/index.html
www.apa.org/act/resources/fact-sheets/index.aspx
https://www.childwelfare.gov/topics/preventing/promoting/parenting/understanding/

Anxiety: https://adaa.org/living-with-anxiety/children/tips-parents-and-caregivers#

ADHD: https://chadd.org/

Positive parenting: https://resourcecentre.savethechildren.net/node/7509/pdf/pdep_2016_4th_edition.pdf

Important point to remember

- Authoritative parents seem to balance the two roles of enforcing rules as well as being responsive and warm. They supportively listen to their children and allow for negotiation as needed while still setting clear limits and high expectations.
- One way the parent–child relationship is built is by the parent seeking to understand the reasons behind a child's behavior without assuming those reasons are negative.
- The purpose of discipline is to teach children how to behave better, not leave them with lasting memories of significant disappointment and anger.
- A nurturing environment is a common factor in the prevention of problems that often cooccur: academic failure, crime, mental illness, drug addiction, risky sexual behavior, and other societal problems.
- Keeping in mind the developmental needs of teens to be with their friends in prosocial activities is important so that parents do not take this privilege away too frequently. Resentment between teen and parent can build to unhealthy levels when this consequence is overused.
- It is important not to trade feeling helpless for becoming punitive toward the child just to prove that something is being done.

References

Adler, A. (1930). *Guiding the child: On the principles of individual psychology.* New York: Greenberg Publisher.

American Psychological Association. (n.d.). *ACT raising safe kids program factsheets and handouts.* Retrieved from <https://www.apa.org/act/resources/fact-sheets/index>.

Anxiety and Depression Association of America. (n.d.). *Tips for parents and caregivers.* Retrieved from <https://adaa.org/living-with-anxiety/children/tips-parents-and-caregivers>.

Armor, D. (2017). *Maximizing intelligence.* New York: Routledge.

Arnett, J. J. (2012). *Human development: A cultural approach.* New Jersey: Pearson.

Barkley, R. A. (2013). *Taking charge of ADHD: The complete, authoritative guide for parents* (3rd ed.). New York: The Guilford Press.

Baumrind, D. (1971). Current patterns of parental authority. *Developmental Psychology, 4*(1, Pt.2), 1–103. Available from https://doi.org/10.1037/h0030372.

Biglan, A., Flay, B. R., Embry, D. D., & Sandler, I. N. (2012). The critical role of nurturing environments for promoting human well-being. *American Psychologist, 67*(4), 257–271. Available from https://doi.org/10.1037/a0026796.

Bodenmann, G., Cina, A., Ledermann, T., & Sanders, M. R. (2008). The efficacy of the triple P - Positive parenting program in improving parenting and child behavior: A comparison with two other treatment conditions. *Behaviour Research and Therapy, 46*, 411–427.

Boeldt, D. L., Rhee, S. H., DiLalla, L. F., Mullineaux, P. Y., Schulz-Heik, R. J., Corley, R. P., ... Hewitt, J. K. (2012). The association between positive parenting and externalizing behaviour. *Infant and Child Development, 21*, 85–106. Available from https://doi.org/10.1002/icd.764.

Burkhart, K., Knox, M., & Brockmyer, J. (2013). Pilot evaluation of the ACT raising safe kids program on children's bullying behavior. *Journal of Child and Family Studies, 22*, 942–951.

Butts, J. A., Bazemore, G., & Meroe, A. S. (2010). *Positive youth justice: Framing justice interventions using the concepts of positive youth development*. Washington, DC: Coalition for Juvenile Justice.

Carroll, P., & Hamilton, W. K. (2016). Positive discipline parenting scale: Reliability and validity of a measure. *The Journal of Individual Psychology, 72*(1), 60–74. Available from https://doi.org/10.1353/jip.2016.0002.

Centers for Disease Control and Prevention. (n.d.).*CDC's developmental milestones*. Retrieved from <https://www.cdc.gov/ncbddd/actearly/milestones/index.html>.

Chen, E., Brody, G. H., & Miller, G. E. (2017). Childhood close family relationships and health. *American Psychologist, 72*(6), 555–566.

Chen, F. R., & Raine, A. (2018). Effects of harsh parenting and positive parenting practices on youth aggressive behavior: The moderating role of early pubertal timing. *Aggressive Behavior, 44*, 18–28. Available from https://doi.org/10.1002/ab.21720.

Collins, W. A., Maccoby, E. E., Steinberg, L., Hetherington, E. M., & Bornstein, M. H. (2000). Contemporary research on parenting: The case for nature and nurture. *American Psychologist, 55*(2), 218–232. Available from https://doi.org/10/1037/003-066X.55.2.218.

Cooley, M. E., Veldorale-Griffin, A., Petren, R. E., & Mullis, A. K. (2014). Parent–child interaction therapy: A meta-analysis of child behavior outcomes and parent stress. *Journal of Family Social Work, 17*(3), 191–208.

Dadds, M. R., & Tully, L. A. (2019). What is it to discipline a child: What should it be? A reanalysis of time-out from the perspective of child mental health, attachment, and trauma. *American Psychologist*. Available from https://doi.org/10.1037/amp0000449, Advance online publication.

Dweck, C. (2006). *Mindset: The new psychology of success*. New York: Penguin Random House.

Eddy, J. M., Reid, J. B., & Fetrow, R. A. (2000). An elementary school-based prevention program targeting modifiable antecedents of youth delinquency and violence: Linking the interests of families and teachers (LIFT). *Journal of Emotional and Behavioral Disorders, 8*(3), 165–176.

Eyberg, S. (1988). Parent-child interaction therapy: Integration of traditional and behavioral concerns. *Child & Family Behavior Therapy, 10*(1), 33–46.

Faber, A., & Mazlish, E. (2002). *How to talk so kids will listen and listen so kids will talk*. New York: Harper Collins.

Feldman, R. (2015). The adaptive human parental brain: Implications for children's social development. *Trends in Neurosciences, 38*(6), 387–399.

Ford, J. D., Chapman, J., Connor, D. F., & Cruise, K. R. (2012). Complex trauma and aggression in secure juvenile justice settings. *Criminal Justice and Behavior, 39*(6), 694–724.

Gfroerer, K., Nelsen, J., & Kern, R. (2013). Positive discipline: Helping children develop belonging and coping resources using individual psychology. *The Journal of Individual Psychology, 69*, 294–304.

Ginott, H. G. (1965). *Between parents and children*. New York: Macmillan.

Gottman, J., & Declaire, J. (1997). *The heart of parenting: Raising an emotionally intelligent child*. New York: Simon and Schuster.

Graham, R. A., & Weems, C. F. (2014). Identifying moderators of the link between parent and child anxiety sensitivity: The roles of gender, positive parenting, and corporal punishment. *Journal of Abnormal Child Psychology, 43*, 885–893. Available from https://doi.org/10.1007/s10802-014-9945-y.

Greene, R. W. (2014). *The explosive child: A new approach for understanding and parenting easily frustrated, chronically inflexible children*. New York: Harper Collins.

Grusec, J. E., Danyliuk, T., Kil, H., & O'Neill, D. (2017). Perspectives on parent discipline and child outcomes. *International Journal of Behavioral Development, 41*(4), 465–471.

Howe, T. R., Knox, M., Altafim, E. R. P., Linhares, M. B. M., Nishizawa, N., Fu, T. J., ... Pereira, A. I. (2017). International child abuse prevention: Insights from ACT raising safe kids. *Child and Adolescent Mental Health, 22*(4), 194–200.

Kaminski, J., Valle, L. A., Filene, J. H., & Boyle, C. L. (2008). A meta-analytic review of components associated with parent training program effectiveness. *Journal of Abnormal Child Psychology, 36*, 567–589. Available from https://doi.org/10.1007/s10802-007-9201-9.

Kelly, J. (2015). Positive youth justice, Part two: Community works, Oakland, Calif. In *The chronicle of social change*. Retrieved from <https://chronicleofsocialchange.org/article/positive-youth-justice-part-two-community-works-oakland-calif>.

Knox, M. (2020). Physical punishment and child maltreatment, In Knox, M. (Ed), Clinician's Toolkit for Children's Behavioral Health, 2020, Elsevier.

Knox, M., & Burkhart, K. (2014). A multi-site study of the ACT raising safe kids program: Predictors of outcomes and attrition. *Children and Youth Services Review, 39*, 20–24.

Lieberman, M. D., Eisenberger, N. I., Crockett, M. J., Tom, S., Pfeifer, J. H., & Way, B. M. (2007). Putting feelings into words: Affect labeling disrupts amygdala activity to affective stimuli. *Psychological Science, 18*, 421–428.

Lippold, M. A., Duncan, L. G., Coatsworth, J. D., Nix, R. L., & Greenberg, M. T. (2015). Understanding how mindful parenting may be linked to mother–Adolescent communication. *Journal of Youth and Adolescence, 44*(9), 1663–1673. Available from https://link.springer.com/article/10.1007/s10964-015-0325-x.

Loren, R. E., Vaughn, A. J., Langberg, J. M., Cyran, J. E., Proano-Raps, T., Smolyansky, B. H., ... Epstein, J. N. (2015). Effects of an 8-session behavioral parent training group for parents of children with ADHD on child impairment and parenting confidence. *Journal of Attention Disorders, 19*(2), 158–166.

Lucas County Community Health Assessment. (2016/2017). Retrieved from <http://www.healthylucascounty.org/wp-content/uploads/sites/2/2017/10/FINAL-2016-17-General-Lucas-County-CHA-Participant-Feedback-Included-10-4-17.pdf>; <http://grantfundamentals.com/?page_id = 28>.

McGonigal, K. (2012). *The willpower instinct*. New York: Penguin.

Miller, G. E., Lachman, M. E., Chen, E., Gruenewald, T. L., Karlamangla, A. S., & Seeman, T. E. (2011). Pathways to resilience: Maternal nurturance as a buffer against the effects of childhood poverty on metabolic syndrome at midlife. *Psychological Science, 22*(12), 1591–1599. Available from https://doi.org/10.1177/0956797611419170.

Nelsen, J. (2006). *Positive discipline*. New York: Penguin Random House.

Neville, H. J., Stevens, C., Pakulak, E., Bell, T. A., Fanning, J., Klein, S., ... Isbell, E. (2013). Family-based training program improves brain function, cognition, and behavior in lower socioeconomic status preschoolers. *Proceedings of the National Academy of Sciences of the United States of America*. Available from https://doi.org/10.1073/pnas.1304437110.

Nielson, L. (2017). Re-examining the research on parental conflict, coparenting, and custody arrangements. *Psychology, Public Policy and Law, 23*(2), 211–231.

Nowak, C., & Heinrichs, N. (2008). A comprehensive meta-analysis of triple P-Positive parenting program using hierarchical linear modeling: Effectiveness and moderating variables. *Clinical Child and Family Psychology Review, 11*, 114–144. Available from https://doi.org/10.1007/s10567-008-0033-0.

Office of Juvenile Justice and Delinquency Prevention. (1998).*Guide for implementing the balanced and restorative justice model (NCJ 167887)*. Retrieved from <https://www.ojjdp.gov/pubs/implementing/accountability.html>.

Office of the Minister for Children and Youth Affairs. (2009). *Parents' perspectives on parenting styles and disciplining children*. Dublin: The Stationery Office.

Ollendick, T. H., Greene, R. W., Austin, K. E., Fraire, M. G., Halldorsdottir, T., Allen, K. B., ... Noguchi, R. J. (2016). Parent management training and collaborative & proactive solutions: A randomized control trial for oppositional youth. *Journal of Clinical Child & Adolescent Psychology, 45*(5), 591–604.

Ordway, M. R., Webb, D., Sadler, L. S., & Slade, A. (2014). Parental reflective functioning: An approach to enhancing parent-child relationships in pediatric primary care. *Journal of Pediatric Health Care, 29*(4), 325–334. Available from https://doi.org/10.1016/j.pedhc.2014.12.002.

Pastorelli, C., Lansford, J. E., Kanacri, B. P. L., Malone, P. S., Di Giunta, L., Bacchini, D., ... Sobring, E. (2016). Positive parenting and children's prosocial behavior in eight countries. *Journal of Child Psychology and Psychiatry, 57*, 824–834. Available from https://doi.org/10.1111/jcpp.12477.

Perry, B. D. (2001). The neurodevelopmental impact of violence in childhood. In D. Schetky, & E. P. Benedek (Eds.), *Textbook of child and adolescent forensic psychiatry*. Washington, DC: American Psychiatric Press.

PEW Charitable Trusts. (2015) *Re-examining juvenile incarceration*. Retrieved from <https://www.pewtrusts.org/en/research-and-analysis/issue-briefs/2015/04/reexamining-juvenile-incarceration>.

Portwood, S. G., Lambert, R. G., Abrams, L. P., & Nelson, E. B. (2011). An evaluation of the adults and children together (ACT) against violence parents raising safe kids program. *The Journal of Primary Prevention, 32*(3–4), 147.

Roben, C. K. P., Cole, P. M., & Armstrong, L. M. (2013). Longitudinal relations among language skills, anger expression, and regulatory strategies in early childhood. *Child Development, 84*(3), 891–905.

Sanders, M. R., Kirby, J. N., Tellegen, C. L., & Day, J. J. (2014). The triple P-positive parenting program: A systematic review and meta-analysis of a multi-level system of parenting support. *Clinical Psychology Review, 34*, 337–357.

Segerstrom, S. C., Boggero, I. A., & Evans, D. R. (2016). Pause and plan: The physiology of self-regulation. In K. D. Vohs, & R. F. Baumeister (Eds.), *Handbook of self-regulation: Research, theory and applications* (3rd ed.). New York: Guilford Press.

Silva, J. (2011). *ACT facilitator manual: ACT raising safe kids program*. Washington, DC: American Psychological Association.

Stromberg, J. (2013). *The neuroscientist who discovered he was a psychopath*. [Review of the book *The psychopath inside*, by Fallon, J.]. Retrieved from <https://www.smithsonianmag.com/science-nature/the-neuroscientist-who-discovered-he-was-a-psychopath-180947814/>.

Waller, R., Gardner, F., Dishion, T., Sitnick, S. L., Shaw, D. S., Winter, C. E., ... Wilson, M. (2015). Early parental positive behavior support and childhood adjustment: Addressing enduring questions with new methods. *Social Development, 24*, 304–322. Available from https://doi.org/10.1111/sode.12103.

Waller, R., Trentacosta, C. J., Shaw, D. S., Neiderhiser, J. M., Ganiban, J. M., Reiss, D., ... Hyde, L. (2016). Heritable temperament pathways to early callous–unemotional behavior. *The British Journal of Psychiatry, 209*, 475–482. Available from https://doi.org/10.1192/bjp.bp.116.181503.

Washington, T., Rose, T., Coard, S. I., Patton, D. U., Young, S., Giles, S., ... Nolen, M. (2017). Family level factors, depression, and anxiety among African-American children: A systematic review. *Child & Youth Care Forum, 46*, 137–156. Available from https://doi.org/10.1007/s10566-016-9372-z.

CHAPTER

3

Promoting healthy weight and managing childhood and adolescent obesity using evidence-based methods

Yazhini Srivathsal[1], *Kimberly Burkhart*[2] and *Michele Knox*[3]

[1]Banner Medical Group/University of Arizona College Of Medicine Phoenix, Phoenix, AZ, United States, [2]Pediatrics & Psychiatry, Rainbow Babies and Children's Hospital, Case Western Reserve University, Cleveland, OH, United States, [3]Department of Psychiatry, University of Toledo College of Medicine and Life Sciences, Toledo, OH, United States

Introduction

Childhood obesity and overweight are and will most certainly continue to be for the coming years, major health problems in the United States (Ward et al., 2017). As such, childhood obesity and overweight are topics that often need to be addressed by the US health-care providers. In some cases, parents and caregivers present questions about these issues and seek to be educated. In other cases, parents and caregivers do not bring up weight as a concern, but the child's weight status makes it a necessary focus of intervention. These issues are best addressed early in development; research shows that early development of obesity predicts obesity in adulthood, especially for children who were severely obese (Ward et al., 2017).

Clinician's Toolkit for Children's Behavioral Health
DOI: https://doi.org/10.1016/B978-0-12-816024-4.00003-6

Primary prevention

There is only limited research regarding the primary prevention of obesity. Most of the studies indicate that the most sustainable and beneficial effect on obesity prevention involves multiple strategies, as opposed to a single-component intervention. These strategies focus on meals, classroom activities, sport and play activities, and involve home, school, and community participants (Lobstein et al., 2015).

When it comes to diet and physical activities, caregivers have questions about what, and how much, are recommended. Table 3.1 is based on both governmental and professional sources and lists recommended diet and physical activity by age.

Methods and timing of feeding also influence the risk of obesity. For example, a study on 8030 infants who were predominantly fed formula for the first 6 months found that such infants were about 2.5 times more likely to be obese at 24 months of age relative to infants predominantly fed breast milk. The early introduction of solid foods (<4 months) and putting the child to bed with a bottle also increased the likelihood of obesity (Gibbs & Forste, 2013). However, another study conducted with 1181 infants followed for 6 years concluded that the timing of introduction of solid foods was not associated with child obesity at 6 years (Barrera, Perrine, Li, & Scanlon, 2016). Given the inconsistent findings from these studies, further research is needed to assess the influence of feeding timing on obesity.

Classification of obesity

Body mass index or BMI is one way of measuring obesity and is defined as an individual's weight in kilograms divided by the square of their height in meters. For example, if someone weighs 100 lb (45.4 kg) and is 4′ tall (1.22 m), then their BMI will be 30.5 (weight in kilogram/square of their height in meters: 45.4/1.49 = 30.5). In children and adolescents, BMI is age and sex specific and is referred to as the BMI-for-age. This is because the child's body composition will vary by age and sex. The child's weight, height, and BMI are determined and assessed as relative to the weight, height, and BMI, respectively, of other children of the same age and sex. According to the Centers for Disease Control and Prevention (CDC) (U.S. Department of Health and Human Services, 2018), in children and teens:

1. underweight is defined as a BMI less than the 5th percentile of the same age and sex.
2. normal or healthy weight is defined as 5th percentile to less than 85th percentile of the same age and sex.

TABLE 3.1 Recommended diet and physical activity by age.

Age	Dietary recommendations	Physical activity recommendations
0–6 Months	*Breastfeeding* Every 1–3 h, as long as the baby is actively feeding, around 8–12 feedings every 24 h *Formula feeding*—2–3 oz every 3–4 h at birth; 4 oz every 4 h at 1 month; 6–8 oz around 4–5 times every 24 h. No more than 32 oz of formula in 24 h	
6–12 Months	• Breast milk or formula • Try to offer breast milk before offering solids at each feeding • Pureed fruits, vegetable, whole grains, meats • Avoid honey, unpasteurized juices, and fortified cow's milk • Limit foods with added sugar and foods high in salt • No 100% juice or sugar added beverages • Water about 4–6 oz per day	
12–24 Months	• Breastfeeding as needed • Something to eat or drink about every 2–3 h, or about 5–6 times a day (around three meals and two to three snacks every day). • Fruits, vegetable, whole grains, meats, dairy • 4 oz or less of 100% juice a day • Fortified cow's milk • Child eats more of the foods the caregivers eat, so eating a healthy diet sets a good example for the toddler	• Provide a minimally structured play environment that is safe, and nurturing • Allow supervised, unstructured exploration of the outdoors, and develop enjoyment of outdoor physical activity
2–3 Years	• 40 calories for every inch of height • Around 1000 calories per day for 2-year olds, 1200–1400 calories per day for 3-year olds • Fruits, vegetable, whole grains, meats, dairy • Child's serving size should be approximately one-quarter of an adult's	• Play actively several times daily • Screen time less than 1 h daily • Caregivers need to role model active lifestyles and limit children's inactivity

(*Continued*)

TABLE 3.1 (Continued)

Age	Dietary recommendations	Physical activity recommendations
4–5 Years	• Depending on activity level 1200–1600 calories for boys, 1200–1600 calories for girls • Fruits: Whole fruits, offer a variety, fresh/frozen/canned/dried (unsweetened such as raisins), limit fruit juices • Vegetables: Offer a variety, fresh/frozen/canned, add a dip • Grains: At least half whole grains, offer a variety with various healthy toppings • Protein: Offer a variety, limit highly processed meat (hot dogs, chicken nuggets), add beans • Dairy: Unflavored, low fat, fat free milk, yogurt, and cheese	• Encourage free and unorganized play with emphasis on fun, playfulness, exploration, and experimentation while being mindful of safety and proper supervision • Play actively several times daily • Screen time less than 1 h daily • Caregivers need to role model active lifestyles and limit children's inactivity
6–8 Years	• Depending on activity level, 1200–2000 calories per day • Based on a 2000-calorie daily food plan: ◦ Vegetables—2.5 cups ◦ Fruits—2 cups ◦ Grains—6 oz ◦ Dairy—2 cups every day ◦ Protein foods—5.5 oz every day	• 60 minutes or more of physical activity daily that are age appropriate, enjoyable, and offer variety. • *Aerobic*: Moderate or vigorous intensity; vigorous intensity at least 3 days a week • *Muscle strengthening*: At least 3 days a week • *Bone strengthening*: At least 3 days a week
9–13 Years	• 1600–3200 calories per day	
14 + Years	• 1600–3200 calories per day	

Adapted from www.choosemyplate.gov; www.usda.gov; www.cdc.gov; www.healthychildren.org from the American Academy of Pediatrics.

3. overweight is defined as a BMI at or more than the 85th percentile and under the 95th percentile of the same age and sex.
4. obesity is defined as a BMI at or above the 95th percentile of the same age and sex.

Epidemiology and comorbidities

Recent studies show that currently, one in three children in the United States is either overweight or obese (Kumar & Kelly, 2017). Overweight status predicts obesity in children. For example, overweight

5-year olds are four times as likely as healthy-weight children to become obese (Cunningham, Kramer, & Narayan, 2014).

Pediatric obesity is associated with an increased likelihood of serious medical conditions. For example, pediatric obesity is linked to the emergence of comorbidities previously considered to be diseases of adulthood, including type 2 diabetes mellitus, hypertension, nonalcoholic fatty liver disease, obstructive sleep apnea, and lipid abnormalities (Kumar & Kelly, 2017). A recent study that compared the cardiovascular risk factors of severely obese youth (defined as Class IV obese, who were over 160% of the 95th percentile of the BMI for age and sex) with youth of lower levels of obesity concluded that the metabolic risk factors associated with obesity in childhood begin to happen well before the child or individual reaches Class IV obesity (Zabarsky et al., 2018).

Risk factors

There are various risk factors for obesity, including genetic; environmental and neighborhood factors; increased intake of sugar-sweetened beverages; consumption of fast food and processed snacks; decreased physical activity; shorter sleep duration; and increased personal, prenatal, or family stress (Brown, Halvorson, Cohen, Lazorick, & Skelton, 2015). Several family factors affect risk and outcomes as well; low familial motivation to change, poor adherence to recommendations, and maladaptive parent management are often significant barriers to decreasing obesity in children and adolescents (Kitzman-Ulrich et al., 2010; Kolagotla & Adams, 2004).

Parental misperceptions also can be risk factors, where many parents do not view their child as obese, or misperceive their child's weight. One study indicated, for example, that parents who misperceived their child's weight were almost 12 times more likely to have an obese child (Mckee, Long, Southward, Walker, & Mccown, 2016). This makes it even more important that clinicians educate the parents and caregivers about healthy weight and childhood obesity. Research shows that most obese children do not have an underlying endocrine or single genetic cause for their weight gain (Kumar & Kelly, 2017).

Assessment and management

The methods of assessing risk include identification of elevated BMI, medical risks, and unhealthy eating and physical activity habits (Barlow, 2007). Screening is recommended to begin at age 6, and this should include screening for psychological comorbidities such as school absences or refusal, poor school performance, peer teasing, bullying, low self-esteem, anxiety, depression, self-injurious behavior, anger outbursts, substance use, eating disordered behaviors, and family attitudes about weight (Pont, Puhl, Cook, & Slusser, 2017; Styne et al., 2017).

The tests for the diagnosis of obesity are calculating the BMI, measuring the skinfold thickness, and waist circumference. There is no conclusive evidence that any test is generally superior to the others, but the BMI is a reliable, simple diagnostic test for identifying childhood adiposity/obesity (Simmonds, Llewellyn, Owen, & Woolacott, 2016), and it can be tracked easily over the lifespan. The BMI must be calculated and plotted annually, and this should be integrated with other information to assess the child's obesity risk, along with the methods to assess diet and physical activity behaviors (Barlow, 2007).

Once obesity is diagnosed, a staged approach to pediatric weight management is recommended with consideration of the age of the child, severity of obesity, and the presence of obesity-related comorbidities in determining the initial stage of treatment (Kumar & Kelly, 2017). Evidence-based approaches to obesity need to be both multifaceted and longitudinal. Research suggests that clinicians should use a longitudinal, developmentally appropriate life-course approach to help identify the children who are at risk and on the path to obesity (Daniels & Hassink, 2015). Clinicians should employ long-term interventions; moderate (26–75 hours) to high (> 75 hours) intensity intervention lasting for 6–12 months is recommended (Barton, 2010). The United States Preventive Services Task Force recommends that children who are meeting criteria for obesity should be referred to comprehensive, intensive, behavioral interventions to improve weight status. Multicomponent interventions including dietary modifications, physical activity changes, behavioral strategies, and active parent involvement should be made available to all children who meet criteria (Whitlock, O'Connor, Williams, Beil, & Lutz, 2010).

A well-established method for addressing obesity in the clinic setting is called "the 5 As of obesity management in the office setting" (Gurnani, Birken, & Hamilton, 2015). These include Ask, Assess, Advise, Agree, and Assist. The clinician should ask for the child's permission to be able to discuss his/her weight. Assessment should involve determining readiness to change, the underlying cause of obesity, physical, and mental health complications that may be present, as well as identifying barriers to weight loss. The clinician should advise the patient on health-related risks and treatment options. The goal of this discussion is to help the child and his/her family choose behavioral goals that are specific, measurable, achievable, relevant, and timely (i.e., SMART goals). Finally, the clinician should summarize the agreed-upon plan, provide resources, and schedule a follow-up.

Family-based behavioral treatment has been studied for over 30 years and is an empirically supported intervention for decreasing childhood obesity. Family-based behavioral treatment involves methods where a parent is treated with a child with obesity. Family weigh-ins are performed, followed by individual and group therapy sessions separately for the parent and the child, provision of a treatment manual including the recommended dietary change, a physical activity program, and information on parenting (Epstein, Paluch, Roemmich, & Beecher, 2007). The results of research on this method indicated that targeting both parents (if the child has two parents) is superior to a nontargeted control group, and both lifestyle and aerobic physical activity programs are superior to a calisthenics control group. In a study evaluating the impact of family-based behavioral treatment 10 years postintervention, those who were treated with their parents showed significant decreases in relative weight in comparison to those who were treated separately from their parents (Epstein, Valoski, Wing, & McCurley, 1990). In keeping, parental weight loss has been shown to be a significant and important predictor of child success in family-based behavioral intervention (Best et al., 2016). Similarly, results of a metaanalysis including randomized trials of pediatric lifestyle interventions indicated that participants experienced a decrease in BMI when the participant's family was involved. When caregivers were not involved, however, the effect on weight loss was not substantial (McGovern et al., 2008).

Systematic reviews suggest that interventions comprising dietary modification, physical activity, behavioral therapy, and education can significantly decrease systolic and diastolic blood pressure, BMI, and triglycerides (Rajjo et al., 2017). Effective behavioral therapy interventions often include self-monitoring, decreased sedentary behavior, dietary modification/decreased exposure to obesogenic foods, designated mealtimes, stimulus control, preplanning, positive reinforcement for making recommended behavioral changes, and modeling of healthy eating and behavioral practices in the home (e.g., Jull & Chen, 2013). Other strategies include a diet free of or including fewer sugar-sweetened beverages; increased intake of fruits and vegetables to five or more servings per day; promoting a lifestyle with reduced sedentary behaviors such as fewer TV sets, removing TV and media from bedroom and kitchen; focusing on bedtime; getting at least 9 hours of sleep; and identifying opportunities for 60 minutes of moderate to vigorous physical activity daily (Daniels & Hassink, 2015). Table 3.2 provides details about each of these strategies.

Some obesity prevention and intervention programs also include learning emotion regulation strategies and how to manage high risk social situations, and challenging and restructuring negative automatic thoughts (Skjakodegard et al., 2016). Emotion regulation involves

TABLE 3.2 Behavioral strategies to prevent or reduce childhood overweight/obesity.

Strategy	Description
Self-monitoring	Children and parents track and record when eating occurs, what has been eaten, and associated mood. The child and the parent can pay particular attention to when the child wants to eat, planning to determine triggers for wanting to eat. Similarly, families can track physical activity, provide regular feedback about activity, and plan to change factors (e.g., time outside of home, media use, time with friends) that lead to greater or lesser involvement in physical activity
Stimulus control	This is defined as behaving in a particular way when a stimulus is present and behaving in a different way in its absence. For example, a child may eat more when the television is on at dinner or while on social media. As a result, media use can be limited or restricted to particular times of day
Preplanning	Parents work with their children to set up designated mealtimes, determine healthy meals in advance, when exercise will occur, possible physical activities, and problem solve potential barriers to follow through
Positive reinforcement	Parents can provide a reinforcer (primary, social, tangible, and/or activities/privileges) if a child meets his/her food and exercise-related goals. Children should be actively involved in choosing rewards to ensure that they are effectively motivating behavior change
Removing TV and media from bedroom	Parents set rules for time and place of media use. This should help promote a more restful sleep. Improved sleep is associated with decreased obesity
Behavior management strategies	Parents and youths can identify specific behavioral targets (e.g., increased number of steps per day, eating fruits at snack time), engaging in planned practice and rehearsal of the behaviors, then record progress toward that goal. Parents immediately, contingently, and frequently reinforce achievement using motivating, novel reinforcers or reinforcing activities. Parents can ignore and not reinforce tantrums or demanding behavior related to unhealthy foods. Parents can distract and engage young children in activities rather than providing snacks
Exposure to new foods	Parents can gradually introduce new healthy foods. This can be done by presenting a nonpreferred food followed by a taste of a preferred food. Reinforcers can also be used in response to trying new foods

Adapted from Jull, A., & Chen, R. (2013). Parent-only vs. parent-child only (family focused) approaches for weight loss in obese and overweight children: A systematic review and metaanalysis. Obesity Review, 14, 761–768 and Daniels, S. R., & Hassink, S. G. (2015). The role of the pediatrician in primary prevention of obesity. Pediatrics, 136(1), e275–e292.

identifying the connection among negative emotions and overeating. Strategies to manage emotions may include using relaxation strategies (e.g., diaphragmatic breathing and progressive muscle relaxation), engaging in problem-solving, and using positive activity scheduling (i.e., engaging in activities enjoyed by the child). The child learns how to work with the family to develop a plan for eating at parties, holidays, and on vacation. The child also learns how to communicate with peers about his/her goals related to living a healthier lifestyle. The patient learns how maladaptive or negative thoughts about his/her self, others, and world can trigger eating. Learning how to think more adaptively, engage in positive self-talk, and to develop a positive self-image and body image is often also addressed in obesity prevention and intervention programs.

Researchers have also recommended that positive behavioral programs (e.g., ParentCorps; Hajizadeh et al., 2017) be adapted to address obesity due to these programs' efficacy in promoting children's healthy lifestyle behaviors. These programs use positive behavior support (PBS) that employ nonaversive techniques that reinforce caregiver–child interactions. The strategies used are (1) proactively structuring the child's environment, such as serving healthy foods, limiting calorie dense, high fat/high sugar foods, ensuring that the child's schedule provides opportunities for physical activities, (2) actively providing positive reinforcement for desired behaviors through verbal praise and other incentives, and (3) actively participating with the child in the physical activities. Child inhibitory control is another target of PBS intervention that plays a role in pediatric obesity. Child inhibitory control involves caregivers intervening by teaching the child the ability to delay gratification and the skills for emotional regulation. Caregivers also provide support by modeling healthy lifestyle behaviors (Smith, George, & Prado, 2017).

Consensus recommendations based on information obtained from the American Academy of Pediatrics Institute for Healthy Childhood Weight and The Obesity Society include the use of a family-based multicomponent behavioral therapy model, an integrated care model, and a multidisciplinary care team to address and manage obesity (Wilfley et al., 2017). Effective delivery should include the use of evidence-based protocols, medical oversight, and a minimum dose of 25 hours of intervention (Wilfley et al., 2017). Moreover, Wilfley et al. (2017) conducted a multisite randomized clinical trial that demonstrated that parent–child dyads who received family-based behavioral weight loss treatment (based on social and learning theory principles) followed by social facilitation maintenance had significantly improved long-term weight loss in comparison to those who received the same intervention followed by behavioral skills maintenance. Social facilitation is a socioecological approach that emphasizes parental facilitation of children's peer networks, as well as coaching on improved body image, how to respond to teasing, and how to maintain behaviors that decrease weight (Wilfley et al., 2007). Furthermore, the findings suggested that interventions greater than 26 hours in total duration resulted in the greatest percentage of weight loss.

Studies have shown that interventions that include linkages to neighborhood resources such as health coaches, periodic reminders (educational materials by text and mail), online community resource maps to identify resources with the family's community that could support behavior change (like local parks, young men's christian association (YMCA)), and healthy grocery shopping programs result in improved family outcomes and reduced child BMI (Elsie et al., 2017). A metaanalysis that evaluated the effectiveness of 139 childhood obesity prevention programs conducted in high-income countries and implemented in various settings concluded that schools are an important setting to implement effective childhood obesity intervention programs. A concomitant involvement of the home, family, and the community is desirable, and improving access to physical activity facilities and healthy food choices both at school and home is effective (Wang et al., 2015).

Motivational interviewing also has been recommended for use in addressing pediatric obesity (Davis et al., 2007). This technique is typically integrated with anticipatory guidance nutrition counseling and behavioral interventions designed to elicit change talk (Resnicow et al., 2016). Motivational interviewing is a client-centered, collaborative decision-making process that encourages patients to develop their own arguments for health change behavior. Change talk is elicited by the clinician asking open-ended questions, making affirmative statements, reflection statements, and summary statements (OARS). Through the use of these and other strategies, the clinician assesses the patient's readiness and confidence to change. The four key principles of motivational interviewing (MI) include expressing empathy, supporting self-efficacy, evoking motivation for change, and developing discrepancies between the patient's goal and current choices/lifestyle. In addition, costs and benefits to making the patient's identified changes are elicited and summarized as a way to help patients address obstacles and become motivated by potential benefits.

The following is an example of a dialogue between a clinician and patient using motivational interviewing techniques:

Clinician:	On a scale 0–10, how ready are you to make changes in your child's diet?
Parent:	6
Clinician:	I'm wondering what made you say 6 and not a lower number
Parent:	I want my child to get healthy. I don't want her to get diabetes like me
Clinician:	You've listed good reasons. It's clear that you love your daughter and want the best for her. What steps do you think you can take to make changes?
Parent:	I can probably buy more fruits and vegetables. I can include a fruit or vegetable at dinner
Clinician:	That sounds great! What do you think could potentially get in the way of meeting this goal?
Parent:	I am often running late after work and don't have time to make dinner. We then just get fast food
Clinician:	I'm wondering whether it's possible to prepare for meals on the weekends...
Parent:	Yes, I suppose I could. It will just take planning, but I can just take it one week at a time
Clinician:	I think that's a great plan. Would it make sense to try your plan, and then meet again sometime soon to review how it went?

Motivational interviewing alone has had mixed results in treating pediatric obesity (Resnicow, Davis, & Rollnick, 2006; Schwartz et al., 2007), and effectiveness may depend on demographic characteristics such as child gender and parent educational level (Davoli et al., 2013). It appears that at least short-term positive results can be achieved when motivational interviewing is combined with other components such as behavior management, but more research is needed to better delineate its effectiveness in the prevention and treatment of childhood obesity (Limbers, Turner, & Varni, 2008).

Preschool-aged children

Obesity in preschool-aged years increases the likelihood of obesity in youth and adulthood, and today, almost 2 million preschool-aged children in the United States meet criteria for obesity (Ogden et al., 2016). Few studies have examined the efficacy of behavioral interventions in preschool-aged children (e.g., Cunningham et al., 2014); however, in the primary care setting, a 6-month family-based intervention comprising 18 sessions, involving both the child and the caregiver, was found to decrease weight compared with an education only control group (Quattrin et al., 2012). A 12-month, seven-session family motivational interviewing program was not found to be more effective than care as usual in decreasing BMI (Taveras et al., 2011). In yet another study, participants in an 18-session clinic and home-based intervention demonstrated a significantly greater decrease in BMI compared with those families who received motivational interviewing and those receiving care as usual (Stark et al., 2018).

Physical activity

Physical activity has been shown to be very helpful in obesity prevention and management. Since risk factors for chronic diseases such as obesity, heart diseases, and metabolic diseases such as diabetes can begin to develop early in life, regular physical activity beginning in childhood makes it more likely that the children will remain healthy both in their childhood and adulthood. Caregivers should make the physical activity enjoyable and age-appropriate to the children, offer a variety of activities, take part in the activity as much as possible, and model healthy behavior. According to the Office of Disease Prevention and Health Promotion's (ODPHP) Physical Activity Guidelines (https://health.gov/paguidelines/second-edition/), children and adolescents should do 60 minutes (1 hour) or more of physical activity daily. This can be aerobic, muscle strengthening, or bone strengthening type of activities.

- *Aerobic*: At least 3 days a week
  - Moderate intensity—Active recreation, such as hiking, skateboarding, rollerblading, bicycle riding, and brisk walking
  - Vigorous intensity—Active games involving running and chasing, such as tag; bicycle riding; jumping rope; martial arts, such as karate; running; sports such as soccer, ice or field hockey, basketball, swimming, tennis, cross-country skiing
- *Muscle strengthening*: At least 3 days a week
  - Games such as tug-of-war; modified push-ups (with knees on the floor); resistance exercises using body weight or resistance bands; rope or tree climbing; sit-ups (curl-ups or crunches); swinging on playground equipment/bar
- *Bone strengthening*: At least 3 days a week
  - Games such as hopscotch; hopping, skipping, jumping; jumping rope; running; sports such as gymnastics, basketball, volleyball, tennis

Other management strategies

Other management strategies for pediatric obesity include medication management and surgical management. Among the group of weight-loss medications, Orlistat (which helps in not digesting/poorly digesting the orally consumed fats) is the only US Food and Drug Administration–approved prescription drug for the treatment of overweight and obese adolescents. Other medications, including metformin, exist, but more and larger studies are needed to establish their role in treatment (Matson & Fallon, 2012). Lastly, bariatric surgery has been found to be effective in decreasing excess weight and improving comorbidities in adolescents with severe obesity. However, there are limited data on the long-term efficacy and safety of bariatric surgery in adolescents (Kumar & Kelly, 2017).

Recommendation for improving clinical practice

Clinicians addressing weight issues need to be very sensitive to the feelings and needs of the patients in their clinical practice. They should create a safe, welcoming, and nonstigmatizing clinic/office space for youth with obesity and their families. They should practice role modeling by having a nonjudgmental, noncritical, nonbiased, and supportive approach with the patients and their families and recognize and acknowledge the complex etiology of obesity rather than place blame and judgment on the patient/family (Pont et al., 2017). One way to achieve this goal is to use sensitive and nonstigmatizing language and words in communication about weight with youths and families. Examples would be to use words such as "weight" and "BMI" over words such as "fat" and "weight problem." Using people-first language (i.e., placing the individual first before the medical condition) such as "a child with obesity" rather than "an obese child" is also recommended (Pont et al., 2017). It is important to help patients and families understand that obesity is a medical diagnosis with real health consequences. This information should be conveyed in a sensitive and supportive manner, even in clinical documentation (Pont et al., 2017). Clinicians should also support and involve their patients in evidence-supported community programs and advocate for policy changes that help combat obesity in childhood (Vine, Hargreaves, Briefel, & Orfield, 2013). Handout 1 provides resources for clinicians and families related to healthy weight, physical activity, and obesity prevention/intervention.

In conclusion, childhood obesity continues to be a major health concern in the United States. Children and their families need the help of clinicians in a multitude of avenues to tackle this. Awareness about childhood obesity seems to be on the rise, thanks to the various initiatives and programs developed in recent years. Though awareness can lead to motivation for healthy lifestyle changes, these changes have to become a habit to bring about sustained results, and evidence suggests that the solution to childhood obesity is a complicated one. Family-based behavioral treatment including a variety of behavior management strategies can bring about positive outcomes. As evidenced by the studies reviewed above, childhood obesity management has optimal results when the family also adopts healthy lifestyle changes. Motivational interviewing can be used with both adolescents and parents; this technique has some preliminary support but needs additional research to better determine effective components and duration of outcomes. Youth-focused interventions include education, behavior therapy, cognitive restructuring, techniques to address emotion regulation, and relaxation training. School-based interventions have received some empirical support, and there is also evidence that interventions designed to connect the family with community programs and resources may be beneficial. In sum, clinicians who work with children and their families should continue to educate, encourage, and emphasize the importance of childhood obesity management and provide them long-term, comprehensive support along their journey.

Handout 1. Resources for information on healthy weight and lifestyle

- Institute for Healthy Childhood Weight from the American Academy of Pediatrics (https://ihcw.aap.org) provides multiple modules for clinicians for continuing education and clinical support and also provides education for parents/caregivers. They provide an algorithm for the assessment and management of childhood obesity in patients 2 years and older at this website: https://ihcw.aap.org/Documents/Assessment%20%20and%20Management%20of%20Childhood%20Obesity%20Algorithm_FINAL.pdf.
- The National Heart, Lung, and Blood Institute, a part of the US Department of Health and Human Services, has the WE CAN (Ways to Enhance Children's Activity and Nutrition https://www.nhlbi.nih.gov/health/educational/wecan/tools-resources/index.htm) program and provides information for parents, including community-based resources.
- The American Psychological Association has the initiative ABCDE (Act Boldly to Change Diet and Exercise) and explains why these changes are important, and how this can be achieved (https://www.apa.org/topics/children/healthy-eating.aspx).
- The ChooseMyPlate program from the US Department of Agriculture (www.choosemyplate.gov) is about various ways to adopt a healthy lifestyle, not limited to nutrition, and physical activity. Some of the resources are at this website https://www.choosemyplate.gov/myplate-tip-sheets that provides resources and tip sheets for making the right food choices; eating on a budget; healthy choices while eating out, at parties, during holidays; healthy eating for various lifestyles; caregivers being role models for healthy food choices; and more information. https://www.choosemyplate.gov/dietary-guidelines—The ChooseMyPlate program's website also has resources on how to create a balanced meal on a plate, and other resources including dietary guidelines.
- The Food and Nutrition Service is a part of the US Department of Agriculture (www.fns.usda.gov) and has resources on nutrition and various programs including the women, infants, and children (WIC) program. Here is an example of the guidelines for feeding healthy infants, and typical daily portion sizes for children up to 12 months of age https://wicworks.fns.usda.gov/sites/default/files/media/document/Guidelines%20for%20Feeding%20Healthy%20Infants%20Job%20Aid%20FINAL_rev6-2017_508c.pdf.
- The American Academy of Pediatrics (www.healthychildren.org) provides information on nutrition, and fitness pertaining to the various stages of life from being a fetus to being a young adult.

Example is https://www.healthychildren.org/English/ages-stages/toddler/nutrition/Pages/Serving-Sizes-for-Toddlers.aspx that shows the average daily intake guide for a toddler.

- The Centers for Disease Control and Prevention provides childhood obesity resources and has multiple resources including information on state and local programs that are funded by the CDC for disease prevention and health promotion (https://www.cdc.gov/obesity/childhood/causes.html).
- The Academy of Nutrition and Dietetics has information on food, health, and fitness, including infographics explaining the details such as portion sizes (www.eatright.org).
- Children's Hospital Los Angeles' Kids N Fitness program is a 6-week, evidence-based weight management program for overweight and obese children ages 8–16 years (https://www.chla.org/kids-n-fitness).
- The Robert Wood Johnson Foundations' Healthy Children Healthy Weight initiative addresses nutrition, energetic play, and positive social and emotional environments (https://healthyeatingresearch.org/who-we-are/healthy-children-healthy-weight/).
- WakeMed Physician Practices ENERGIZE! Program focuses on risk assessment, family-centered education, and promotion of sustainable lifestyle change (https://www.wakemed.org/childrens-energize-program#about).
- Louisiana State University Agricultural Center's Smart Choices for Healthy Families program provides education and support to families with limited resources on how to improve dietary practices and more effectively manage limited resources (https://snaped.fns.usda.gov/library/materials/smart-choices-community-nutrition-education-program).
- Eat Smart, Move More, NC (https://www.eatsmartmovemorenc.com/) is a North Carolina statewide movement that promotes increased opportunities for healthy eating and physical activity.
- Examples of community health education programs:
  1. SWITCH program (http://www.physicalactivitylab.org/switch-school-wellness-programming.html) includes a community awareness campaign to modify key health behaviors, increasing physical activity, improving nutrition, and reducing screen time.
  2. Tioga County Fit for Life initiative (http://tiogapartnership.org/collaborations/) is a comprehensive primary prevention program that uses school-based health education classes, a virtual wellness club, and community health fairs to promote healthy nutrition and physical activity.

- Examples of multisector community initiatives:
  1. Shape Up Somerville (https://www.somervillema.gov/departments/health-and-human-services/shape-somerville) trains medical professionals on childhood obesity guidelines and current BMI screening practices as part of a community-wide effort in Somerville, Massachusetts, to increase daily physical activity and healthy eating through programming, physical infrastructure improvements, and policy work.
  2. North Carolina Institute of Medicine's task force on early childhood obesity prevention initiative aims to improve education in obesity prevention and treatment for future health professionals as well as practicing health professionals, to ensure adherence of insurers and payers to the Affordable Care Act requirements for coverage of obesity prevention, diagnosis, and treatment of obesity and to compile state and local services, resources, and supports for families.
  3. Healthy weight (https://www.nichq.org/project/collaborate-healthy-weight) is a national quality improvement effort to share and spread promising and evidence-based practices to prevent and treat obesity among children, and this provided an environment for rapid-cycle testing and the robust exchange of ideas with the support of world-class obesity and quality improvement experts.

References

Barlow, S. E. (2007). Expert Committee Recommendations Regarding the Prevention, Assessment, and Treatment of Child and Adolescent Overweight and Obesity: Summary report. *Pediatrics, 120*(Supplement 4), S164–S192.

Barrera, C. M., Perrine, C. G., Li, R., & Scanlon, K. S. (2016). Age at introduction to solid foods and child obesity at 6 years. *Childhood Obesity, 12*(3), 188–192.

Barton, M. (2010). Screening for obesity in children and adolescents: US Preventative Services Task Force recommendation statement. *Pediatrics, 125*(2), 361–367.

Best, J. R., et al. (2016). Shared weight and dietary changes in parent-child dyads following family-based obesity treatment. *Health Psychology, 35*(1), 92–95.

Brown, C. L., Halvorson, E. E., Cohen, G. M., Lazorick, S., & Skelton, J. A. (2015). Addressing childhood obesity. *Pediatric Clinics of North America, 62*(5), 1241–1261.

Cunningham, S. A., Kramer, M. R., & Narayan, K. M. (2014). Incidence of childhood obesity in the United States. *New England Journal of Medicine, 370*, 403–411.

Daniels, S. R., & Hassink, S. G. (2015). The role of the pediatrician in primary prevention of obesity. *Pediatrics, 136*(1), e275–e292.

Davis, M. M., et al. (2007). Recommendations for prevention of childhood obesity. *Pediatrics, 120*(Suppl 4), 5229–5253.

Davoli, A. M., Broccoli, S., Bonvicini, L., Fabbri, A., Ferrari, E., D'Angelo, S., & Romani, G. (2013). Pediatrician-led motivational interviewing to treat overweight children: An RCT. *Pediatrics, 132*(5), e1236–e1246.

Elsie., et al. (2017). Comparative effectiveness of clinical-community childhood obesity interventions: Childhood obesity interventions: A randomized clinical trial. *JAMA Pediatrics, 171*(8), 1–8.

Epstein, L. H., Paluch, R. A., Roemmich, J. N., & Beecher, M. D. (2007). Family-based obesity treatment, then and now: Twenty-five years of pediatric obesity treatment. *Health Psychology, 26*(4), 381–391.

Epstein, L. H., Valoski, A., Wing, R. R., & McCurley, J. (1990). Ten-year follow-up of behavioral, family-based treatment for obese children. *JAMA, 264*(19), 2519–2523.

Gibbs, B. G., & Forste, R. (2013). Socioeconomic status, infant feeding practices and early childhood obesity. *Pediatric Obesity, 9*(2), 135–146.

Gurnani, M., Birken, C., & Hamilton, J. (2015). Childhood obesity: Causes, consequences, and management. *Pediatric Clinics, 62*(4), 821–840.

Hajizadeh, N., Stevens, E. R., Applegate, M., Huang, K. Y., Kamboukos, D., Braithwaite, R. S., & Brotman, L. M. (2017). Potential return on investment of a family-centered early childhood intervention: A cost-effectiveness analysis. *BMC Public Health, 17*(1), 796.

Jull, A., & Chen, R. (2013). Parent-only vs. parent-child only (family focused) approaches for weight loss in obese and overweight children: A systematic review and meta-analysis. *Obesity Review, 14*, 761–768.

Kitzman-Ulrich, H., Wilson, D., George, S., Lawman, H., Segal, M., & Fairchild, A. (2010). The integration of a family systems approach for understanding youth obesity, physical activity, and dietary programs. *Clinical Child and Family Psychology Review, 13*(3), 275–283.

Kolagotla, L., & Adams, W. (2004). Ambulatory management of childhood obesity. *Obesity Research, 12*(2), 275–283.

Kumar, S., & Kelly, A. S. (2017). Review of childhood obesity. *Mayo Clinic Proceedings, 92*(2), 251–265.

Limbers, C. A., Turner, E. A., & Varni, J. W. (2008). Promoting healthy lifestyles: Behavior modification and motivational interviewing in the treatment of childhood obesity. *Journal of Clinical Lipidology, 2*(3), 169–178.

Lobstein, T., Jackson-Leach, R., Moodie, M. L., Hall, K. D., Gortmaker, S. L., Swinburn, B. A., ... Mcpherson, K. (2015). Child and adolescent obesity: Part of a bigger picture. *The Lancet, 385*(9986), 2510–2520.

Matson, K. L., & Fallon, R. M. (2012). Treatment of obesity in children and adolescents. *Journal of Pediatric Pharmacology and Therapeutics, 17*(1), 45–57.

McGovern, L., et al. (2008). Clinical review: Treatment of pediatric obesity: A systematic Review and meta-analysis of randomized trials. *Journal of Clinical Endocrinology Metabolism, 93*(12), 4600–4605.

Mckee, C., Long, L., Southward, L. H., Walker, B., & Mccown, J. (2016). The role of parental misperception of child's body weight in childhood obesity. *Journal of Pediatric Nursing, 31*(2), 196–203.

Office of Disease Prevention and Health Promotion. *Active children and adolescents.* (2018). Retrieved from <https://health.gov/paguidelines/second-edition/>.

Ogden., et al. (2016). Trends in obesity prevalence among children and adolescents in the United States, 1988–1994 through 2013–2014. *JAMA, 315*, 2292–2299.

Pont, S. J., Puhl, R., Cook, S. R., & Slusser, W. (2017). Stigma experienced by children and adolescents with obesity. *Pediatrics, 140*(6)), e20173034.

Quattrin., et al. (2012). Efficacy of family-based weight control program for preschool children in primary care. *Pediatrics, 130*, 660–666.

Rajjo., et al. (2017). Treatment of pediatric obesity: An umbrella systematic review. *Journal of Clinical Endocrinology Metabolism, 102*(3), 763–775.

Resnicow, K., et al. (2016). Advances in motivational interviewing for pediatric obesity. *Pediatric Clinics of North America, 63*(3), 539–562.

Resnicow, K., Davis, R., & Rollnick, S. (2006). Motivational interviewing for pediatric obesity: Conceptual issues and evidence review. *Journal of American Diet Association, 106* (12), 2024–2033.

Schwartz., et al. (2007). Office-based motivational interviewing to prevent childhood obesity: A feasibility study. *Archives of Pediatric and Adolescent Medicine, 161*(15), 495–501.

Simmonds, M., Llewellyn, A., Owen, C. G., & Woolacott, N. (2016). Simple tests for the diagnosis of childhood obesity: A systematic review and meta-analysis. *Obesity Reviews, 17*(12), 1301–1315.

Skjakodegard, H. F., et al. (2016). Study protocol: A randomized controlled trial evaluating the Effect of family-based behavioral treatment of childhood and adolescent obesity – The FABO-study. *BMC Public Health, 16*, 1–9.

Smith, J. D., George, S. M., & Prado, G. (2017). Family-centered positive behavior support interventions in early childhood to prevent obesity. *Child Development, 88*(2), 427–435.

Stark., et al. (2018). Clinic and home-based behavioral intervention for obesity in preschoolers: A randomized trial. *The Journal of Pediatrics, 192*, 115–121.

Styne, D. M., Arslanian, S. A., Connor, E. L., Farooqi, I. S., Murad, M. H., Silverstein, J. H., & Yanovski, J. A. (2017). Pediatric obesity—Assessment, treatment, and prevention: An Endocrine Society Clinical Practice guideline. *The Journal of Clinical Endocrinology & Metabolism, 102*(3), 709–757.

Taveras., et al. (2011). Randomized controlled trial to improve primary care to prevent and manage childhood obesity: The high five for kids study. *Archives of Pediatric and Adolescent Medicine, 165*, 714–722.

U.S. Department of Health and Human Services. *Defining childhood obesity.* (2018). Retrieved from <https://www.cdc.gov/obesity/childhood/defining.html>.

Vine, M., Hargreaves, M. B., Briefel, R. R., & Orfield, C. (2013). Expanding the role of primary care in the prevention and treatment of childhood obesity: A review of clinic- and community-based recommendations and interventions. *Journal of Obesity, 2013*, 1–17.

Wang, Y., Cai, L., Wu, Y., Wilson, R. F., Weston, C., Fawole, O., ... Segal, J. (2015). What childhood obesity prevention programmes work? A systematic review and meta-analysis. *Obesity Reviews, 16*(7), 547–565.

Ward, Z. J., Long, M. W., Resch, S. C., Giles, C. M., Cradock, A. L., & Gortmaker, S. L. (2017). Simulation of growth trajectories of childhood obesity into adulthood. *New England Journal of Medicine, 377*(22), 2145–2153.

Whitlock, E. P., O'Connor, E. A., Williams, S. B., Beil, T. L., & Lutz, K. W. (2010). Effectiveness of weight management interventions in children: A targeted systematic review for the USPSTF. *Pediatrics, 125*(2), e396–418.

Wilfley, D. E., et al. (2007). Efficacy of maintenance treatment approaches for childhood overweight: A randomized controlled trial. *JAMA, 298*(14), 1661–1673.

Wilfley, D. E., et al. (2017). Dose, content, and mediators of family-based treatment for childhood obesity: A multisite randomized clinical trial. *JAMA Pediatrics, 171*(12), 1151–1159.

Zabarsky, G., Beek, C., Hagman, E., Pierpont, B., Caprio, S., & Weiss, R. (2018). Impact of severe obesity on cardiovascular risk factors in youth. *The Journal of Pediatrics, 192*, 105–114.

CHAPTER

4

Expectations and recommendations for toileting

Kimberly Burkhart[1], *Carrie Cuffman*[2] *and Catherine Scherer*[2]

[1]Pediatrics & Psychiatry, Rainbow Babies and Children's Hospital, Case Western Reserve University, Cleveland, OH, United States, [2]Department of Pediatrics, Division of Developmental-Behavioral Pediatrics & Psychology, Rainbow Babies and Children's Hospital, Cleveland, OH, United States

Introduction

This chapter focuses on toilet training and the most common problems associated with toileting, such as encopresis and enuresis. The focus of this chapter is on "normative" child development, but it is important to note that the time and speed with which each child moves through the various stages of toilet training differ. Different expectations and recommendations may be appropriate for a child with a neurodevelopmental disorder such as autism spectrum disorder or a severe developmental delay. Medical and behavioral recommendations are provided within this chapter for children who are experiencing toileting problems. If toileting problems do not resolve, it is recommended that parents consult with a healthcare and/or a behavioral health provider.

Toilet training

Toilet training should be initiated when a toddler meets specific physical, behavioral, and developmental milestones. For example, the ability to identify sensation of fullness in the rectum and interest in toileting tend to appear at predictable ages. Children typically begin to

Clinician's Toolkit for Children's Behavioral Health
DOI: https://doi.org/10.1016/B978-0-12-816024-4.00004-8

identify the sensation of fullness between 12 and 18 months of age. Many toddlers show interest in toilet training around 2 years of age. While many parents start toilet training before age 2, some research suggests that there is little benefit of starting training before 27 months of age (Blum, Taubman, & Nemeth, 2003).

Readiness for toilet training is evidenced by children asking questions about diapers, the toilet, and wearing underwear. Females typically show interest and master toilet training earlier than males. Children with developmental delays are ready to train later than typically developing children. To determine whether a toddler is ready to begin toilet training, please see Handout 1. Having the ability to sense the urge to go, keeping a diaper dry for at least 2 hours and following basic instructions are essential to the toilet training process. If the child is unable to walk to the toilet (e.g., due to a motor disability) or is unable to pull up or down his or her pants or diaper, toilet training can still be initiated, but the child will require more caregiver assistance.

Once the child appears ready, it is recommended that the child be involved in choosing a potty chair. The potty chair or seat should be put in the bathroom so the child can become familiar with it. The child should have the opportunity to sit on the potty chair with his/her clothes on. The child may prefer to use a toilet over a potty chair to model a parent or sibling. If that is the case, then a step stool, and possibly also a modified toilet seat, should be used. The child should have his/her feet resting on the floor or on a stool. The child should have the opportunity to get comfortable with the toilet and to play with a toy or look at a book while sitting. The parent's goal should be to make the bathroom a fun place for the child.

To begin the toilet training process, using the toilet to urinate should be the primary focus. Once daytime competency for using the toilet to urinate is accomplished, a parent can then focus on the child having bowel movements in the toilet. A parent should instruct the child to sit on the potty chair or toilet without a diaper for a few minutes at 2-hour intervals including when the child first wakes up in the morning, after meals, and before and after naptime. For boys, it is typically easiest to master urination sitting down. The process can gradually move toward urinating standing up after bowel training has been completed. Parents should track when their child goes to the bathroom to begin to facilitate a regular schedule. When a child stools in a diaper, the parent can help the child to dump the content of a dirty diaper in the toilet. The child can further participate in this process by flushing the toilet, which can be reinforcing for the child. Parents should look for behavior changes to indicate when stooling needs to take place. The potty chair should be brought with parents to facilitate practice away from home. Immediate verbal praise and small reinforcers such as stickers are often helpful in positively shaping toileting behavior. Positive reinforcement is described in more detail in Handout 4.

Parents should be coached to be patient, to remember that many accidents are expected to happen, and to understand that this process takes months, and sometimes over a year (Blum et al., 2003). Parents should stay calm when accidents occur, and children should not be punished for accidents.

Toilet training should be initiated when there is not going to be a major life change such as the family moving or the arrival of a sibling. Parents should be aware that toileting competency during naptime and nighttime takes longer to achieve. Most children will fully achieve dry sleep times between ages 5 and 7. Until then, disposable training pants and mattress covers can be used.

Constipation and encopresis

Definition and prevalence

Constipation is a common problem among children with worldwide prevalence estimates ranging between 0.7% and 29.6%. It is cited as the reason for 3%–5% of primary care visits and 25% of the referrals to gastroenterologists (Colombo, Wassom, & Rosen, 2015; Madani, Tsang, & Kamat, 2016; van den Berg, Benninga, & Di Lorenzo, 2006). Constipation is defined as having bowel movements that occur less often than usual or consist of hard, dry stools that are difficult to pass. A child who has not had a bowel movement in 4 days is considered constipated. More specifically, Rome III criteria are often used by medical providers to determine whether a patient is meeting criteria for functional constipation. Functional constipation is defined as meeting at least two of the following criteria every week for the past 2 months: two or fewer defecations in the toilet per week, at least one episode of fecal incontinence each week, history of painful or hard bowel movements, presence of large fecal mass in the rectum, and/or history of large diameter stools obstructing the toilet. Patients and their caregivers are often asked to rate the child's stool consistency through the use of the Bristol stool chart, which provides a chart of seven stool types with Type 1 being indicative of constipation and Type 7 being indicative of watery, entirely liquid stool (Heaton & Lewis, 1997).

Encopresis is less common than constipation. Encopresis is estimated to occur in approximately 3% of 4-year-olds and 1.6% of 10-year-olds (Har & Croffie, 2010). According to the Diagnostic and Statistical Manual of Mental Disorders (5th ed.; DSM–5; American Psychiatric Association, 2013), an individual meets criteria for encopresis when there has been repeated passage of feces into inappropriate places whether involuntary or intentional, at least one such event has occurred each month for at least 3 months, and the chronological age or developmental age of the individual is at least 4-years-old. This behavior cannot be attributable to physiological effects of a substance (e.g., laxative) or another medical condition except through a mechanism involving constipation. Criteria for encopresis involve either experiencing constipation with overflow incontinence or without constipation and overflow incontinence, which is determined by physical examination or by history (American Psychiatric Association, 2013). Rome III criteria are often used by medical providers to distinguish between retentive fecal incontinence and nonretentive fecal incontinence. Fecal incontinence is defined as the involuntary passage of stool in inappropriate places after toileting skills have been acquired. The retentive type is associated with functional constipation and impaction, which typically occurs when liquid stool leaks around an impacted stool ball. Nonretentive type occurs in the absence of constipation. The patient must meet all of the following criteria for the past 2 months to be diagnosed with nonretentive fecal incontinence: defecation into places that are inappropriate to the social context at least once a month, no evidence of inflammatory, anatomic, metabolic, or neoplastic process that explains the symptoms, and no evidence of fecal retention (Rasquin, Di Lorenzo, & Forbes, 2006). Nonretentive type is characterized by voluntary stooling into a diaper or clothes and is typically behavioral in etiology (Har & Croffie, 2010).

Etiology

Functional constipation, or constipation without an identified organic etiology, is the most common type of childhood constipation. Functional constipation often presents at times of transition. In infancy, constipation often occurs when switching from breast milk to cow's milk or pureed foods to solid foods. In toddlers, constipation typically presents at the time of toilet training. In young children, constipation may present when entering school (Madani et al., 2016).

Many factors contribute to and can worsen functional constipation, including inadequate hydration, a limited diet, stool withholding, externalizing behavior, a sedentary lifestyle, and slow intestinal transit or motility issues (Colombo et al., 2015). Just as functional constipation is the most common cause of constipation, functional encopresis is the most common cause of encopresis and represents about 90% of all encopresis. The most common cause of functional encopresis is overflow incontinence associated with constipation (Har & Croffie, 2010).

Stool withholding plays a significant role in both childhood functional constipation and retentive encopresis. The cycle of stool withholding often begins when the child does not recognize or does not respond to the urge to defecate. This results in stool remaining in the rectum and the rectum stretching. The longer the child goes without defecating, the more stool accumulates; and as this occurs, stool becomes harder, drier, and more difficult and painful to pass. If this happens repeatedly, encopresis may occur as stool becomes impacted and subsequent peristaltic movement of the colon pushes liquid stool around the impaction. The reasons why a child may start the cycle of stool withholding are varied and typically include a painful bowel movement, not wishing to stool at school, and/or being unwilling to interrupt a preferred activity to use the toilet (Colombo et al., 2015).

While the majority of constipation and encopresis in children is functional, there are organic causes that should be assessed. Less common causes of constipation include Hirschsprung's disease (in which the absence of ganglion cells in the intestinal wall leaves the colon in constant contraction), anterior displacement of the anus, hypothyroidism, celiac disease, irritable bowel syndrome, and the use of medications such as anticholinergics and narcotics (Madani et al., 2016). Organic causes of encopresis overlap with organic causes of constipation and include anatomic causes such as poorly functioning anorectum after the correction of imperforate anus or anal stenosis, disruption of neural pathways after bowel resection, neurologic causes such as Chagas disease, Hirschsprung's disease, or spinal cord injury, and medications such as tricyclic antidepressants (Har & Croffie, 2010). Warning signs indicating that further evaluation is needed to rule out a medical condition include failure to stool within 48 hours of birth, poor growth, neurologic abnormalities (particularly of lower extremities), poor bladder control, bloody stools, severe abdominal pain, vomiting, or fever (Colombo et al., 2015; Madani et al., 2016).

Behavioral health treatment of constipation and encopresis

Psychosocial assessment of encopresis involves meeting with caregivers to evaluate the child's current stooling patterns. The clinician also should assess whether the child has the ability to communicate the need to use the toilet and if he/she has the prerequisite skills necessary to use the toilet (e.g., unbutton/pull down pants, sit, wipe, and pull-up pants). Additional information that needs to be obtained includes determining whether the child is stooling daily or withholding the stool, giving behavioral indications of stool retention, complying with using the toilet to stool, and information on the child's type of stool and overall toileting habits. Caregivers should be asked whether the child stools in the toilet, uses a pull-up, stools in his/her pants, complies with sit times, when and where fecal episodes occur, whether parents have implemented sit times, and if the child is compliant.

Behavioral assessment also involves determining what methods have been used to encourage the child to use the toilet, how the child has responded to the methods that have been tried, environmental contingencies that have been established, and the emotional, social, and behavioral functioning of the child (Cunningham & Banez, 2006). Based on the child's developmental level, he/she should be asked about the frequency with which he/she stools (poops), if and how he/she can tell that he/she needs to stool, where stooling occurs, whether it hurts, if there is difficulty in having it come out, whether the child wants to learn how to use the toilet (potty), whether (and why) the child dislikes stooling, and if he/she has stomachaches (Cunningham & Banez, 2006).

The next step is to provide psychoeducation on diagnostic criteria and treatment. Parent response to toileting problems can create emotional and behavioral problems in the child such as anxiety and/or disruptive behavior. For example, if parents are overly emotional or punitive in their response, this could negatively impact the child's mental health and parent–child interactions and inadvertently cause the behavior to be maintained.

If fecal incontinence is due to a medical or developmental disorder, issues affecting stooling, such as the child's motivation and compliance, should be further evaluated. If the child meets criteria for retentive fecal incontinence, education about appropriate intake of dietary fiber and water, digestion, and elimination should be provided to the parent and child (if the child is able to understand), a structured behavioral toileting program should be established, and any needed treatment of oppositional behavior should be provided. Relaxation strategies should be taught and used prior to stooling to minimize pain. Moderate exercise on a regular basis should be recommended as it can facilitate the passage of stool. For nonretentive fecal incontinence a structured behavioral toileting program needs to be established, and treatment of oppositional behavior is often needed (Cunningham & Banez, 2006). A structured behavioral plan consists of collecting baseline data, modeling/practicing sit times, implementing sit times at regular intervals, teaching the child to strain, and positive reinforcement for stooling on the toilet. Please see Handouts 2–5 for more information.

Biofeedback

Another method of addressing defecation disorders is biofeedback that for constipation uses anorectal monitoring to make physiological information accessible to the patient including when and how to engage in relaxation. Mixed results of research on this method have been attributed to small sample size, uncontrolled designs, simultaneous use of laxatives, and differences in identifying successful treatment outcomes. Biofeedback may be considered helpful as an adjunctive treatment, but intense conventional laxative treatment with behavioral intervention is recommended as best practice (e.g., Bleijenberg & Kuijers, 1994; Fernandez-fraga, Azpiroz, Casaus, Aparici, & Malagelada, 2005; Loening-Baucke 1995; van der Plas et al., 1996).

Medical treatment of constipation

In addition to behavioral treatments for constipation, medical treatments can play a key role. If fecal impaction is present, the first step in treatment is for a medical professional to perform a disimpaction (bowel cleanout). Removal of fecal impaction allows decompression of the rectum and normal passage of stool. Without disimpaction a child with fecal impaction cannot return to normal stooling patterns and may have fecal soiling. There are numerous ways to perform a cleanout, but oral laxatives are typically the preferred method. The medical professional prescribes a large amount of laxative to be taken over several days. Osmotic laxatives are often used by themselves or may be used in combination with stimulant laxatives, such as senna or bisacodyl. Enemas or rectal irrigations are used, as well, by some healthcare providers. If prior at-home cleanouts have failed or the patient is severely impacted, a healthcare provider may choose to admit the child to the hospital for administration of laxatives via nasogastric tube. As a last resort, manual disimpaction under anesthesia may be used (Colombo et al., 2015; Har & Croffie, 2010; Tabbers et al., 2014).

After disimpaction has been successfully completed, the child should be placed on maintenance laxative therapy. This prevents recurrent fecal impaction and enables continued painless passage of bowel movements. Maintenance treatment can continue for months to years depending on the child's needs. PEG 3350 is the most common medication used for maintenance therapy due to its ease of use and improved efficacy compared to other oral laxatives (Colombo et al., 2015). Of the other oral laxatives, lactulose is generally preferred over mineral oil or milk of magnesia due to limited research on the latter two (Tabbers et al., 2014). Stimulant laxatives, such as senna and bisacodyl, are sometimes used in conjunction with an osmotic laxative or stool softener. In addition to pharmacologic treatment, healthcare providers also frequently counsel their patients on diet changes as a treatment for constipation, particularly increasing fiber and fluid intake. While these diet changes are widely recommended, there is limited evidence of their effectiveness (Tabbers et al., 2014). Tables 4.1 and 4.2 provide details on treatment recommendations for healthcare professionals.

TABLE 4.1 Recommendations for an initial visit for constipation (Colombo et al., 2015).

- Evaluate for red flags on history and physical exam and if present evaluate further or consider referral to a pediatric GI specialist
- If impacted: Perform cleanout
- If not impacted: Start maintenance regimen with oral medication
- For all patients: Provide education, discuss behavioral modifications, and counsel on diet changes

TABLE 4.2 Typical dosing of frequently used oral laxatives.

PEG 3350	Maintenance: 0.2–0.8 g/kg/day
	Disimpaction: 1–1.5 g/kg/day (max 100 g/day, max 6 days)
Lactulose	1–2 g/kg, once to twice/day[a]
Mineral oil	1–18 years: 1–3 mL/kg/day (max 90 mL/day)[a]
Bisacodyl	3–10 years: 5 mg/day[a]
	>10 years: 5–10 mg/day[a]
Senna	2–6 years: 2.5–5 mg once to twice/day[a]
	6–12 years: 7.5–10 mg/day[a]
	>12 years: 15–20 mg/day[a]

[a]*Maintenance dosing.*
Adapted from Tabbers, M., DiLorenza, C., Berger, M., Faure, C., Langendam, M., Nurko, S., et al. (2014). Evaluation and treatment of functional constipation in infants and children: Evidence-based recommendations from ESPGHAN and NASPGHAN. Journal of Pediatric Gastroenterology and Nutrition, 58(2), 258–274.

Associations and outcomes

Research indicates that encopresis is associated with lower self-esteem, decreased academic performance, greater social isolation, family disruption, and higher rates of engaging in bullying and antisocial behaviors (Har & Croffie, 2010; Joinson, Heron, Butler, & von Gontard, 2006; Kovacic et al., 2015). It is not yet known whether these factors are causal, whether they result from the many difficulties associated with encopresis, or whether the relationships are bidirectional. In the educational setting, accommodations are often needed, which include toileting breaks, ensuring bathroom accessibility, and providing classroom modification (Garman & Fica, 2012).

Children with ADHD are more likely to have constipation and fecal incontinence. It is possible that this is attributed to an altered peripheral or enteric nervous system (McKeown, Hisle-Gorman, Eide,

Gorman, & Nylund, 2013). Moreover, 10%–20% of children with autism spectrum disorder have comorbid encopresis (Hardy, 2009). Abuse and other forms of stress have also been shown to be associated with constipation and encopresis (Philichi, 2008). Problems with toileting in children for whom medical causes have been ruled out and competency has already been achieved should serve as a warning sign that additional assessment around trauma and abuse should be considered. Approximately 25% of the children who suffer from constipation continue to have constipation into adulthood (Rajindrajith, Devanarayana, Perera, & Benninga, 2016).

Enuresis

Definition and prevalence

The International Children's Continence Society developed standardized definitions for lower urinary tract (LUT) dysfunction (Austin et al., 2014; Neveus et al., 2006). LUT dysfunction falls under the broader term bladder bowel dysfunction. Comorbid bowel problems often include constipation and encopresis. If bowel problems are not present, the term LUT dysfunction is used. LUT dysfunction can include storage problems such as incontinence, as well as voiding abnormalities related to frequency, hesitancy, and straining (Kuwertz-Broking & von Gontard, 2018).

Urinary incontinence is defined as the involuntary leakage of urine in children equivalent to a chronological or developmental age of 5-years-old with at least one episode of leaking per month for the past 3 months (Roth & Austin, 2014). Incontinence can be further defined as continuous or intermittent. Continuous incontinence usually occurs with anatomic urinary abnormalities or following urologic surgeries. Intermittent incontinence includes both diurnal and nocturnal enuresis. According to the DSM-5, enuresis is defined as repeated voiding of urine into the bed or clothes whether voluntary or unintentional with a frequency of at least twice a week for at least 3 consecutive months or the presence of clinically significant distress or impairment in social, academic, or other important areas of functioning (American Psychiatric Association, 2013).

Approximately 15% of children experience daytime incontinence at 4.5-years-old. Between 10% and 15% of 7-year-old, children meet criteria for enuresis with a decrease of 15% with each year of age thereafter (Maternik, Krzeminska, & Zurowska, 2015). At 15-years-old, only 1% of children will meet criteria (Bayne & Skoog, 2014). When a child has never obtained continence, it is referred to as primary. Primary enuresis occurs in 75% of the children who meet criteria for enuresis.

In secondary enuresis, wetting has resumed after a dry period that has lasted 6 months or greater and is commonly associated with LUT and/or constipation.

Etiology

The etiology of nocturnal enuresis is multifactorial and often includes overactive bladder, underactive bladder, dysfunctional voiding, vesicovaginal reflux, extraordinary daytime frequency (at least hourly voiding of small volumes of urine), and/or anatomic abnormalities, such as ectopic ureter and posterior urethral valves (Maternik et al., 2015). Approximately 75% of children meet criteria for nocturnal enuresis, which is also referred to as monosymptomatic enuresis (MSE). Non-MSE (NMSE) refers to the presence of LUT symptoms, such as daytime incontinence or voiding abnormalities along with nocturnal leaking. NMSE accounts for 30% of all cases of enuresis.

MSE is thought to be largely inherited in an autosomal dominant pattern (Kuwertz-Broking & von Gontard, 2018). The risk for meeting criteria for MSE is 77% when both parents have a history of MSE (Kuwertz-Broking & von Gontard, 2018; Traisman, 2015). Another cause of MSE is polyuria or excess nighttime urine production (defined as urine production greater than 130% of the expected bladder capacity for age). In some children, this is related to an abnormal diurnal pattern of vasopressin secretion, which causes increased urine production at night (Kuwertz-Broking & von Gontard, 2018). Nocturnal bladder overactivity and decreased capacity are additional causes. Approximately 30% of the children with enuresis meet criteria for NMSE (Roth & Austin, 2014). The etiology of NMSE is often the same as MSE, but many times constipation is present, which can be the main cause of enuresis (Roth & Austin, 2014).

Behavioral health treatment of enuresis

The first step in treating enuresis is to determine whether constipation is present. If constipation is present, then behavioral and medical intervention should be implemented to address this problem. A detailed history should be taken with the following questions asked (Bayne & Skoog, 2014):

1. The age at which the child was toilet trained for both urine and stool (if applicable)
2. The child's dietary habits
3. History of urinary tract infections, urologic surgeries, or abnormalities

4. Whether there have been urine or stool control problems in the past
5. If the child has been dry at night for greater than 6 months
6. If recent stressors have presented

The following questions related to voiding should be asked (Kuwertz-Broking & von Gontard, 2018):

1. How often does the child urinate during the day?
2. How many nights per week does the child wet?
3. What is the volume of urine that the child leaks or wets?
4. Have there been any changes in frequency?
5. Are there signs of urgency, hesitancy, straining, or holding maneuvers (standing on tip toes, crossing legs, grabbing, or squatting with the heel pressed to the perineum)?
6. Have there been complaints of incomplete emptying, postvoid dribbling, and/or pain?

A dietary history should include drinking habits (amount and time of day), caffeine use, and amount of dairy and carbonated beverages consumed. History of urinary tract infections, urologic surgeries, or abnormalities also is needed.

Diurnal wetting should be targeted before nocturnal wetting. A voiding diary should be kept to determine patterns. Simple behavioral interventions are often the first line of treatment for enuresis. These simple treatments, such as fluid restriction, rewarding dry nights, lifting and waking, and bladder training, are more effective than no treatment, but less effective in comparison to the use of enuresis alarm therapy and medication.

There is not one simple behavioral intervention, however, that seems to be more effective than another (Caldwell, Nankivell, & Sureshkumar, 2013). There are simple behavioral interventions to address incontinence, which are as follows:

Fluid restriction—Fluid restriction, particularly before bedtime, may decrease bladder volume. Fluids should be restricted 1–2 hours prior to going to bed.

Lifting—Caregivers lift the child while the child is still asleep to put the child on the toilet to urinate. It has been argued, however, that this method does not give the child the opportunity to recognize the sensation of a full bladder, which is a skill needed for successful toileting behavior.

Scheduled wakening—Caregivers wake the child to urinate. Baseline data on typical wetting times can be obtained to assist the caregiver in deciding when best to wake the child. It is often recommended that caregivers wake up children 1.5–2 hours after falling asleep. Older children can use an alarm to engage in scheduled wakening and toileting.

Positive reinforcement—Children are rewarded when they remain dry for the night or get up to use the toilet. See Handout 4 for details on the effective use of positive reinforcers.

Stop–start method—Children with weak pelvic muscles are taught and asked to repeatedly interrupt their urine stream to strengthen pelvic muscles.

Complex behavioral interventions often involve the use of an enuresis alarm. Alarms often consist of sensors in the child's underwear or in a bed pad. When the child urinates, a buzzer, vibration, or light goes off. This then serves as a trigger for the child to stop urinating and to get up to use the toilet. After alarm training has been successful, overlearning can be implemented. Overlearning is a reinforcement procedure in which extra drinks are given at bedtime to ensure that the bladder is full and that the child learns to wake up to void.

Dry bed training involves waking the child up every hour the first night to go to the bathroom. If an accident occurs, the child engages in cleanliness training and positive practice. Full spectrum training involves a combination of positive reinforcement, enuresis alarm training, retention control training, overlearning, and cleanliness training.

The first-line treatment of daytime incontinence is urotherapy, which involves education on bladder functioning, regular voiding habits, fluid intake, pelvic muscle training, and behavior modification (Maternik et al., 2015). Research indicates that after 3 months of intervention, children's health-related quality of life significantly improves following urotherapy (Equit, Hill, Hubner, & von Gontard, 2014).

Biofeedback has been used to treat children with symptoms of bladder dysfunction. There is little research to support its effectiveness, and studies are based on small sample sizes. Meta-analyses indicate that there is no support for the effectiveness of biofeedback for the treatment of children with enuresis. Additional research using randomized controlled trials is needed to better address the effectiveness of this method (Fazeli, Lin, Nikoo, Jaggumantri, & Afshar, 2015).

Medical evaluation and treatment of enuresis

The physical exam should include abdominal exam to look for masses, distension, palpable stool, or organomegaly. The genital area should be examined for irritation, dampness, or urethral polyps. The exam should also include the sacral region for potential anatomical abnormalities such as sacral dimple, gluteal cleft, lipoma, or hair tuft (Roth & Austin, 2014), as well as an overall neurologic assessment of tone, muscle strength, and reflexes. Laboratory studies should include a urinalysis.

Medications for enuresis can be considered when urotherapy has not been successful. Medications can help control symptoms but do not lead to the resolution of enuresis (Kuwertz-Broking, & von Gontard, 2018; Traisman, 2015). Desmopressin (DDAVP), a synthetic analog of vasopressin, is used to reduce urine production at night and is approved for children older than 6 years of age (Kuwertz-Broking & von Gontard, 2018; Traisman, 2015). It can be used alone or with a bedwetting alarm. Success rates with using DDAVP are between 60% and 70%, with 30% of patients responding fully and 40% responding partially. Tablets are given 30–60 minutes prior to bed. The medication lasts for approximately 8–10 hours. If it is successful, it can be used in 3-month intervals. Since enuresis resolves at a rate of 15% per year without intervention, it is important to stop the medication and check for resolution. DDAVP is considered safe; however, it can have a serious side effect of water intoxication and hyponatremia. This can present with headache, nausea, vomiting, and convulsions.

Oxybutynin is an anticholinergic medication that is most effective when used with DDAVP (Kuwertz-Broking & von Gontard, 2018; Traisman, 2015). Children with decreased functional bladder capacity may benefit from this medication. It comes in both short- and long-acting forms. Side effects include dry mouth, flushing, constipation, and blurred vision.

Imipramine, a tricyclic antidepressant, has anticholinergic, antispasmodic, and CNS effects. It is approved for children ages 6 years and older for enuresis. Imipramine is a third-line treatment due to its potential side effects, particularly cardiotoxicity. It should only be prescribed by a specialist. It has a 40% success rate, and many children relapse when it is stopped. Common side effects include dry mouth and changes in mood. Table 4.3 lists steps for healthcare providers to follow when a patient presents with enuresis.

TABLE 4.3 Recommendations for an initial visit for enuresis.

- When possible, a 1-week bowel and bladder diary should be done prior to the visit
- A careful history should include asking about leaking, voiding patterns, and stooling patterns
- Treat constipation first and then address daytime urinary symptoms and then nighttime voiding
- For all patients: provide education and discuss urotherapy

Associations and outcomes

Enuresis is associated with lower self-esteem and academic performance, increased social isolation and sibling teasing, and decreased family quality of life (Caldwell et al., 2013; Kuwertz-Broking & von Gontard, 2018; National Clinical Guideline Centre, 2010). It is not yet known whether these factors are causal, result from the many difficulties associated with enuresis, or the relationships are bidirectional. Those who have ADHD and conduct problems are more likely to have enuresis (Maternik et al., 2015; National Clinical Guideline Centre, 2010; Roth & Austin, 2014). Also, constipation, daytime incontinence, encopresis, developmental problems, male gender, and young age are associated with enuresis (National Clinical Guideline Centre, 2010).

Emotional stressors and social concerns are associated with moderate enuresis (Sureshkumar, Jones, Caldwell, & Craig, 2009). Secondary enuresis is often associated with having experienced a stressful event (e.g., divorce, trauma, or abuse), which serves as a precipitant (Sinha & Raut, 2016). An association has been found between stressful early childhood events and nocturnal enuresis occurring at least twice per week up to several years later (Joinson, Sullivan, von Gontard, & Heron, 2016). Children who have been exposed to disturbing events (e.g., family breakdown, moving, or separation from parent) in the first 4 years of life, especially between the age of 3 and 4 years, have an increased prevalence of having nocturnal enuresis up to age 15 years. Children exposed to 4 or more disturbing events have double the risk of experiencing nocturnal enuresis (Douglas, 1973). Delayed or inadequate toilet training has been shown to put children at risk for nocturnal enuresis, as well (Franco, von Gontard, & DeGennaro, 2013). Enuresis is more common at all ages in lower socioeconomic groups (Sinha & Raut, 2016). There is evidence to suggest that enuretic children are at a high risk for experiencing physical punishment and children whose parents had enuresis are at even higher risk for being physically punished (Sá et al., 2016).

Conclusion

Toilet training is a targeted major developmental milestone for children between the age of 2 and 3 years. Successful toilet training typically starts once the child shows signs of readiness and interest and can last for many months. Several toileting problems also can present in childhood. For example, constipation among children is common. Encopresis is the voluntary or intentional, repeated passage of feces into inappropriate places. While the majority of constipation and encopresis in children is functional, there are organic causes which should be assessed. Enuresis is characterized by voluntary or unintentional repeated voiding of urine into the bed or clothes. Its etiology is often multifactorial, with a strong genetic component. Both encopresis and enuresis can be associated with stress, trauma, or child maltreatment. Medical treatment and behavioral health intervention often go hand in hand in the treatment of constipation, encopresis, and enuresis. Psychosocial assessment is needed, a structured and consistent approach to toileting should be developed, and reinforcement for targeted behavior should be provided.

Handout 1. Is the child ready to toilet train?

Toilet training (potty training) is best started only when children are able to do certain things.

If the answers to the following are "yes," then your child may be ready to toilet train.

1. Can the child sense the urge to go?
2. Can the child walk to and sit on the toilet?
3. Can the child keep a diaper dry for at least 2 hours?
4. Can the child follow basic instructions?
5. Can the child pull down his/her pull-up, diaper, training pants, and/or underwear? If not, toilet training can still be initiated, but with caregiver assistance with steps.

Handout 2. Using sit times for constipation and encopresis

First figure out when your child's bowel movements usually occur. You can do this by monitoring for a bowel movement:

- Check your child's clothing at least three times a day for poop.
  - If your child pooped in their clothes, he or she should rinse and wash his/her clothing if able to do so, or help you do these things. You should then bathe your child (or have them bathe/shower by themselves if they are able). The child should put on clean clothes. Stay calm during this process.
  - Praise and consider providing a reward if your child stools in the toilet.
- Document the time and consistency of each stool in the stool diary.

Then start doing sit times:

- Use your stool diary to determine when your child usually poops.
- Have your child sit on the toilet at the times they typically poop.
- If your child doesn't seem to follow a regular pattern of pooping, choose two to three times during the day, which will work best. Children often have bowel movements after meals, so after eating is a good time to try.
- Have your child sit for 5–10 minutes.
- Praise your child for sitting.

Other tips:

- Make sure your child is sitting in the right position: feet firmly on a flat surface with the knees at the same height as the hips.
- Avoid distractions.
- Have your child relax and try to make sit times pleasant.

If your child poops in the toilet,

- Check the toilet for stool consistency and amount.
- Provide a reward when they poop in the toilet.
- Document the stool in the stool diary.

Handout 3. Stooling diary

Date	Time	Stool on toilet (Y or N)?	If no, participated in cleanup (Y or N)?	Amount of stool (small, medium, or large)	Consistency (soft, medium, or hard)	Medication (type and time)

Handout 4. Rewarding stooling in the toilet

Rules for giving rewards

1. Immediate—Give the reward within minutes of the toileting behavior.
2. Consistent—Give the reward every time the behavior occurs.
3. Predictable—Inform the child about the rewards in advance.
4. Contingent upon the behavior occurring—Give the reward only for the targeted behavior.
5. Special/new—The reward should be desirable to the child and novel; rewards may need to be changed over time.
6. Motivating to the child.

Types of rewards

1. Primary (food or drink)
2. Social (hugs, high fives, praise, or other positive social attention)
3. Tangible (stickers or small toys)
4. Activities/privileges (going to the park, riding bikes, special play time with a parent, watching television, or a short period of time with electronics)
5. Tokens (small objects such as poker chips or points earned for the child to purchase a primary, social, tangible, or activity reinforcer)

Handout 5. Behavioral strategies for addressing toileting problems and challenging behavior

Difficulty transitioning from a diaper to the toilet

1. Identify a reinforcer/reward.
2. Use backward chaining (i.e., breaking a skill down into smaller steps, then teaching and reinforcing the last step in the sequence first, then the second to the last step, and so on). For example, have the child wash his/her hands in the sink near the toilet. Provide a reinforcer. Continue to work backward by choosing the next step, such as pulling up his/her pants while standing near the toilet followed by flushing the toilet, and wiping. Allow the child several trials of each step before proceeding to the next, and reinforce completion every time.
3. Provide a diaper when asked, but only when the child is in the bathroom. Reinforce successful voiding in the bathroom.
4. Once your child is doing this, it is required that he/she sit on the toilet while wearing the diaper in order to get the reinforcer.
5. Cut a hole in the diaper so the child can void in the toilet.
6. Continue practice with the previous step until the diaper can be removed and voiding in the toilet is successful.

Challenging behavior at sit times

1. Use shaping—Have your child sit on the toilet to determine a baseline of how long your child will sit. It is not expected that children will sit for longer than 5 minutes. Gradually increase this amount of time using a positive reinforcer after completion of sit times. If your child gets up before the time is up, do not give the reinforcer. Provide your child with a relaxing activity to make the toilet a positive experience.
2. Escape behavior—If your child tantrums when toileting requests are made, set a timer for a short period of time (e.g., 10 seconds) and place the child on the toilet. Keep the child there until the timer rings. The child can engage in enjoyable activities while waiting. Once the child sits for 10 seconds cooperatively, gradually increase the amount of time. If your child refuses to even go in the bathroom, then move the child closer and closer to the bathroom by setting a timer and using a reinforcer at each step. The child could first be reinforced for standing in the doorway and then in front of the sink. Close approximations should be reinforced until the child is using the toilet.

Handout 6. Recommended resources

The Poo in You, a YouTube video about "poo accidents," constipation, and encopresis for youths, produced by Children's Hospital of Colorado; available at https://www.youtube.com/watch?v=SgBj7Mc_4sc

It's Potty Time, Tracey Corderoy, 2014—toilet training and using the potty

The Princess and the Potty, Wendy Cheyette Lewison, 2015—toilet training

Uh, Oh Gotta Go, Bob McGraph, 1996—toilet training

International Children's Continence Society Resources for Families: http://i-c-c-s.org/parents/

Important points to remember

- While many parents start toilet training before age 2, some research suggests that there is little benefit of starting training before 27 months of age (Blum et al., 2003).
- Parents should stay calm when accidents occur, and children should not be punished for accidents.
- Functional constipation often presents at times of transition. In infancy, constipation often occurs when switching from breast milk to cow's milk or pureed foods to solid foods. In toddlers, constipation typically presents at the time of toilet training. In young children, constipation may present when entering school (Madani et al., 2016).
- Warning signs indicating that further evaluation is needed to rule out a medical condition include failure to stool within 48 hours of birth, poor growth, neurologic abnormalities (particularly of lower extremities), poor bladder control, bloody stools, severe abdominal pain, vomiting, or fever (Colombo et al., 2015; Madani et al., 2016).
- Simple behavioral interventions are often the first line of treatment for enuresis. These simple treatments, such as fluid restriction, rewarding dry nights, lifting and waking, and bladder training, are more effective than no treatment, but less effective in comparison to the use of enuresis alarm therapy and medication.

References

American Psychiatric Association. (2013). Elimination disorders. In *Diagnostic and statistical manual of mental disorders* (5th ed.). Washington, DC: American Psychiatric Publishing.

Austin, P. F., Bauer, S. B., Bower, W., Chase, J., Franco, I., Hoebeke, P., & Nevéus, T. (2014). The standardization of terminology of lower urinary tract function in children and adolescents: Update report from the standardization committee of the international children's continence society. *The Journal of Urology, 191*(6), 1865. e13.

Bayne, A. P., & Skoog, S. J. (2014). Nocturnal enuresis: An approach to assessment and treatment. *Pediatrics in Review/American Academy of Pediatrics, 35*(8), 327–335. Available from https://doi.org/10.1542/pir.35-8-327.

Bleijenberg, G., & Kuijers, H. C. (1994). Biofeedback treatment of constipation: A comparison of two methods. *American Journal of Gastroenterology, 89*, 1021–1026.

Blum, N. J., Taubman, B., & Nemeth, N. (2003). Relationship between age at initiation of toilet training and duration of training: A prospective study. *Pediatrics, 111*(4), 810–814.

Caldwell, P. H. Y., Nankivell, G., & Sureshkumar, P. (2013). Simple behavioural interventions for nocturnal enuresis in children (review). *Cochrane Database of Systematic Reviews, 7*, 1–65.

Colombo, J. M., Wassom, M. C., & Rosen, J. M. (2015). Constipation and encopresis in childhood. *Pediatrics in Review, 36*(9), 392–401.

Cunningham, C. L., & Banez, G. A. (2006). Defecation disorders. In C. L. Cunningham, & G. A. Banez (Eds.), *Pediatric gastrointestinal disorders* (pp. 127–159). New York: Springer.

Douglas, J. W. B. (1973). Early disturbing events and later enuresis. In I. Kolvin, R. C. MacKeith, & S. R. Meadow (Eds.), *Bladder control and enuresis* (pp. 109–117). London: William Heinemann Medical Books.

Equit, M., Hill, J., Hubner, A., & von Gontard, A. (2014). Health-related quality of life and treatment effects on children with functional incontinence and their parents. *Journal of Pediatric Urology, 10*, 922–928.

Fazeli, M. S., Lin, Y., Nikoo, No., Jaggumantri, J. P. C., & Afshar, K. (2015). Biofeedback for nonneuropathic daytime voiding disorders in children: A systematic review and meta-analysis of randomized controlled trials. *Journal of Urology, 193*, 274–280.

Fernandez-fraga, X., Azpiroz, F., Casaus, M., Aparici, A., & Malagelada, J. (2005). Responses of anal constipation to biofeedback treatment. *Scandinavian Journal of Gastroenterology, 1*, 20–27.

Franco, I., von Gontard, A., & DeGennaro, M. (2013). Evaluation and treatment of nonmonosymptomatic nocturnal enuresis: A standardization document from the International Children's Continence Society. *Journal of Pediatric Urology, 9*, 234–243.

Garman, K., & Ficca, M. (2012). Managing encopresis in the elementary school setting: The school nurse's role. *The Journal of School Nursing, 28*(3), 175–180.

Har, A. F., & Croffie, J. M. (2010). Encopresis. *Pediatrics in Review, 31*(9), 368–374.

Hardy, L. T. (2009). Encopresis: A guide for pediatric nurses. *Archives of Psychiatric Nursing, 23*, 351–358.

Heaton, K. W., & Lewis, S. J. (1997). Stool form scale as a useful guide to intestinal transit time. *Scandinavian Journal of Gastroenterology, 32*(9), 920–924.

Joinson, C., Heron, J., Butler, U., & von Gontard, A. (2006). Psychological differences between children with and without soiling problems. *Pediatrics, 117*(5), 1575–1584.

Joinson, C., Sullivan, S., von Gontard, A., & Heron, J. (2016). Stressful events in early childhood and developmental trajectories of bedwetting at school age. *Journal of Pediatric Psychology, 41*(9), 1002–1010.

Kovacic, K., Sood, M. R., Mugie, S., Di Lorenzo, C., Nurko, S., Heinz, N., ... Silverman, A. H. (2015). A multicenter study on childhood constipation and fecal incontinence: Effects on quality of life. *The Journal of Pediatrics, 166*(6), 1482–1487.

Kuwertz-Broking, E., & von Gontard, A. (2018). Clinical management of nocturnal enuresis. *Pediatric Nephrology, 33*(7), 1145–1154.

Loening-Baucke, V. (1995). Biofeedback treatment for chronic constipation and encopresis in childhood: Long-term outcomes. *Pediatrics, 96*, 105–110.

Madani, S., Tsang, L., & Kamat, D. (2016). Constipation in children: A practical review. *Pediatric Annals, 45*(5), 189–196.

Maternik, M., Krzeminska, K., & Zurowska, A. (2015). The management of childhood urinary incontinence. *Pediatric Nephrology, 30*(1), 41–50.

McKeown, M. D., Hisle-Gorman, E., Eide, M., Gorman, M. D., & Nylund, C. M. (2013). Association of constipation and fecal incontinence with attention-deficit/hyperactivity disorder. *Pediatrics, 132*, 1210–1215.

National Clinical Guideline Centre. (2010). *Nocturnal enuresis: The management of bedwetting in young people*. London: Royal College of Physicians.

Neveus, T., von Gontard, A., Hoebeke, P., Hjalmas, K., Bauer, S., Bower, W., ... Djurhuus, J. C. (2006). The standardization of terminology of lower urinary tract function in children and adolescents: Report from the standardization committee of the International Children's Continence Society (ICCS). *Journal of Urology, 176*, 314–324.

Philichi, L. (2008). When the going gets tough. *Gastroenterology Nursing, 31*, 121–130.

Rajindrajith, S., Devanarayana, N. M., Perera, B. J., & Benninga, M. A. (2016). Childhood constipation as an emerging public health problem. *World Journal of Gastroenterology, 22*(30), 6964–6975.

Rasquin, A., Di Lorenzo, C., Forbes, D., et al. (2006). Childhood functional gastrointestinal disorders: Child/Adolescent. *Gastroenterology, 130*, 1527–1537.

Roth, E. B., & Austin, P. F. (2014). Evaluation and treatment of nonmonosymptomatic enuresis. *Pediatrics in Review/American Academy of Pediatrics, 35*(10), 430–438.

Sá, C. A., Gusmão Paiva, A. C., de Menezes, M. C., de Oliveira, L. F., Gomes, C. A., de Figueiredo, A. A., ... Netto, J. M. (2016). Increased risk of physical punishment among enuretic children with family history of enuresis. *The Journal of Urology, 195*(4), 1227–1230.

Sinha, R., & Raut, S. (2016). Management of nocturnal enuresis –Myths and facts. *World Journal of Nephrology, 5*(4), 328–338.

Sureshkumar, P., Jones, M., Caldwell, P., & Craig, J. C. (2009). Risk factors for nocturnal enuresis in school-age children. *Journal of Urology, 182*, 2893–2899.

Tabbers, M., DiLorenza, C., Berger, M., Faure, C., Langendam, M., Nurko, S., ... Benninga, M. (2014). Evaluation and treatment of functional constipation in infants and children: Evidence-based recommendations from ESPGHAN and NASPGHAN. *Journal of Pediatric Gastroenterology and Nutrition, 58*(2), 258–274.

Traisman, E. S. (2015). Enuresis: Evaluation and treatment. *Pediatric Annals, 44*(4), 133.

van den Berg, M. M., Benninga, M., & Di Lorenzo, C. (2006). Epidemiology of childhood constipation: A systematic review. *American Journal of Gastroenterology, 101*, 2401–2409.

van der Plas, R. N., Benninga, M. A., Buller, H. A., Bossuyt, P. M., Akkermans, L. M., Redekop, W. K., & Taminiau, J. A. (1996). Biofeedback training in treatment of childhood constipation: A randomised controlled study. *The Lancet, 348*(9030), 776–780.

CHAPTER

5

Finding the right fit: schooling options for children

J. Ann Lentini

Doc Ann Counseling, Hendersonville, NC, United States

Defining the issue: how does a clinician advise on choosing the best schooling option?

Parents or guardians often present to the office of a clinician with questions about how to choose the "best school" or educational option for their children. Advisors must determine how to direct the parent with issues such as how to choose a school for a child, whether to stay with a current situation or look at other options, and how to ask for special services. As concluded by Borghans, Golsteyn, and Stenberg (2015), expert advice may lead to a significant and positive influence on the quality of school choice for students, especially for those students who are male or who have parents with lower education levels.

Clinicians may, however, find it difficult to advise parents and guardians on schools and school selection for their children, as education has changed drastically in the recent past. In the 21st century, parents and guardians have many options for schooling. There are schooling options available now that did not exist a generation ago. Therefore advisors may not be up-to-date in what might be best for their clients and patients. Parents may be unaware of all possible opportunities, though they may have children who could benefit from a specialized experience. Options in education have greatly expanded—both for typical and atypical educational tracks.

Parents can choose between district public schools, charter public schools, magnet schools, private schools, and home-based schooling. Advising parents about how to go about the selection of a school is not

Clinician's Toolkit for Children's Behavioral Health
DOI: https://doi.org/10.1016/B978-0-12-816024-4.00005-X

immediately straightforward. In addition, some families may find themselves virtually excluded from certain schools based on location or socioeconomic status (SES) (Villavicencio, 2013; Siegel-Hawley, 2013). In some urban areas, such as New York City, school choice may be well established. In fact, there is a handbook on best public high schools (Hemphill, 2015) that states, "For [this] third edition I looked for schools that spark students' curiosity, broaden their horizons, and help them develop into thoughtful, caring adults" (Preface, page v). School choice is, however, not limited to metropolitan areas. Even rural areas have experienced an explosion in school choice due to changing laws and vouchers that allow students greater access to private schools (Ham, 2017).

Key terms: brief overview of schooling options

District public school: Traditional school supported by taxes. Children go to school based on where they live. National, local, and state governments control curriculums.

Charter public school: Supported by public taxes and some community fundraising. Children selected by application through a lottery process. Curriculum determined by school. Legal regulations vary from state to state with respect to charter schools; some state laws may not require 100% of teachers to be certified or may allow private firms involved in school design/curriculum. Charter public schools may have independence from some regulations that govern district public schools but are accountable through the state assessment systems.

Magnet public school: Supported by taxes. Children selected by application or lottery process. Curriculum determined by school. School may be specialized in a certain way, for example, with a special focus on the arts or STEM (Science, Technology, Engineering, and Mathematics).

Early college: A type of public education for high school students where students may attend a local college at no cost and be able to pursue or obtain an associate's degree while finishing high school.

Online public school: Same as traditional district public school but online. Gives teachers and students more flexibility with schedule and place.

Home-based schooling: Parents are responsible for children's education. Must register with the state as a homeschool and follow state guidelines. Many include homeschool co-ops that are study opportunities organized by homeschooling families.

Private school: Funding directly from students' families. May have scholarship options for students based on need or merit. May be religious, nonreligious, or directed toward a certain pedagogy (e.g., Montessori, Roggiero, or Outdoor Learning). May be directed toward students with certain developmental or learning difficulties (e.g., autism spectrum disorder, attention deficit hyperactivity disorder (ADHD)). May be a boarding or day school.

Inpatient and day treatment center: For children with serious behavioral or developmental issues. May be day school only or boarding school. May be affiliated with a hospital or behavioral health center.

Legal considerations

Enrollment

Recently in the United States, some states passed laws that allow parents greater flexibility in schooling options for their children. For example, dual enrollment is allowed in some states. This means that the child attends public school for half of the day and the parent provides education for the other half of the day. With this option the child can homeschool and have the benefits of local public school as well. Another type of dual enrollment allows a public high school student to attend college courses. Take note of local, state, and national laws that may allow more (or fewer) options in your area (e.g., Education Commission of the States, 2018; North Carolinians for Home Education, 2018).

Special needs

When advising parents, it is important to be aware of special laws that may give parents extra support. The IDEA (*Individuals with Disabilities Education Act*) is a law put in place by Congress in 1986. This program provides free public education to children with disabilities starting at age 3. Some children may start receiving services shortly after birth if their need is recognized. Advisors to families should be aware of these services and refer families as early as possible for information and resources on the *IDEA website* (sites.ed.gov/idea/parents-families/) or the National Center for Learning Disabilities (NCLD) (ncld.org/wp-content/uploads/2014/11/IDEA-Parent-Guide1.pdf) website for more information.

Hirano and Rowe (2016) found that it was important to emphasize the involvement of parents of children with disabilities in academic choice, not only in primary and secondary school but also in postschool success. If child has special needs, or may need special education services, this may be an additional consideration for parents and guardians. Some types of schools are obligated to provide these special services, but others may not. For example, charter and magnet schools are public schools and must follow state and federal laws concerning disabilities. If a parent has a child with a behavioral disorder, learning disability, or developmental disability, this may be a consideration, as private schools may not be obligated to follow these laws.

Barriers: poor school fit may relate to suboptimal social, educational, mental, and physical health outcomes

If parents and guardians are not able to secure a good school to fit the needs of their child, there may be social, educational, mental health, and physical health outcomes that are less than optimum. Bullying, educational and social mismatches, and lack of school resources can result in problems that could have been avoided if parents and guardians had appropriate guidance and information.

Factors influencing choices about schools

It must be recognized that some families may not have the resources or time to go through a school-choice process. They may perceive that there are fewer options available than there are in reality. They may not have the same access to information as other families. They also may consider other factors such as social capital (rather than individual student opportunity) in decision-making. For example, Villavicencio (2013) found that approximately 50% of the parents interviewed at a New York City charter school had shown "little or no search behaviors" prior to choosing schools. Ham (2017) discussed several ways that parents go about choosing a school. Personal experience with the school, discussion with friends and family, and conversation with principals and teachers made the most impact on their decisions.

Other studies showed that parents may consider issues other than academic standing when making school choices. A study by Bosetti (2004) indicated that the top three considerations for their sample of 1500 parents who chose private nonreligious, private religious, public traditional, and public alternative schools were (1) that the child liked the school, (2) that the school was safe, and (3) that the teachers were caring. These factors did not vary by type of school chosen. A different study by Burgess, Greaves, Vignoles, and Wilson (2015) demonstrated that while most parents valued academics in school choice, this preference was modified by commuting distance and socioeconomic composition of the school. Burgess also found that parents of higher SES may prefer schools that report the best academic outcomes. If parents with higher SES consistently choose schools with stronger academics, then a possible result is that children of high SES may end up with an academic advantage. In contrast, Allen, Burgess, and McKenna (2014) found that some parents may support even a "failing" school with lower academic scores. This may occur due to loyalty toward the school for reasons of tradition or location. If this occurs, a school may have higher admissions than "deserved," and parents may not be aware of the school's failing status. It may be particularly important to encourage the parents/guardians of children in lower SES environments to fully consider all options (Burgess et al., 2015).

Methods to practically and effectively address school choice with families including important topics to consider in education

Reviewing research on teaching methods, learning environments, and children's academic and social outcomes is beneficial when searching for the best possible fit for a child's specific needs.

Gauge parent interest and student needs

If parents/guardians appear not to be interested in choosing a school for their child, it is useful to ask questions about whether they feel they have a choice and if not, why not? Perhaps the most important role of the clinician is to empower parents to advocate for their children and inform them of options. If parents are made aware of choices and shown how their involvement may positively affect their child, they may make time for engagement. Some research suggests that parent involvement in schools may affect student achievement (El Nokali, Bachman, & Votruba-Drzal, 2010; See & Gorard, 2015). It is advantageous to emphasize to parents the potential positive impacts of their involvement. Reading about how other parents make decisions about choosing a school may be of service to some parents. In a study on educational choices, Valentine (2016, p. 75) asked parents these questions: "What characteristics about your child aid in your decision making? To what extent do you feel comfortable making decisions about your child's school? Are you satisfied with the variety of school choices available to you? What types of schools or programs would you suggest for your school district?" Valentine discovered that parent *expectations* in academics/curriculum, culture/safety, and school reputation were of primary consideration in school choice decisions. *Access* (or perceived access) to a school was the secondary consideration in school choice. The tertiary consideration in determining the school of choice was parent perceived *responsibility* in meeting the child's needs, knowing the child, and their own parenting roles. Parent dissent may also be helpful in motivating schools toward improvements and better outcomes. For example, parents opting children out of testing and demanding alternative curriculums have led to school changes (Stitzlein, 2015).

Make a game plan

It is worthwhile to have a game plan when speaking about school options. For example, one might encourage parents to do the following:

- Read the definitions of charter school, magnet school, home-based school, etc. (see Handout 2).
- Learn which options are available locally and what state and local laws allow.
- Look at each child as an individual and consider his/her strengths and weakness (e.g., perhaps shy but great at math).
- Consider the strengths and challenges of the family (perhaps able to afford an expensive private school, but not able to volunteer in class).
- Consider the unique language and cultural factors of the family, if any.
- Learn if there is any way to address barriers to attend certain desirable schools (e.g., scholarships for low-income families or carpools for longer commuting distances).
- Discuss preferences with child/children. Understand and take into consideration their concerns and preferences.
- List in order of preference each school—considering what is best for child and family overall.
- Visit top considerations. Observe classes and meet with teachers, if possible.
- Speak to and get to know the families at preferred schools. If possible, attend parent organization meetings to get information. Ask other parents about the schools' strengths and weaknesses.
- Educate oneself on the process of admission (e.g., charter schools may have a lottery).
- Make a first choice and have a second and third option back-up plan.

Handouts that may be given to parents are included at the end of the chapter. The first one assesses parent interest in school choice, and the second defines different options. The third is a list of links that may be useful in evaluating schools. The fourth is a checklist to guide parents/guardians to make the best choice for a good fit.

Review important topics in assessing schools

Following is an evidenced-based overview of 19 topics that are relevant when making decisions about schooling options, which are: school grade, teacher qualifications, graduation rates/rankings, classroom size, pre-school, healthy living, community atmosphere, diversity and culture, bullying, discipline, school security, parent involvement, donations and expected contributions, academically/intellectually gifted programs, special curriculums, homework, extracurricular activities, school counselors, and finally future plans and anticipated changes. This brief review should provide some useful tools to evaluate educational options.

School grade. If a parent or guardian chooses to appraise a school, one helpful source of data may be the school's grade. Under the No Child Left Behind Act, all districts are required to distribute annual reports of achievement about their schools (Chingos, Henderson, & West, 2010). The Education Commission of the States made recommendations to help parents clearly understand "report cards" on schools. They found that, to make evaluating schools easier, the reports should be easy to find and easy to understand. In addition, they should measure the following: readiness for career or postsecondary education, student achievement, closure of the achievement gap, growth in student academics, and graduation rates (Mikulecky & Christie, 2014). Parent and guardians should be aware that schools with higher grades may spend a greater part of the school year practicing skills test. They should evaluate if this is a good fit for their child. Parents can search the grade for the schools in their areas at the School Grades website (schoolgrades.org).

Teacher qualifications. Parents may find it helpful to know what qualifications teachers in their schools possess. Do special education teachers have master's level training? What certifications do academically gifted teachers have? The organization, "All Education Schools," has a resource to explain what kinds of teaching education are required for each state (alleducationschools.com/teacher-certification/). In addition, most states have a public educator lookup site at the site for National Association of State Directors of Teacher Education and Certification (NASDTEC) (nasdtec.net/general/custom.asp?page = PublicEducatorCert).

Graduation rates/rankings. Detailed information about a school's drop out and graduation rates is useful. Also data about how students in a school perform on average on college board exams (such as American college testing (ACT) or scholastic assessment tests (SATs)) are informative. These data may be available at the state's department of education. A search by state is necessary to get this information. A parent must search their state department of education site for the test averages desired for the year desired. There is not a central organizing site for all states' data.

Classroom sizes. Parents may intuitively believe that the smaller the classroom size, the better communication. However, in a review of the literature, Gladwell (2013) found that there may be an optimum class size, but that smaller is not always better. Some reports suggest that classroom size does matter (smaller *is* sometimes better), especially in populations with low-income and minority students (Schanzenbach, 2014). Parents must take into account the unique situation of their child to make the best choice.

Preschool. For families that choose to place their children in a preschool, selection is quite important as these are formative years in a child's development. For parents interested in more information on this subject, *zerotothree.org* is a good place to start. Camilli, Vargas, Ryan, and Barnett (2010) found academic and social benefits for children who attended a preschool prior to kindergarten. In addition, Barnett and Hustedt (2005) found modest lasting benefits for children in Head Start programs. Recently, online preschools have been marketed to parents to meet the demand for preschool. However, there is little evidence for benefits of online education, and experts have expressed concern for harm due to increased screen time in this population (Campaign for a Commercial Free Childhood, 2018).

Healthy living. Diet and exercise are factors that parents may consider when making school choices. Schalkwijk et al. (2015) describe the prevalence of obesity and poor diet in today's children and state that schools may be helpful in dealing with these problems by promoting physical activity and serving healthy and nutritional lunches. However, while school-based approaches to obesity prevention sound promising, clear evidence of the effectiveness of this approach does not exist, and such programs may be ineffective without changes in social norms and the home environment (Pbert et al., 2016). Parents concerned about physical activity should inquire about physical education and recess, as students' access and involvement in these can differ greatly by school or district.

Community atmosphere. The social atmosphere in a school may aid in a student's achievement. Community can be defined as the quality or character of human relationships in an area. It may be described as having four elements: membership, influence, integration and fulfillment of needs, and a shared emotional connection (McMillan & Chavis, 1986). The sense of a student's belonging to the group may be a consideration in school choice. Osterman (2000) emphasizes the importance of community in schools and benefits thereof for students. Osterman reports that organizational, instructional, and interpersonal strategies that enhance positive interaction among and between students enhance the sense of community and thereby may improve students' motivation, behavior, and learning. Parents may ask other parents and students and teachers about what they believe constitutes the atmosphere at a particular school. They may also wish to spend a day at the school observing to get a personal sense of how the school environment works.

Diversity/Culture. As diversity and school culture are often important topics in assessing schools, there are resources to help parents understand school demographic characteristics. The Public School Review (publicschoolreview.com/diversity-rankings/national-data) lists schools according to state and ranks them with a diversity score.

Bullying. Experience with bullying can negatively affect students in multiple ways (e.g., increased anxiety, depression, health complaints, and decreased academic achievement and school attendance). Schools may have various ways of addressing this problem. Some schools may have proactively set into place antibullying programs (Ansary, Elias, Greene, & Green, 2015). For example, one study showed that "active caring exercises" in second–sixth grade reduced bullying incidents and increased students' self-esteem (McCarty, Teie, McCutchen, & Geller, 2016). It is important to know if the school is using responses to bullying that have been shown to be ineffective or harmful. For example, the Stop Bullying government site (Stopbullying, 2019) (stopbullying.gov/prevention/at-school/index.html) lists interventions that are not effective such as group therapy, "zero-tolerance" approaches including suspension or expulsion, or mediation sessions between the bully and the victim. It also lists evidence-based programs shown to be effective. The Olweus Bullying Prevention Program (OBPP) is one evidence-based bullying prevention program that parents may find useful if they encounter this problem in their schools (violencepreventionworks.org/public/index.page).

Discipline. Another key criterion in choosing the best educational fit for a child is behavior management. It is advisable for parents to be aware of whether the school is using evidence-based disciplinary methods. There are effective disciplinary methods such as token economy and level systems based on positive reinforcement of targeted behaviors and positive behavioral interventions and supports (PBIS) (pbis.org/school/pbis-in-the-classroom). The metaanalysis by Korpershoek, Harms, de Boer, van Kuijk, and Doolaard (2016) found a variety of behavior management programs were effective, but the strongest effects were found for programs that targeted social–emotional development and student-centered learning.

Some programs may not have been studied or may have been shown to be ineffective or even harmful (e.g., confinement, Scared Straight interventions; Lilienfeld, 2007). Asking whether, and to what extent, teachers receive training in behavior management may provide additional helpful information. Schools' suspension and expulsion policies are also important to know.

One method of managing children's behavior is corporal punishment, defined as "the use of physical force with the intention of causing a child to experience pain, but not injury, for the purpose of correction or control of the child's behavior" (Straus, 2000, p. 1110). Nineteen US states, mainly in the southeast, allow corporal punishment. According to the US Alliance (2018), "Ironically, students are being hit on a frequent basis in the very schools that promote zero-tolerance policies toward violence. Each year, conservatively 166,807 children are paddled, spanked, or otherwise struck by public school faculty." It is notable that there exists racial disparity in school corporal punishment.

For example, Gershoff and Font (2016) found that in southeastern states, Black children were disproportionately spanked when compared to Caucasian children.

Some recently developed discipline programs may involve teachers using cell phone apps in a surveillance-type method for classroom control. These apps may require the teacher to carry a smartphone during the day in order to mark minute to minute incidents of students' good and poor behavior. Synchronous audible negative and positive tones may be associated with these marks. With some programs, parents may access this information at any time in the day to see real-time updates on how their child is behaving. Third-party companies may also have access to this information. These methods have not been thoroughly empirically validated to date. Further, concerns have been raised about the use of such technology in the classroom and the protection of private student information (Singer, 2014). Despite the privacy concerns, many states do not yet have laws concerning the use of internet-based disciplinary methods in the classroom. Soroko (2016) cited some concerns about one app including repetitive distracting sounds, modeling unwanted behavior, possibility of public shaming and embarrassment, anxiety about constant surveillance, and negative feedback tactics that use fear and intimidation. Parents can inquire about discipline methods with the principal or head of school, but it is important to note that there may be significant variation among teachers or classrooms in the type and level of behavior management used.

School security. Given the high rates of school violence in the United States, it would be remiss not to address school security. Many schools conduct various types of safety drills in an effort to train children in safe and effective responding in the event of an emergency. Standard safety drills include fire and tornado drills. More recently, schools have implemented lockdown drills to attempt to prepare for an active shooter. These types of drills are more controversial (Blad, 2017; Tipton, 2015). Parents and guardians, especially those with anxious children, should be advised to ask about what kind of safety drills are in place and how they are conducted. Children who might be sensitive to this kind of drill should be identified and then taken steps to address those concerns. Some schools may allow a child to have an alternate safety training on parent request.

Also meaningful to address in school security is the school location, presence or absence of police or security officers on campus, and security features such as cameras, special security windows, fencing, and ease of accessibility. Parents may assess many of these issues with a simple day visit during school hours. A discussion on these issues with the principal or head of school also may be helpful.

Parent involvement. Schools vary greatly in how much parent involvement is welcomed, expected, and encouraged. Some schools require monthly parent volunteer hours; other schools have no delineated expectations of parents. The type of volunteer hours available may be of interest to the parent or guardian. Parent/Teacher organizations exist in many schools. These help parents and teachers stay in contact on a regular basis and aid the school in meeting students' needs. In addition, some schools may encourage parents to come into the classroom and teach something in their area of specialty or interest. Others may ask parents to read with students. Some schools may want help with office work or special events. Other schools may want help with maintaining grounds and general upkeep. It is good to know before choosing a school what kind of help from parents the school expects, allows, or encourages.

Donations and expected contributions. Prior to enrollment, parents may not be aware of what kind of fundraising the school does. Some schools may do little to no fundraising, while others have several fundraising events throughout the year. Some public charter schools may need to do many fundraising events in order to balance their budgets. Parents and guardians, especially those considering private school options, may wish to consider how comfortable they are with fundraising activity (Anderson, 2012). If this is a concern, parents also may learn about nonprofit private schools at the National Association of Independent Schools, an organization that provides information and support to nonprofit private schools nationally (nais.org).

Many parents may not anticipate the impact of fundraising efforts. For example, one group of researchers (Caparosa et al., 2014) noted that fundraising created a significant source of unhealthy foods on school campuses. Another group (Ward, Kippen, Buykx, Gilligan, & Chapman, 2015) found that although 60% of the parents objected to the use of alcohol at fundraising events when children were present, there was an increasing trend to sell alcohol at school fundraising events. Posey-Maddox (2016) noted that while white-advantaged parents who financially supported their public school nominally encouraged diversity, practically they had challenges actually meeting this stated goal. Given budget gaps and government deficits in supporting education and the financial needs of schools, it is important to consider the many aspects of school fundraising.

Academically/Intellectually gifted programs. Parents of creative and high-achieving children may wish to investigate whether the school has academically/intellectually gifted programs. When such programming is not available, gifted students' outcomes can be less than optimal. For example, Chinnis (2016) described the problem of underperformance in academically gifted children. While there were many contributing factors, some of these were failing to identify these students and also failing to offer them challenging work. Academically gifted children often do not receive supplementary academic support or individual attention because they are able to complete their work. Unfortunately, they then may become less enthusiastic about learning and school. However, gifted enrichment programs have been found to have a significant positive influence on students' academic achievement as well as their social–emotional development (Kim, 2016). For these reasons, parents should ask how children are assessed for academically/intellectually gifted programs and how the programs are implemented.

Special curricula. Some schools use special curricula to teach state-required subjects or subjects that supplement typical educational curricula in meaningful ways. Some examples of special curricula are project-based learning (a hands-on approach), exploratory learning (out of classroom activities), arts or music-based curricula, STEM-based curricula, foreign language–based curricula, and language arts–based curricula.

Homework. Some elementary schools have a "no homework" policy. Others start homework in kindergarten. Some researchers report overall benefits of homework even in elementary school (Marzano & Pickering, 2007). One review of the literature on homework identified a positive influence on achievement that was stronger for students in later grades (7–12) than for students in lower grades (Cooper, 2016; Cooper, Robinson, & Patall, 2006). Further, the amount of time spent on homework matters; for junior high students, the research supports no more than 90 minutes per night, and for high school students, no more than 90–150 minutes (Cooper, 2008). Parents may want to inquire if homework is required, and if so how much, especially in situations where school days and extracurricular activities leave children with few unscheduled hours.

Extracurriculars: music and sports. For some parents the availability of music classes or sports in school may greatly affect their preference for a certain school. Children's involvement in extracurriculars may have important benefits. Research such as Kelley and Demorest's (2016) study showed that (controlling for family SES), students at schools (both charter and district public schools) in Chicago that offered music had better rates of attendance and increased test scores. A study on sports in school by Kniffin, Wansink, and Shimizu (2015) suggested that high school student–athletes had higher status careers and higher levels of leadership later in life and showed more prosocial behavior such as late-in-life volunteerism and charitable giving.

However, some research suggests that the impact of extracurriculars on academic outcomes may be smaller than parents realize. Marshall's (2015) metaanalysis identified a small effect size for the influence of extracurricular activities on academics and suggested the subject needed further study. In keeping, Shulruf's (2010) metaanalysis also identified small effects for the influence of extracurricular activities on educational outcomes.

School counselors. School counselors can be helpful in dealing with issues such as bullying, school atmosphere, academic challenges, diversity and cultural issues, school security, healthy living, and many other issues (Kyle & DeVoss, 2015; Abreu, Black, Mosley, & Fedewa, 2016;

Mau, Li, & Hoetmer, 2016; Williams, Greenleaf, Albert, & Barnes, 2014). Parents and guardians may wish to inquire about whether or not school counselors are available on campus to help children resolve issues. Some schools have full-time school counselors, and other schools have only part-time school counselors or no school counselors. Parents should know about the policies and ethical considerations on school counseling. They should know who the school counselor is and how referrals are made. In addition, parents/guardians should inquire whether or not parent permission is needed for a child to be seen by the counselor. The American School Counselor Association (2016) is a good resource for information on school counseling.

Anticipated changes and policies. Parents should make themselves aware of potentially impactful changes to staff, school structures, or policies. A beloved principal may be retiring. A new curriculum may be on the horizon. An expansion may be in planning stages. Parents and guardians should anticipate that schools go through many changes from year to year. They should be advised to ask teachers, administrators, and other parents what changes may be expected in the near future. The National Association of State Boards of Education (NASBE) (nasbe.org/healthy_schools/hs/map.php) is a great resource for finding out what the policies are in health education, social/counseling education, violence prevention, etc. in the local area. For example, for grades K-8, 30 minutes of vigorous exercise daily may be a state mandated policy. The NASBE site can inform both parents and students about state mandates and curriculum requirements.

Conclusion

If parents and guardians consider the above mentioned issues and options in choosing schools, they can potentially avoid a mismatch and increase the likelihood of positive outcomes for their child. A child who has a "good fit" in their school can develop and maintain healthy social attachments with peers, develop positive relationships with teachers and administrators, and have stability and continuity in their education. The importance of these elements cannot be overemphasized. A good advisor to parents can be an invaluable influence to facilitate, encourage, and educate parents and guardians about school choice for their children.

Four handouts for advisors to use with parents and guardians are included in this chapter. These handouts can help advisors (1) assess parents' interest in school choice, (2) inform parents with an overview about what educations options may be available, (3) provide links for more resources, and (4) guide parents with a checklist for making a good choice about schooling options for their children.

Handout 1. Questions for parents to assess interest in school choice

1. *Do you have any options for schools in your area? Yes/No/Not sure*
   List options:

   ____
   ____
   ____

2. *Are you interested in learning about the importance of school choice for your child?*
   Rate level of interest: (little interest) 1/2/3/4/5 (great interest)

   ____
   ____
   ____

3. *Have you already picked a school or educational option for your child? Yes/No*
   If yes, do you feel happy/confident about this choice?

   ____
   ____
   ____

4. *Does your child have any special interests, needs, or are their other considerations unique to your child? Yes/No*
   If yes, describe...

   ____
   ____
   ____

5. *Do you feel that your financial situation, location, or other issues limit your child's options or your choices as a parent? Yes/No*
   Describe...

   ____
   ____
   ____

**Other questions/comments/concerns about school*

Handout 2. Brief overview of schooling options

District public school: Traditional school supported by taxes. Children go to school based on where they live. National, local, and state governments control curriculums.
Charter public school: Supported by public taxes and some community fundraising. Children selected by application through a lottery process. Curriculum determined by school. Legal regulations vary from state to state with respect to charter schools; some state laws may not require 100% of teachers to be certified or may allow private firms to be involved in school design/curriculum. Charter public schools may have independence from some regulations that govern district public schools but are accountable through the state assessment/accountability systems.
Magnet public school: Supported by taxes. Children selected by application or lottery process. Curriculum determined by school. School may be specialized in a certain way, for example, with a special focus on the arts or STEM.
Early college: A type of public education for high school students whereby students may attend a local college at no cost and be able to pursue or obtain an associate's degree while finishing high school.
Online public school: Same as traditional district public school but online. Gives teachers and students more flexibility with schedule and place.
Home-based Schooling: Parents are responsible for children's education. Must register with the state as a homeschool and follow state guidelines. Many include homeschool coops, study opportunities organized by homeschooling families.
Private school: Funding directly from students' families. May have scholarship options for students based on need or merit. May be religious, nonreligious, or directed toward a certain pedagogy (e.g., Montessori, Roggiero, and Outdoor Learning). May be directed toward students with certain developmental or learning difficulties (e.g., autism spectrum, ADHD). May be a boarding or day school.
Inpatient and day treatment center: For children with serious behavioral or developmental issues. May be day school only or boarding school. May be affiliated with a hospital or behavioral health center.
Note: Some of these may or may not be available in your area. Check local sources and laws. See the US Department of Education (2017) *for recent updates.*

Handout 3. Helpful links for parents and guardians to aid in school selection

- School grades—Ratings/Reviews for local schools: schoolgrades.org
- School choices for parents—Defines types of schools: www2.ed.gov/parents/schools/choice/definitions.html
- Early development—Importance of a child's early years: *zerotothree.org*
- The National Association of State Boards of Education—Lists curriculum requirements for schools: nasbe.org/healthy_schools/hs/map.php
- States that allow corporal punishment: ncbi.nlm.nih.gov/pmc/articles/PMC5766273/
- PBIS: *pbis.org/school/pbis-in-the-classroom*
- NCLD information: *dredf.org/wpcontent/uploads/2014/04/preschool_brief.pdf*
- IDEA Parent Guide for students with disabilities: *ncld.org/wp-content/uploads/2014/11/IDEA-Parent-Guide1.pdf*
- Stop bullying site: stopbullying.gov/prevention/at-school/index.html
- OBPP: violencepreventionworks.org/public/index.page
- Educator certification lookup: nasdtec.net/general/custom.asp?page = PublicEducatorCert
- Required teacher training by state: alleducationschools.com/teacher-certification/
- National Association of Independent Schools—Nonprofit providing support: nais.org
- The Public School Review diversity rankings: *publicschoolreview.com/diversity-rankings/national-data*
- School counseling—Roles and responsibilities: *schoolcounselor.org*

Handout 4. Checklist for school selection

1. *Read the definitions handout to understand of types of schools.*
2. *Consider the following*:
   a. *School grade*. Parents can search the grade for the schools in their areas at the School Grades website (*schoolgrades.org*).
   b. *Teacher qualifications*. Get to know what qualifications teachers in the school possess. Do special education teachers have master's level training? What certifications do academically gifted teachers have? The organization, "All Education Schools," has a resource to explain the required teacher education for each state (*alleducationschools.com/teacher-certification*). In addition, most states have a public educator lookup site that can be found at the site for NASDTEC (*nasdtec.net/general/custom.asp?page = PublicEducatorCert*).
   c. *Graduation rates/rankings*. Look at information about the school's drop out and graduation rates, students' performance on college board exams (such as ACT/SATs or performance in different domains). These data may be available at the state's department of education website (e.g., see "School-Level Results"; *education.alaska.gov/assessments/results/results2018*).
   d. *Classroom sizes*. If you feel your child would benefit from being taught in a smaller classroom, ask about typical classroom size per grade.
   e. *Preschool*. If you choose to enroll your child in preschool, the quality of the school is paramount, as the first years of a child's development are very important.
   f. *Healthy living*. Ask the school about access to food, types of food choices, as well as required and optional exercise, gym classes, and recess.
   g. *Community atmosphere*. The sense of a student's belonging to the group should be a consideration in school choice. Ask about community activities and school environment.
   h. *Diversity/Culture*. Understand the school's diversity and school culture to be sure the school is conducive to your child's learning and social functioning. The Public School Review (*publicschoolreview.com/diversity-rankings/national-data*) lists schools according to state and ranks them with a diversity score.
   i. *Bullying*. Request information about the school's bullying prevention program. What is the school's typical response to bullying? Is the program supported by research showing that it is effective? Is the school using approaches that are not supported by research, such as peer mediation and zero-tolerance approaches?

j. *Discipline.* Ask about what types of behavior management the school uses. There are effective disciplinary methods such as token economy and level systems based on positive reinforcement and PBIS (*pbis.org/school/pbis-in-the-classroom*). Also determine if schools are using methods known to be ineffective or even harmful (e.g., confinement, Scared Straight interventions). Did teachers receive training in behavior management? What are schools' policies on corporal punishment (paddling/spanking), suspension and expulsion?
k. *School security.* Does the school conduct safety drills? If so, what kind and how often? Is the school location safe for children and are police or security officers on campus?
l. *Parent involvement.* Find out how much parent involvement is welcomed, expected, and encouraged, and how much you wish to or are able to contribute.
m. *Donations and expected contributions.* Ask about how much and what types of fundraising are required or expected of families.
n. *Academically/Intellectually gifted programs.* Parents of creative and high-achieving children may wish to investigate whether the school has academically/intellectually gifted programs.
o. *Special curricula.* If important to your family, find out of the school has special curricula such as project-based learning (a hands-on approach), exploratory learning (out of classroom activities), art or music–based curricula, STEM-based curricula, foreign language–based curricula, and language arts–based curricula.
p. *Homework.* Inquire whether the school has a homework or "no homework" policy, and how much time students spend on such activities.
q. *Extracurriculars.* Inquire about music, arts, sports, and other activities that suit your child's skills and interests.
r. *School counselor.* Does the school have full time, on-site counselors to help children deal with bullying and other issues? What are the credentials of the counselors? What are the school policies on counseling for students?
s. *Anticipated changes and policies.* Ask teachers, administrators, and other parents what changes to the school structure, staff, curricula, or policies may be expected in the near future. The National Association of State Boards of Education is a great resource for information about policies for your local area (www.nasbe.org).

Next steps:

- ☐ *Consider each child as an individual with his/her strengths/challenges.*
- ☐ *Consider the strengths and challenges of the family.*
- ☐ *Consider unique cultural and language factors of the family.*
- ☐ *Learn if there are any way to address barriers (scholarships? carpools?).*
- ☐ *Discuss preferences with child.*
- ☐ *List schools in order of preference (considering child and family overall).*
- ☐ *Visit top considerations and get to know families at those schools.*
- ☐ *Learn about the application or admission requirements.*
- ☐ *Make a first choice and have a second and third option back-up plan.*
- ☐ *Apply/Enroll.*

Important points to remember

- Parents can search for the "grade" for the schools in their areas at the School Grades website (www.schoolgrades.org).
- See stopbullying.gov for more information on evidence-based antibullying programs in your area.
- There are effective disciplinary methods such as token economy and level systems based on positive reinforcement of targeted behaviors and PBIS (pbis.org/school/pbis-in-the-classroom). A variety of behavior management programs are effective, but the strongest effects are for programs that target social–emotional development and student-centered learning.
- See US Alliance (endhitting.org) for more information on corporal punishment in the United States.
- The NASBE is a great resource for information about school policies (www.nasbe.org).

References

Abreu, R. L., Black, W. W., Mosley, D. V., & Fedewa, A. L. (2016). LGBTQ youth bullying experiences in schools: The role of school counselors within a system of oppression. *Journal of Creativity in Mental Health, 11*(3–4), 325–342.

All Education Schools. Retrieved from <www.alleducationschools.com/teacher-certification/> Accessed 12.08.19.

Allen, R., Burgess, S., & McKenna, L. (2014). *School performance and parental choice of school: Secondary data analysis*. Department for Education, Retrieved from <dera.ioe.ac.uk/19631/1/RR310_-_School_performance_and_parental_choice_of_school.pdf>.

American School Counselor Association. *ASCA Ethical Standards for school counselors*. (2016). Retrieved from <www.schoolcounselor.org/asca/media/asca/Ethics/EthicalStandards2016.pdf>.

Anderson, J. (2012). Private schools mine parents' data, and wallets. *New York Times*. Retrieved from <www.nytimes.com/2012/03/27/nyregion/private-schools-mine-parents-data-and-wallets.html>.

Ansary, N. S., Elias, M. J., Greene, M. B., & Green, S. (2015). Guidance for schools selecting antibullying approaches: Translating evidence-based strategies to contemporary implementation realities. *Educational Researcher, 44*(1), 27–36. Retrieved from <https://doi.org/10.3102/0013189X14567534>.

Barnett, W. S., & Hustedt, J. T. (2005). Head start's lasting benefits. *Infants & Young Children, 18*(1), 16–24.

Blad, E. (2017). Do schools' 'active-shooter' drills prepare or frighten? Many parents oppose such instruction. *Education Week, 37*, 1–11. Available from www.edweek.org.

Borghans, L., Golsteyn, B. H., & Stenberg, A. (2015). Does expert advice improve educational choice? *PLoS One, 10*(12), e0145378. Retrieved from <http://journals.plos.org/plosone/article?id = 10.1371/journal.pone.0145378>.

Bosetti, L. (2004). Determinants of school choice: Understanding how parents choose elementary schools in Alberta. *Journal of Education Policy, 19*(4), 387–405.

Burgess, S., Greaves, E., Vignoles, A., & Wilson, D. (2015). What parents want: School preferences and school choice. *The Economic Journal, 125*(587), 1262–1289.

Camilli, G., Vargas, S., Ryan, S., & Barnett, W. S. (2010). Meta-analysis of the effects of early education interventions on cognitive and social development. *Teachers College Record, 112*(3), 579–620.

Campaign for a Commercial-Free Childhood. *Defending the early years.* (2018). Retrieved from <www.commercialfreechildhood.org/sites/default/files/devel-generate/pha/online_pre-k_statement.pdf?eType = EmailBlastContent&eId = c0f2d68d-1078-407e-8d69-7d14e3eafd30>.

Caparosa, S. L., Shordon, M., Santos, A. T., Pomichowski, M. E., Dzewaltowski, D. A., & Coleman, K. J. (2014). Fundraising, celebrations and classroom rewards are substantial sources of unhealthy foods and beverages on public school campuses. *Public Health Nutrition, 17*(6), 1205–1213.

Chingos, M. M., Henderson, M. B., & West, M. R. (2010). Grading schools. *Education Next, 10*(4). Retrieved from <http://educationnext.org/grading-schools/>.

Chinnis, K.L. (2016). *The underperformance of gifted elementary school students* (Doctoral dissertation). The University of North Carolina at Charlotte.

Cooper, H. (2008). Does homework improve academic achievement?: If so, how much is best. *SEDL Letter, 20*(2). Retrieved from <http://www.sedl.org/pubs/sedl-letter/v20n02/homework.html> Accessed 12.08.19.

Cooper, H. *Duke University Center for Child and Family Policy.* (2016). Retrieved from <childandfamilypolicy.duke.edu/2016/03/homeworks-benefits-are-age-dependent/>.

Cooper, H., Robinson, J. C., & Patall, E. A. (2006). Does homework improve academic achievement? A synthesis of research, 1987–2003. *Review of Educational Research, 76*(1), 1–62.

Education Commission of the States. (2018). Retrieved from <www.ecs.org/dual-concurrent-enrollment-policies/> Accessed 12.08.19.

El Nokali, N., Bachman, H. J., & Votruba-Drzal, E. (2010). Parent involvement and children's academic and social development in elementary school. *Child Development, 81*(3), 988–1005. Retrieved from <https://doi.org/10.1111/j.1467-8624.2010.01447.x>.

Gershoff, E. T., & Font, S. A. (2016). Corporal punishment in U.S. public schools: Prevalence, disparities in use, and status in state and federal policy. *Social Policy Report, 30*(1), 1–37. Retrieved from <www.ncbi.nlm.nih.gov/pmc/articles/PMC5766273/>.

Gladwell, M. (2013). *David and Goliath: Underdogs, misfits, and the art of battling giants* (1st ed.). New York: Little, Brown and Company.

Ham, R.C. (2017). *School choice in rural North Carolina: Understanding parents' experiences navigating the school choice process* (Doctoral dissertation). The University of North Carolina at Greensboro. Retrieved from <https://search.proquest.com/openview/fc30e4917403bc2705b67020384f83b0/1?pq-origsite = gscholar&cbl = 18750&diss = y>.

Hemphill, C. (2015). *New York City's best public high schools: A parents' guide.* Teachers College Press. Retrieved from <books.google.com/books>.

Hirano, K. A., & Rowe, D. A. (2016). A conceptual model for parent involvement in secondary special education. *Journal of Disability Policy Studies, 27*(1), 43–53.

Kelley, J., & Demorest, S. M. (2016). Music programs in charter and traditional schools: A comparative study of Chicago elementary schools. *Journal of Research in Music Education, 64*(1), 88–107.

Kim, M. (2016). A meta-analysis of the effects of enrichment programs on gifted students. *Gifted Child Quarterly, 60*(2), 102–116.

Kniffin, K. M., Wansink, B., & Shimizu, M. (2015). Sports at work: Anticipated and persistent correlates of participation in high school athletics. *Journal of Leadership & Organizational Studies, 22*(2), 217–230.

Korpershoek, H., Harms, T., de Boer, H., van Kuijk, M., & Doolaard, S. (2016). A meta-analysis of the effects of classroom management strategies and classroom management programs on students' academic, behavioral, emotional, and motivational outcomes. *Review of Educational Research, 86*(3), 643–680.

Kyle, P. B., & DeVoss, J. A. (2015). The professional school counselor's role as change agent in school. *School Counseling Research & Practice, 3*, 7–16.

Lilienfeld, S. O. (2007). Psychological treatments that cause harm. *Perspectives on psychological science, 2*(1), 53–70.

Marshall, J.D. *Is there an academic benefit to participating in extracurricular activities? A systemic review and meta-analysis.* (2015). Retrieved from <wp.cune.org/jillmarshall/files/2015/02/Is-there-an-Academic-Benefit-to-Participating-in-Extracurricular-Activities-A-Systemic-Review-and-Meta-analysis.pdf>.

Marzano, R. J., & Pickering, D. J. (2007). The case for and against homework. *Educational Leadership, 64*(6), 74–79.

Mau, W. C. J., Li, J., & Hoetmer, K. (2016). Transforming high school counseling: Counselors' roles, practices, and expectations for students' success. *Administrative Issues Journal: Connecting Education, Practice, and Research, 6*(2), 83–95.

McCarty, S., Teie, S., McCutchen, J., & Geller, E. S. (2016). Actively caring to prevent bullying in an elementary school: Prompting and rewarding prosocial behavior. *Journal of Prevention & Intervention in the Community, 44*(3), 164–176.

McMillan, D. W., & Chavis, D. M. (1986). Sense of community: A definition and theory. *Journal of Community Psychology, 14*(January 1986), 6–23.

Mikulecky, M., & Christie, K. (2014). *Rating states, grading schools: What parents and experts say states should consider to make school accountability systems meaningful.* Education Commission of the States. Retrieved from <www.ecs.org/docs/rating-states,grading-schools.pdf>.

National Association of Independent Schools. (2018). Retrieved from <www.nais.org> Accessed 12.08.19.

National Association of State Boards of Education (NASBE). (2019). Retrieved from < (nasbe.org/healthy_schools/hs/map.php) > Accessed 13.08.19.

National Association of State Directors of Teacher Education and Certification (NASDTEC). <www.nasdtec.net/general/custom.asp?page = PublicEducatorCert> Accessed 12.08.19.

National Center for Learning Disabilities (NCLD). (2018). Retrieved from <dredf.org/wp-content/uploads/2014/04/preschool_brief.pdf>. Accessed 12.08.19.

North Carolinians for Home Education. (2018). Retrieved from <www.nche.com/high-school/additional-sources> Accessed 12.08.19.

Olweus Bullying Prevention Program (OBPP). (2018). Retrieved from <www.violencepreventionworks.org/public/index.page> Accessed 12.08.19.

Osterman, K. F. (2000). Students' need for belonging in the school community. *Review of Educational Research, 70*(3), 323–367.

Pbert, L., Druker, S., Barton, B., Schneider, K. L., Olendzki, B., Gapinski, M. A., ... Osganian, S. (2016). A school-based program for overweight and obese adolescents: A randomized controlled trial. *Journal of School Health, 86*(10), 699–708.

Posey-Maddox, L. (2016). Beyond the consumer: Parents, privatization, and fundraising in US urban public schooling. *Journal of Education Policy, 31*(2), 178–197.

Schalkwijk, A., Bot, S., de Vries, L., Westerman, M., Nijpels, G., & Elders, P. (2015). Perspectives of obese children and their parents on lifestyle behavior change: A qualitative study. *International Journal of Behavioral Nutrition and Physical Activity, 12*(102), 2–8.

Schanzenbach, D.W. (2014). *Does class size matter?.* National Education Policy Center. Retrieved from <http://nepc.colorado.edu/files/pb_-_class_size.pdf>.

See, B., & Gorard, S. (2015). The role of parents in young people's education—A critical review of the causal evidence. *Oxford Review of Education, 41*(3), 346–366.

Siegel-Hawley, G. (2013). Educational gerrymandering? Race and attendance boundaries in a demographically changing suburb. *Harvard Educational Review*, *83*(4), 580–612.
Shulruf, B. (2010). Do extra-curricular activities in schools improve educational outcomes? A critical review and meta-analysis of the literature. *International Review of Education*, *56* (5–6), 591–612.
Singer, N. (2014). Privacy concerns for ClassDojo and other Tracking Apps for schoolchildren. *New York Times*. Retrieved from <www.nytimes.com/2014/11/17/technology/privacy-concerns-for-classdojo-and-other-tracking-apps-for-schoolchildren.html>.
Soroko, A. *No child left alone: The ClassDojo app. Our schools/Ourselves*. (2016). Retrieved from <www.researchgate.net/publication/304627527_No_child_left_alone_The_ClassDojo_app>.
Stitzlein, S. (2015). Improving public schools through the dissent of parents: Opting out of tests, demanding alternative curricula, invoking parent trigger laws, and withdrawing entirely. *Educational Studies*, *51*(1), 57–71.
Stop Bullying. (2019). Retrieved from <https://www.stopbullying.gov/>. Accessed 13.08.19.
Straus, M. A. (2000). Corporal punishment and primary prevention of physical abuse. *Child Abuse & Neglect*, *24*(9), 1109–1114.
Tipton, J. (2015). Lockdown high: When the schoolhouse becomes a jailhouse. *Contemporary Justice Review*, *18*(1), 95–97. Retrieved from <https://doi.org/10.1080/10282580.2015.1007280>.
US Alliance. (2018). Retrieved from <http://www.endhitting.org/home/paddling/#>. Accessed 12.08.19.
US Department of Education. (2017). Retrieved from <https://www2.ed.gov/parents/schools/choice/definitions.html> Accessed 12.08.19.
Valentine, D.N. (2016). *How do parents engage in school-choice decisions?* (Doctoral dissertation). The George Washington University. Retrieved from <search.proquest.com/openview/4517dde335e92613d3e262207be071a7/1?pq-origsite = gscholar&cbl = 18750&diss = y>.
Villavicencio, A. (2013). "It's our best choice right now": Examining the choice options of charter school parents. *Education Policy Analysis Archives*, *21*(81). Retrieved from <http://epaa.asu.edu/ojs/article/view/1274>.
Ward, B., Kippen, R., Buykx, P., Gilligan, C., & Chapman, K. (2015). Parents' level of support for adults' purchase and consumption of alcohol at primary school events when children are present. *Drug and Alcohol Review*, *34*(2), 202–206.
Williams, J. M., Greenleaf, A. T., Albert, T., & Barnes, E. F. (2014). Promoting educational resilience among African American students at risk of school failure: The role of school counselors. *Journal of School Counseling*, *12*(9), n9.

Further reading

Machado, D. (2018). *What is a charter school?*. Office of Charter Schools. <www.ncpublicschools.org/charterschools/>.
Schaefer, D. R., Simpkins, S. D., Vest, A. E., & Price, C. D. (2011). The contribution of extracurricular activities to adolescent friendships: New insights through social network analysis. *Developmental Psychology*, *47*(4), 1141.
Stop Bullying. (2018). Retrieved from <www.stopbullying.gov/prevention/at-school/index.html>.

CHAPTER

6

Helping children succeed in school: a guide to special education services

Luke Johnson

Clinical Therapist, Mercy Health Toledo Trauma Recovery Center, Toledo, OH, United States

As professionals tasked with helping families with their daily functioning, including at school, it is important for us to know how to advise parents and guardians on obtaining special education services for their children and ensuring the efficacy and delivery of these services. Therefore we are responsible to know the rights of parents and the best strategies to utilize when working with schools so that we can effectively inform our families.

There are a multitude of reasons that access to special education services is crucial to a child who may have a disability. In general, children with disabilities are more likely to have academic, personal, and learning issues in the school setting (Lee, Clinton, Rispoli, & Lee, 2017). Children with disabilities often have reduced access to education and worse academic and behavioral outcomes than children without disabilities as well (Sacks & Haider, 2017). Although children with disabilities are seemingly fighting an uphill battle compared to their developmentally typical peers, these children can receive special education services which can help provide students with an Individualized Education Program, also known as an IEP (see The Council for Disability Rights' website, http://disabilityrights.org/glossary.htm, for definitions of key terms related to school accommodations). This approach can be highly effective; in fact, the Office of Special Education and Rehabilitative

Clinician's Toolkit for Children's Behavioral Health
DOI: https://doi.org/10.1016/B978-0-12-816024-4.00006-1

Services stated, "The IEP process is one of the most critical tools in ensuring that effective teaching, learning, and increased achievement occurs for all students with disabilities" (La Salle, Roach, & McGrath, 2013, p. 137). It is imperative that we work to understand these children and their struggles. Far too many of our clients lack formal supports to help them navigate the confusing and difficult process of interacting with school systems. Meanwhile, these same clients also face additional barriers to accessing appropriate education for their children. As clinicians, it is our duty to take on the roles of advocate, supporter, and guide.

Children with disabilities are, by law, entitled to special education services, accommodations, and support in public school systems to help meet their educational needs. For a variety of reasons, these services too often go unprovided and the child's needs go unmet.

Epidemiological research suggests that many children are likely to need special education services. In 2002 for example, roughly 8% of the children ages 3–17 were identified as having a learning disability (Dey, Schiller, & Tai, 2004) and 17.4% of the US children ages 2–8 had a diagnosed mental, behavioral, or developmental disorder in a 2016 survey (Cree et al., 2018). Children with mental health diagnoses often qualify for special education services. For example, attention deficit–hyperactivity disorder (ADHD) and anxiety disorders affect a significant amount of children ages 3–17 (Green et al., 2017), and such disorders frequently lead to disruption in school, reduced academic functioning, and poor social interactions (Fabiano et al., 2010).

The entire process of working with schools starts with parents having regular, positive and open communication with school personnel. This helps to ensure that parents are immediately aware of any academic or behavioral concerns in the classroom. It is a good idea for parents to "check in" with the child's teachers every so often in order to understand how his or her learning is progressing and to identify concerns or obstacles. There are also certain circumstances in which it is imperative for the parent to immediately contact the school. Handout 1 lists circumstances that warrant an immediate response by parents, and Handout 2 describes general tips and strategies when working with schools.

If at any time, a parent becomes aware of persistent or impairing behavior or learning concerns, it is a good idea to seek out mental/behavioral health assessment and consultation or intervention. This may seem like a drastic first step, but it is simply a way to gather as much information about your child that can be used to increase their chances of success in and out of school. Many cities have agencies that can complete a psychological assessment of children. A psychological assessment can evaluate a child's IQ and academic achievement skills and assess for possible mental/behavioral health disorders, such as ADHD, anxiety, depression, developmental delays, autism spectrum disorders, and others. Furthermore, many psychological reports have a section that provides specific recommendations to the child's school based on the findings. A thorough psychological assessment can reveal extremely important information that can be shared with the school so that appropriate interventions can be put in place to best meet the child's unique needs.

Whether or not psychological assessment is pursued, if there is a serious concern about the child's ability to learn in the classroom, it is important for the parent to communicate with the school and begin discussing if the child may qualify special education services. The Individuals with Disabilities Education Act (IDEA) was originally passed in 1975 and amended in 2004 to address the educational concerns of these children. IDEA protects the rights of students with disabilities and their guardians. It is the guiding legislation regarding the process in which students receive special education services in public schools and works to provide free, specifically designed instruction to meet the needs of a child with a disability.

Unfortunately, obtaining special education services through IDEA can be a complex and confusing process and one that does not always result in adequate support for children. Handout 3 provides a link to the IDEA statute with details on how this process should take place.

If any party (school personnel, parent, professional, etc.) believes that there is an educational concern, the next step is to request a multifactored evaluation (MFE) from the school to determine if the child meets criteria for special education services. Regardless if previous psychological assessment has been completed outside the school setting, the school district must complete their own version of an evaluation.

To request the MFE, the parent should write a formal letter to the school. This letter should include the request for special education evaluation, consent for the child to be evaluated, and why the parent would like the child to be evaluated. The letter should be signed, dated, and the parent should keep a copy for their records. Handout 3 provides a website with an example template of the MFE request letter.

Once the request has been submitted, the school has 30 days to respond. The school can respond in a few different ways. For example, the school personnel may say that they would like to complete a response to intervention (RTI) plan to see if the student can make progress through more informal interventions. An effective RTI will state appropriate objectives for the student that can be measured and a timeline for when the objectives should be accomplished. For example, "Johnny will successfully identify 24/26 letters by the end of the first quarter." The second part of the RTI will provide concrete interventions that the teacher will use to support the child reaching their objective.

For example, "Johnny's teacher will use repetition, visual cues, and Johnny's favorite storybook to remind him what each letter looks like." The teacher will then begin monitoring and measuring Johnny's progress throughout the quarter. At the end of the quarter, a meeting will be held in which the parent and relevant school staff will be informed of the outcome of the RTI. If the RTI is successful and Johnny has met his objectives, the interventions used will be recorded and used in future learning opportunities. No further action steps are typically taken if this occurs. However, if the RTI is unsuccessful, the school may try different and more intense interventions for another period of time (another RTI), or they may agree that the concern is severe enough that an evaluation for special education services is now warranted.

If the school responds to the parent's request for a special education evaluation with an RTI instead, the parent can ask them to try the RTI, while evaluating for special education services so that time is not lost and the child does not fall further behind. However, the school could deny this request and state that they will only evaluate for special education services after they have tried other options, such as an RTI. If at any point in this process a parent does not agree with the school's decision (such as the school refusing to evaluate until an RTI is completed), the parents can begin the dispute resolution process (this will be covered in another section).

The school's response may be that they agree to the request to evaluate for special education services. If they do, they must provide prior written notice about what action they intend to take and gain the parent's consent. Once the school gains parental consent, they have 60 days to complete the evaluation, also known as the Evaluation Team Report or ETR. School staff will complete evaluations to test the student's IQ, learning abilities, speech, language, hearing ability, social and emotional development, motor skills, and/or other areas of learning/behavior that may impact a child's education. Also, any independent evaluations such as the psychological assessment previously mentioned can be included and considered within this evaluation. Handout 3 includes a link to a website with a sample ETR.

To qualify for special education services under IDEA, a student must have a disability in one or more of the following areas: intellectual disability, hearing impairment, speech or language impairment, visual impairment, emotional disturbance, orthopedic impairment, autism, traumatic brain injury, other health impairment, specific learning disability, deafness, deaf-blindness, multiple disabilities, or developmental delay. For example, a child with an IQ of 60, who has borderline intellectual functioning, would likely qualify for special education services under the category of "intellectual disability." A child with ADHD may qualify under the "other health impairment" category. If a child is having significant behavior concerns that stem from anxiety, they may qualify under "emotional disturbance." If a child has difficulty grasping basic math concepts and numbers, they may suffer from dyscalculia, a specific learning disability.

Once the school personnel complete the child's evaluation, they typically come to one of two decisions. One determination is that the student does not qualify for special education services. In this case the parent can initiate the dispute resolution process (which will be covered later). Alternatively, the school district may find that the child meets criteria under IDEA for a disability that qualifies the child for special education services. If a child qualifies for special education services, the next step is the writing of an IEP. An IEP is a legal, working document that is composed of specific goals and objectives that are individualized to meet the particular child's educational needs. The IEP also includes a list of special education services and accommodations that the school must provide to ensure the child meets the goals and objectives on the IEP. IEPs should include a student's present levels of educational performance, measurable goals and objectives, the plan to measure a child's progress, and how/when parents will be informed of progress. The IEP must be written within 90 days of the initial request for evaluation. Handout 3 includes a website that shows an example of an IEP.

A few of the key sections of an IEP describe the current level of academic achievement and functional performance, measurable annual goals, and specially designed instruction. These sections are described below.

"The present level of academic achievement and functional performance" section helps the team understand how the child is learning compared to grade-level standards. This section should break down the needs that the child has based on assessment outcomes and related data. Observation, outside assessment (such as psychological testing), and special education evaluation information should be included here. Well-written and effective IEPs will have specific, measurable data and contain information regarding all areas of performance, such as academics and behavior. For example, an appropriate summary of a student's performance in the area of math may be:

> As observed in class, [student] was able to identify the essential information (type of problem: addition, subtraction, multiplication, etc.) within her math problems on 1/5 occasions without direct guidance. [Student] needs to be prompted to correct errors on 5/5 occasions, otherwise errors will be left incorrect. The teacher or intervention specialist may have to repeat more than once in order to assist with her problem solving. [Student] needs to continue working on identifying key words and essential information in order to understand the mathematic process/concepts she is currently working on as well as independently receive feedback in order to correct any errors. Typical peers are able to make sense of problems and persevere in solving them.

As shown in the example, this section contains measurable data regarding client's present level of performance, her education needs based on her performance, and information regarding typical grade level or peer performance.

The "Develop measurable annual goals" section should be based on the information contained in "The present level of academic achievement and functional performance" section. Each need that has been identified should have at least one corresponding goal. If it is determined that problem areas include reading comprehension, math computation, and behavior in the classroom, for example, then the IEP should have at least one reading goal, math goal, and behavior goal. These goals should be specific, measurable, and reviewed annually. Each goal should also have multiple, measurable objectives that help the child reach the goal and used as a way to evaluate their progress.

Inappropriate goals and objectives are broad, general statements that are difficult to measure, such as:

> [Student] will make progress on her writing skills throughout the year.

In contrast, an example of a well-written academic goal in the area of writing could be:

> [Student] will utilize strategies to identify and clearly communicate relationships between presented information in writing, on 4/5 occasions, as measured by work samples, and earning at least 80% on final drafts.

An effective objective to coincide with this goal could be:

> When composing a paragraph, [Student] will clearly identify the main idea, at least 3-4 supporting details, and a concluding thought in logical order, on 4/5 occasions, as measured by work samples by the end of the IEP cycle.

Children who qualify for special education services under categories such as "Emotional Disturbance" or "Other Health Impairment" often have IEPs that are focused on their behavioral functioning. An inappropriate behavior goal would be:

> [Student] will listen better to her teachers.

An example of an appropriate behavior goal could be:

> [Student] will increase her ability to follow teacher-directed cues, with no more than one additional prompt from an adult, on 4 out of 5 occasions, as measured by documented observations, by the end of the IEP cycle.

An effective objective to coincide with this goal could be:

> [Student] will begin and continue to stay on task during all in-class assignments, with no more than one additional prompt from an adult, on 4/5 occasions, as measured by documented observations, by the end of the IEP cycle.

Additional types of goals that one may see on an IEP include Speech Therapy and Occupational Therapy. An example of an appropriate Speech Therapy goal is:

> By the end of the IEP, given a verbal or visual prompt [student] will produce targeted speech sounds without errors in 5-6 word sentences with 90% accuracy measured through observation in 80% of data collection opportunities per semester.

An example of an appropriate Occupational Therapy goal is:

> During classroom and therapy handwriting activities, [student] will improve handwriting legibility by writing the lower case letters with a distinct height difference between short and tall letters, place the letters "g, j, p, q and y" below the writing line, place letters within one-sixteenth inch of the baseline and leave adequate space (1/2 inch) between words, 85% of the time when measured once a month for 3 consecutive months.

"Identify specially designed instruction" is the section of the IEP that describes supports and accommodations that the school will provide to help the student achieve the goals of the IEP. Such specially designed instruction can be provided in the form of classroom accommodations, school staff changes, and assistive technology.

A few examples of appropriate specially designed instruction would be the following:

- Presenting information using multisensory approaches (e.g., presenting material auditorily and visually) to aid in attention, auditory working memory, and understanding material.
- Encouraging [student] to use coping strategies when she is upset (e.g., deep breathing) to aid in emotional control.
- Providing an additional explanation of instructions and using faded interventions of organizational and problem-solving skills to aid in difficulties with executive functioning.
- Use of verbal and nonverbal prompts to remind [student] to start a task and remain on-task.
- Providing access to graphic organizers, assistance with spelling, and direct instruction of the writing process to aid in difficulties with written expression skills.

- Direct instruction of mathematical concepts, clarified directions, and checking work when finished, to address difficulties with math reasoning skills.
- Use of a small group to reteach academic information, as needed.

A few examples of appropriate classroom accommodations/modifications would be as follows:

- Tests and quizzes presented in recognition styles (e.g., multiple choice), when possible.
- Use of task planning sheets (e.g., writing down how much time each step of an assignment should take).
- Use of self-monitoring checklists (e.g., checklists for double-checking answers).
- Use of systems for organizing materials.
- Breaking down/chunking assignments into smaller steps.
- Extended time on in-class assignments and tests up to one additional class period.
- Use of movement breaks, when needed.
- Testing in environments with minimal distractions.

In addition, school staff changes written into an IEP could provide a student with one-on-one instruction or a paraprofessional that is assigned to the student to assist with each part of their school day. Finally, assistive technology that could be provided includes the use of voice-to-text technology, proofreading software, and calculators.

Once the IEP is complete, the IEP Team reviews the IEP once a year and completes ETRs every 3 years. IEPs also can be reviewed at the parents' request due to lack of expected progress, or due to new information, new needs, etc. If not satisfied with the implementation of the IEP, parents may pursue dispute resolution. The following are warning signs that an IEP is not as effective or that it is not being implemented correctly:

- If a child continues to receive failing grades. IEPs are designed to be individualized and to provide instruction at the student's current level of learning, as well as providing supports for areas of need. Therefore if the IEP is working as intended, the child's grades should gradually improve. If a few weeks go by and there is no improvement in grades, it is time to call a meeting with the school and review the IEP.
- If IEP goals and objectives are not being met. A student's grades can improve for a variety of reasons, but if they are still not meeting their goals of the IEP, then the IEP is failing and should be revisited.
- If a child continues to be frequently disciplined through referrals, suspensions, or other actions. IEPs with behavior goals are designed to provide support and accommodations so that negative behaviors

are reduced. If the same issues do not improve, it is time for the parents to meet with the school to see what else can be done.

A specific part of special education law that should be considered if a child is on an IEP for behavior concerns is the "Manifestation Determination." A Manifestation Determination Review must be conducted if a child with a suspected disability has been suspended from school for over a total of 10 days within the current school year. At a Manifestation Determination Review the special education team determines if the behavior causing the suspensions is directly caused by the child's disability OR caused by a failure to implement the IEP. If either of these scenarios is true, the school cannot suspend or expel the student. If this is the case, the school should conduct a functional behavior assessment and create a behavior intervention plan (BIP). More information regarding these two tools is detailed below.

If anyone believes that an IEP is ineffective or not being implemented correctly, there are additional steps to ensure a child is receiving the appropriate support, education, and instruction:

- The first step is always to communicate concerns with the school. Parents should be specific with their concerns. For example, "It has been 5 weeks since the implementation of my child's IEP and she is still failing the majority of subjects," or "I noticed from the teacher's report that my child is not making progress on his benchmark objectives on his reading goal."
- The second step is requesting a meeting to address the concerns. If the current IEP is not effective the school is required to consider more intensive and frequent supports and services. Smaller classrooms, more one-on-one instruction, or even shorter school days are all examples of more intensive interventions that can be explored if an IEP is not working as intended. However, it should be noted that IEPs are designed to provide what is called the "Least Restrictive Environment" for students. Essentially, according to IDEA, children should spend as much time as possible with peers who do not receive special education. It is important for parents to keep this in mind if accommodations promote overly restrictive or isolated learning contexts.
- An additional step, specifically with regard to behavior goals not being met, is the school conducting a Functional Behavioral Assessment or FBA. An FBA is a thorough assessment tool used to better understand problem behaviors. The FBA includes an "antecedent," "behavior," and "response" section. Data from these sections promote a more thorough understanding about what was happening before the problem behavior, which can pinpoint possible triggers. The "response" section helps us understand what interventions are being used and whether they are effective at

reducing the behavior. Once the FBA has been conducted and reviewed by the team, a BIP, is created. The BIP is a plan designed to teach and reward positive behaviors.

An example of information one may see in a simple FBA would be the following:

1. Antecedent: Teacher begins math instruction.
2. Behavior: Student ignores the teacher and begins talking to another student.
3. Consequence: Student is redirected back to material.
4. Outcome: Student becomes angry and begins yelling at teacher.

Once this information is gathered and the FBA is developed, the team can then use this information to create the BIP. From the example FBA above, several hypotheses can be made, such as the following:

- The child may have significant difficulty with math and wants to avoid "looking stupid," so he tries to do something else, like socialize with a friend.
- The child may be seated next to his best friend during math class and just wants to talk about their weekend together.
- The child may feel embarrassed when the teacher redirects him in front of the class and therefore lashes out at the teacher.

These hypotheses should be considered when developing the BIP. The BIP should address these hypotheses one at a time. For example:

- If there is a concern with the child's ability to learn in math, additional assessment can be conducted to check for a specific learning disability. Also, an intervention can be put into place that uses an additional school staff member to provide one-on-one support to the student during math.
- If the child is seated next to his best friend, an intervention could be to arrange seating so they are not as distracted by one another. It may also be helpful to allow the students 5 minutes to socialize with one another before instruction begins.
- If the child feels embarrassed when redirected in front of the class, additional redirection interventions can be tried, such as a gentle tap on the desk, or a certain signal from the teacher so that the child knows to begin focusing on his math.

Unfortunately, there are many opportunities throughout the entire special education process for a school and parents to disagree. If the child continues to struggle behaviorally or academically, even after the previously mentioned steps are taken, it may be time to begin the dispute resolution process. Different types of dispute resolution include "facilitation," "mediation," "state complaint," and "due process complaint."

Facilitation. Facilitation is the proactive or preventative approach when there are concerns that conflict or disagreement MAY arise. It is typically the first step of any type of dispute resolution process in special education services. Facilitation can take place in any meeting with the school and is done by a neutral, third party, to ensure that the student's needs are the focus of discussion. To request facilitation, parents should contact the school district's special education director to see if the district is willing to participate in this process. Once agreed, the parent should contact the state's Department of Education's Office for Exceptional Children.

Mediation. Mediation is typically the next step in the dispute resolution process and focuses on conflict resolution. Mediation is also done by a neutral, third party. If there is disagreement between the school and the parent, the mediator helps settle the dispute and works to have all parties come to a written agreement. All parties must sign and follow this agreement. As with requesting facilitation, parents should contact the special education director and then the Department of Education.

State complaint. Another option is to make a state complaint. To make a formal state complaint, parents must call the Department of Education's Office for Exceptional Children and request a complaint form. The complaint must include a statement regarding the alleged violation of federal of state special education requirements. It must also state specific action or inaction the district took that parents believe to be in violation of special education requirement. Finally, the complaint should include facts to support why parents think the district violated special education requirements (Lee, 2019). The complaint must be sent to the Department of Education's Office for Exceptional Children and the school district's superintendent. The department will review and investigate the alleged violation and resolve the complaint within 60 calendar days.

Due process complaint. A final option for dispute resolution, and often the most intensive, is called a due process complaint. The due process complaint should contain the same information as the state complaint and be sent to the school district superintendent and Department of Education's Office for Exceptional Children. The "Resolution Period" is 30 days from the date the due process complaint was filed and is an opportunity for the school district to facilitate a resolution meeting to attempt to resolve the issues. If disputes are still not settled within 30 days, then a due process hearing must be conducted and a decision made within 45 more days. An impartial hearing officer will conduct the meeting and decision will be made within the 45 days.

Sometimes, a child may be struggling in school and they need a few accommodations to help them succeed, but an IEP is not necessary or they do not qualify for special education services. In these cases a "504 plan" may be appropriate. Section 504 is a civil rights law that was enacted to protect individuals with disabilities from discrimination. Section 504 is designed to provide students with disabilities the same opportunities as students who do not have disabilities.

Evaluating for a 504 plan is generally simpler and less intensive than the IEP process. The evaluation involves gathering information from different sources, including reviewing tests and evaluations completed by various professionals. If an individual has a mental or physical impairment that limits one or more major life activity, such as learning, reading, writing, speaking, or caring for oneself, they may qualify for 504 services.

If a child is determined to qualify for a 504 services, a plan will be developed that provides necessary accommodations and modifications such as preferential seating, extra time to complete assignments, shortened assignments, or schedule modifications (e.g., lunch beginning at a different time if a student has diabetes or different options for recess if a child has severe asthma).

Conclusion

Advocating for special education services can be frustrating, confusing, intimidating, and tedious. It is complex and extensive. It is also worth it. Special education is designed to meet the unique needs of each child and often leads to a student experiencing success in school for the first time. When done correctly, special education can easily be the difference between a child graduating or dropping out.

As clinicians, it is our responsibility to know and understand the information presented in this chapter so that we are best prepared to advocate for the rights of the individuals we serve. We must be knowledgeable regarding the specific laws and policies that influence special education. We must be aware of the different processes that occur when pursuing special education, such as evaluations, accommodations, and implementation. Finally, we must strive for competency and professionalism in how we interact with schools so that the children we serve are in the best position to succeed.

Handout 1: Circumstances that warrant immediate attention

- If a child's grades suddenly drop. For example, if you receive a midterm report and the child's grade in science went from a "B" to a "D" in just a few short weeks, you should contact the school/teacher to find out possible reasons why this has happened. Did the child just have a bad test day and the teacher is not worried about their ability to bring the grade up? If so, you should continue to monitor the grades but any additional action steps at this time may not be necessary. However, could the dropping of grades be part of a larger problem? Has the child suddenly seemed to have lost all interest in completing work? Does the child seem to be constantly distracted or having difficulty focusing? Is the child "just not getting it" when it comes to the subject matter? These types of concerns should prompt further discussion on where the issues lie and what should be done to get the child back on track.
- If a teacher reaches out to you with concerns. Teachers are often overwhelmed themselves. They can have packed classrooms with as many as 30 other children, which can make it difficult for them to keep track of each child's individual needs and concerns. This means that if a teacher has a concern that is serious enough for them to make time to contact a parent, we should be listening and be ready to help find ways to support the child. The fact that teachers have so many other kids to look after is another reason why it is important for parents and other professionals to communicate with schools frequently. We are not always immediately made aware of possible concerns simply because teachers do not always have the time and resources to do so. Be proactive! Communicating with teachers/schools often can help "catch" issues early and address them before a child gets too far behind.
- If a child begins receiving referrals or disciplinary action. If your child starts getting sent to the office or is given detentions or other punitive measures, it is time to call the school to figure out what is going on. Is there another student in the classroom that does not get along with your child which is causing disruption and disciplinary action? If so, it may be as simple suggesting the school staff find a way to keep them separated. Or is the child becoming disruptive, defiant, or disrespectful on a daily basis? If this is the case, there may be underlying issues that require additional intervention and support.
- If a child has difficulty learning from the start, even when putting in significant time and effort. It is important to closely monitor if a child is "falling behind" as the school year progresses. This may indicate a

cognitive or learning disability. Certain learning disabilities can occur in the areas of reading, writing, or math. If it is noticed that a child struggles significantly more in one area than the rest, it may be a warning sign of one of these learning disabilities and should be further assessed.

- Other potential warning signs of a learning disability early in a child's life include: if a child has concerns with language, such as difficulty with learning new words, pronunciation, or understanding questions; concerns with literacy, such as difficulty with naming objects or understanding written text; problems with memory; or difficulty with motor, social, or attention skills (Rief, 2017).

Handout 2: General tips and strategies when working with schools

- "We are all on the same team" mindset. When working with a school, it is important to have the mindset that all parties involved are on the same team and working toward the same goals. It is helpful to actively see the school as wanting what is best for a child, just as you do. Approaching interactions with a school in a supportive way can help reach results that "are best for everyone." If everyone works as a cohesive team to help a child succeed in school, everyone's job becomes much easier (school staff, the parent, and definitely the child's).
- Active and positive communication. Consistent and frequent communication with a child's school leads to a multitude of positive results. Primarily, communication helps build a positive relationship with the school. Showing school staff that you are engaged and an active participant in your child's education can make it more likely that the staff reach out to you with important information, whether that be academic progress, behavioral concerns, or just a friendly reminder that an important test is coming up. In addition, voicing concerns about your child's education can lead to a prompt response and intervention to the issues.
- Listening to the entire story. This is part of the "active and positive communication" strategy but is important enough to highlight on its own. It can be difficult to not get emotional, defensive, or angry if it seems like your child is struggling in school or not receiving the support they need, which are valid reactions. However, when communication with the school regarding concerns, it is crucial to listen to and gather all information available. It can be challenging to refrain from interrupting or switching topics during a conversation regarding your child's progress in school. Instead, wait to hear the whole story. Any information provided from school staff has the possibility of being useful in future interventions or planning. It is also common to only have "one side of the story". Often, the school has their side, the child has their own unique perspective, and the guardian has an additional view. It is important for every party to share their piece and listen to the others because the "truth" of the situation is typically somewhere in the middle of all of the stories.
- Documentation. It is extremely important to document any interactions that occur with a school. Having notes to review and prepare for future meetings can help keep all parties on the same page and act as reminders for what has already been discussed and what plans are currently in place. The IEP process has multiple

deadlines that the school is required to meet. It can be useful to document when certain steps of special education occur so that the school can be held accountable and that services are provided to the child in a timely manner.

Handout 3: Useful resources on school accommodations

- The Council for Disability Rights website, with definitions of key terms related to school accommodations: http://disabilityrights.org/glossary.htm
- US statute on education of individuals with disabilities: https://sites.ed.gov/idea/statute-chapter-33
- Council of Parent Attorneys and Advocates. Information on reaching out to legal resources and understanding education rights: https://www.copaa.org
- Wrightslaw website with links to articles and resources to assist with special education rights and advocacy: https://www.wrightslaw.com/
- National Disability Rights Network provides information specific to special education rights: http://www.ndrn.org/en/
- U.S. Department of Education website: https://sites.ed.gov/idea/
- U.S. Department of Education searchable list of contacts the department of education, the higher education agency, special education agency and adult education agency in each state: https://www2.ed.gov/about/contacts/state/index.html
- MFE request letter template: http://www.disabilityrightsohio.org/letter-writing-requesting-multi-factored-evaluation
- An example of how an ETR is written and a description of each section: http://www.norwoodschools.org/Downloads/etrannotations09.pdf
- An example of an IEP: http://www.nasdse.org/portals/0/standards-basediepexamples.pdf
- Information regarding Ohio's special education dispute resolution processes can be found at the Ohio Department of Education website or https://education.ohio.gov/getattachment/Topics/Special-Education/A-Guide-to-Parent-Rights-in-Special-Education/ODE_ParentRights_040617.pdf.aspx
- Parent Training and Information Centers: https://www.parentcenterhub.org/find-your-center/
- Other parent/family resource centers such as the Ohio Coalition for the Education of Children with Disabilities: https://www.ocecd.org/
- Public Interest Law Centers, such as Advocates for Basic Legal Equality: http://www.ablelaw.org

Important points to remember

- Children with disabilities are, by law, entitled to special education services, accommodations, and support in public school systems to help meet their educational needs. For a variety of reasons, these services too often go unprovided and the child's needs go unmet.
- The Individuals with Disabilities Education Act protects the rights of students with disabilities and their guardians. It is the guiding legislation regarding the process in which students receive special education services in public schools and works to provide free, specifically designed instruction to meet the needs of a child with a disability.
- If any party (school personnel, parent, professional, etc.) believes that there is an educational concern, the next step is to request a multifactored evaluation from the school to determine if they meet criteria for special education services.

References

Cree, R. A., Bitsko, R. H., Robinson, L. R., Holbrook, J. R., Danielson, M. L., Smith, C., ... Peacock, G. (2018). Health care, family, and community factors associated with mental, behavioral, and developmental disorders and poverty among children aged 2-8 years - United States, 2016. *Morbidity and Mortality Weekly Report*, *67*(50), 1377–1383. Available from https://doi.org/10.15585/mmwr.mm6750a1.

Dey, A. N., Schiller, J. S., & Tai, D. A. (2004). *Summary health statistics for U.S. children: National health interview survey, 2002*.

Fabiano, G. A., Vujnovic, R. K., Pelham, W. E., Waschbusch, D. A., Massetti, G. M., Pariseau, M. E., ... Volker, M. (2010). Enhancing the effectiveness of special education programming for children with attention deficit hyperactivity disorder using a daily report card. *School Psychology Review*, *39*(2), 219–239.

Green, J. G., Comer, J. S., Donaldson, A. R., Elkins, R. M., Nadeau, M. S., Reid, G., & Pincus, D. B. (2017). School functioning and use of school-based accommodations by treatment-seeking anxious children. *Journal of Emotional and Behavioral Disorders*, *25*(4), 220–232. Available from https://doi.org/10.1177/1063426616664328.

La Salle, T. P., Roach, A. T., & McGrath, D. (2013). The relationship of IEP quality to curricular access and academic achievement for students with disabilities. *International Journal of Special Education*, *28*(1), 135–144.

Lee, A. M. I. (2019). *What to include in a state complaint*. Retrieved from understood, for learning & attention issues website <https://www.understood.org/en/school-learning/your-childs-rights/dispute-resolution/what-to-include-in-a-state-complaint>.

Lee, K., Clinton, M., Rispoli, K., & Lee, J. (2017). Individualized education programmes and parental behaviours for children with disabilities: Moderation effects of head start on children's developmental outcomes. *Child & Family Social Work*, *22*(2), 1000–1014. Available from https://doi.org/10.1111/cfs.12320.

Rief, S. (2017). Heads up, teachers: Red flags for possible LD. In *ADDitude: Inside the ADHD mind*.

Sacks, L. H., & Haider, S. (2017). Challenges in implementation of individualized educational plan (IEPs): Perspectives from India and the United States of America. *Indian Journal of Health & Wellbeing*, *8*(9), 958–965.

CHAPTER

7

Bullying: the role of the clinician in prevention and intervention

Kimberly Burkhart[1] *and Robert D. Keder*[2]

[1]Pediatrics & Psychiatry, Rainbow Babies and Children's Hospital, Case Western Reserve University, Cleveland, OH, United States, [2]Developmental & Behavioral Pediatrics, Connecticut Children's Medical Center, University of Connecticut School of Medicine, Farmington, CT, United States

Introduction

Bullying is identified as a public health problem and an adverse childhood experience due to its negative and possibly long-lasting effects on both physical and mental health. Prevalence estimates of bullying vary greatly and remain largely unknown due to the lack of use of a consistent and universal definition, differences in measuring the frequency of occurrences, and the majority of studies focusing on middle school and high school–aged children (National Academies of Science, Engineering, and Medicine, 2016). For the purpose of this review, bullying will be defined consistently with what has been proposed by the World Health Organization and the Centers for Disease Control and Prevention (CDC). A person is bullied when he or she is repeatedly exposed to negative actions by one or more other persons. Bullying often occurs when there is a real or perceived power difference. Bullying includes actions such as threatening, teasing, name-calling, ignoring, sending hurtful messages, spreading rumors, and excluding others on purpose (Gladden, Vivolo-Kanto, Hamburger, & Lumpkin, 2014; Nansel et al., 2001). Bullying has been documented as occurring as

Clinician's Toolkit for Children's Behavioral Health
DOI: https://doi.org/10.1016/B978-0-12-816024-4.00007-3

young as 4 years of age (Burkhart, Knox, & Brockmyer, 2013; Ilola, Lempinen, Huttunen, & Sourando, 2016).

Bullying can be categorized as verbal, physical, relational (e.g., hurting another's standing with a group by excluding or isolating), or cyber (e.g., using electronic communication to cause embarrassment, humiliate, intimidate, or threaten). Physical bullying is more common in males. Physical and verbal bullying are most common in young children. Research has shown that in adolescents, prevalence rates for cyberbullying are lower than traditional forms of bullying. Cyberbullying and traditional forms of bullying are highly correlated, suggesting that polyaggression is common and should be a focus for intervention (Modecki, Minchin, Harbaugh, Guerra, & Runions, 2014).

There are typically four critical roles that are highlighted when assessing and evaluating bullying. These roles include the child who bullies, the target of bullying, the bully-victim (an individual who initially was a target of bullying and now also engages in bullying behavior, usually to other perceived weaker targets while continuing to be bullied), and the bystander who is an observer of the bullying behavior. The bystander's behaviors can range from being neutral to supporting one or more of the individuals in the bullying behavior dyad. The bystander can also support the victim by intervening or reporting the bullying behavior (National Academies of Science, Engineering, and Medicine, 2016). There are several other terms used in the literature to reference to bullying such as peer victimization, perpetrator, and victim. While the authors acknowledge these variations, a decision was made to use child/patient/client-centered language in acknowledgment that clinicians work with children involved in various roles of bullying.

Prevalence rates

Based on the National Center for Educational Statistics (2016), approximately 20% of US children are bullied, and only 30% of these children tell an adult.

In the general population, 30% of children report the involvement in bullying as either a bully, victim, or bully-victim, with 10% reporting chronic victimization (Molcho et al., 2009). Prevalence of bullying, however, has generally declined among 4th to 12th graders over the past decade (2005–14), which may be attributed to increased school policies and empirically supported program implementation (Waasdorp, Pas, Zablotsky, & Bradshaw, 2017). Bullying tends to decrease with age following the transition to high school (Craig, Harel-Fisch, & Fogel-Grinvald, 2009).

Risk factors for being the target of bullying

Students with disabilities and special needs are two to three times more likely to get bullied than their typically developing peers. Prevalence is highest for students with emotional disturbances. It is believed that between 40% and 60% of youth with autism spectrum disorder are bullied (National Autistic Society, 2017). When evaluating the prevalence rates of bullying in youth with intellectual disabilities, approximately 15% were reported to engage in bullying, 36% were identified as being victimized, and 25% were categorized as bully-victims.

Research has assessed why students believe peers are being targeted. The most frequent perceived reasons by students include a classmate's looks (e.g., unattractiveness, short stature, physical anomalies; 55%), body shape (37%), and race (16%) (Davis & Nixon, 2010). Metaanalyses indicate that overweight and obese youth are at greater risk than normal weight youth to be the victims of bullying with results not being mediated by gender (Van Geel, Vedder, & Tanilon, 2014). More than 70% of the LGBTQ community report being verbally bullied what is more, they are twice as likely to commit suicide after being bullied.

Youth with chronic illnesses, such as food allergies, asthma, inherited bleeding disorders, and osteogenesis imperfecta, are also at heightened risk for being bullied. It is believed that not being able to fully engage in activities with their peers is a contributing factor to the victimization of these youth (Faith et al., 2015). Furthermore, youth who receive physical, occupational, or speech/language therapy are at significantly greater risk of being bullied as these services can differentiate them from typically developing peers (Van Cleave & Davis, 2006). While maltreated children are more likely than other children to bully others, maltreatment also places children at risk for bully victimization (Shields & Cicchetti, 2001).

Characteristics of children who bully

Research has shown that children who bully tend to have greater conduct problems, truancy, rule-breaking behavior, substance use, anxiety, academic difficulties, and passive-aggressive behaviors than their same-age counterparts. They are also are more likely to experience physical punishment at home. Some children who bully have similar aggressive behaviors modeled at home. Adolescents who identify as heterosexual and who bully or are bully-victims are more likely to engage in casual sex and sex under the influence of alcohol and drugs (Holt, Matjasko, Espelage, Reid, & Koenig, 2013).

Those who engage in bullying behaviors are more likely to use cigarettes, drink, and have poorer academic performance and attitude toward school climate but have an easier time making friends (Nansel et al., 2001). Children who bully are more likely to have increased levels of aggression and violence with higher rates of criminal conviction and increased incidence of alcohol and cigarette use as adolescents (Bender, 2010; Wolke, Copeland, Angold, & Costello, 2013). Children who bullied others are more likely to have an antisocial personality disorder in adulthood (Wolke et al., 2013).

Mental and physical health implications

Compared to same-age peers, youth who are targets of bullying are more likely to be anxious or depressed, feel that they do not belong at school and have lower academic performance, poorer social and emotional functioning, greater difficulty establishing and maintaining friendships, and greater loneliness (Fekkes, Pijpers, & Verloove-Vanhorick, 2004; McKenna, Hawk, Mullen, & Hertz, 2011; Nansel et al., 2001; Moore et al, 2017). Youth who are bullied are at least two times as likely to experience psychosomatic problems (e.g., headaches, nausea, and fatigue) in comparison to those who are not bullied (Gini & Pozzoli, 2013). Bullying has also been associated with sleep disturbances, abdominal pain, gastrointestinal complaints, bedwetting, dizziness, and skin problems (Fekkes, Pijpers, & Verloove-Vanhorick, 2004; Gini & Pozzoli, 2013; NAS, 2016). Poor social skills and passive/avoidant coping have also been shown to increase the risk of being bullied (Compas, Jaser, Dunn, & Rodriguez, 2012).

Metadata from the most comprehensive review available to date (Moore et al., 2017), which analyzed 165 studies, suggest a significant association between being the target of bullying and increased alcohol use and tobacco use. This review also found an increase in somatic symptoms, including stomachache, sleep difficulties, headache, dizziness, and back pain. Overall, there was an association between victimization and poorer general health. Despite these findings, there was no consistent increase in utilization of health services in this population. Findings on overall school functioning and social functioning were inconsistent. There also was a greater likelihood of poor academic achievement, loneliness, and poor life satisfaction. Being the target of bullying was found to have increased the odds of reduced quality of life. Metaanalysis found *dose–response* relationships between being the target of bullying and depression, anxiety, suicidal ideation, suicide attempts, nonsuicidal self-injury, medication use, smoking cigarettes, and loneliness (Moore et al., 2017).

There are several studies that have investigated the longitudinal effects of bullying involvement. Results indicate that peer victimization predicts poorer perception of body composition up to 2 years after the bullying has occurred (Frisén, Lunde, & Hwang, 2009). When assessed 7 years after the victimization was reported, youth who were bullied were more likely to have generalized anxiety and panic disorders. Moreover, research has found associations between chronic peer victimization during childhood and adulthood body dissatisfaction, eating disturbances, depression, anxiety, self-criticism, fear of negative evaluation, loneliness, and suicidal behavior (Faith, Malcolm, & Newgent, 2008; Isaacs, Hodges, & Salmivalli, 2008).

In one prospective population study, being a childhood target of bullying or a bully/victim was associated with later negative effects on health, socioeconomic status, and personal relationships in early adulthood. It was discovered that compared to those not involved, children who are the targets of bullying are more likely to have agoraphobia, generalized anxiety, and panic disorder (Wolfe, 2013). In prospective cohort study being the target of bullying during childhood was associated with a limited social relationships, economic hardship, and poor perceived quality of life at age 50 (Takizawa, Maughan, & Arseneault, 2014).

Suicide and deliberate self-harm

According to the CDC, there is a strong relationship between bullying and suicide-related behaviors. However, this relationship is often mediated by other factors including depression and delinquency (Hertz, Donato, & Wright, 2013). There is a dose–response relationship between suicidal ideation and bully victimization (Klomek, Marrocco, Kleinman, Schonfeld, & Gould, 2007) with lower levels of social connectedness and increased severity of bullying involvement (as either a victim or perpetrator) associated with increased suicide risk (Arango, Opperman, Gipson, & King, 2016). Victims, perpetrators, and bully-victims are three to five times more likely to have suicidal ideation and attempts than their uninvolved peers (Espelage & Holt, 2013). There is some evidence to suggest that, in comparison to traditional bullying, cyberbullying is more strongly related to suicidal ideation (Van Geel et al., 2014). When involvement in bullying is suspected or known, it is critical to assess suicidality, as suicide is the second leading cause of death in individuals aged 10–34 years (Centers for Disease Control and Prevention, 2017).

In a metaanalysis investigating deliberate self-harm, 68 effect sizes were calculated using data from 156,284 adolescents. Results indicated that traditional victimization and bullying, as well as cyberbullying, were associated with deliberate self-harm (Heerde & Hemphill, 2018). Status as a bully-victim is associated with many negative outcomes. For example, females who are bully-victims are more likely to have a core phobia, and males are more likely to have suicidality in comparison to same-age peers (Wolke et al., 2013). Children identified as bully-victims have higher probabilities of young adulthood depression, panic disorder, and suicidality (Copeland, Wolke, Angold, & Costello, 2013; Wolfe, 2013).

Bullying and weapon carrying

One in six adolescents report bringing a weapon to school within the past 30 days (Shetgiri, Lin, Auila, & Flores, 2012) and adolescents who are involved in bullying are more likely to carry weapons than adolescents who are not involved in bullying (Nansel, Craig, Overpeck, Saluja, & Ruan, 2004). Bully-victims in the United States are more likely to carry weapons than victims or bullies (Van Geel et al., 2014). Perpetrators who commit school homicides are more likely to be victims of bullying (Anderson et al., 2001; Leary, Kowalski, Smith, & Phillips, 2003).

Characteristics of parents and home environment

Home-related risk factors may also play a role in bullying. For example, there is a relationship between academic difficulties and being the target of bullying, particularly for children who have low parental support and low perceived social connectedness (Beran, 2008; Loukas & Pasch, 2012; Swearer, Espelage, Koening, & Barry, 2012). Hostile, inconsistent parenting and controlling, and overprotective parenting also can place youth at risk for being bullied (Duncan, 2011; Lawson, Lawson, Downder, & Anderson, 2013). Youth with one or both parents who have suboptimal mental health also have a greater likelihood of being a perpetrator of bullying (Shetgiri, Lin, & Flores, 2015). Physical and emotional violence in the home including witnessing domestic violence has been associated with victimization and perpetration (Lucas, Jernbro, Tindberg, & Janson, 2016).

Youth who bully are more likely to demonstrate ambivalent relationships with their siblings and parents; whereas children who do not bully are more likely to display positive relationships with family members

(Connolly & O'Moore, 2003). Harsh parenting and maltreatment also relate to bullying in youths. For example, in a large retrospective study, corporal punishment in the home was associated with experiences of bullying (Vaughn et al., 2011). When peer victimization is separated from the effects of child maltreatment, peer victimization accounts for an incremental proportion of the variance in psychopathology, suggesting that peer victimization is an independent predictor (Sansen, Iffland, & Neuner, 2014). Moreover, in comparison to victims and those who bully, bully-victims are more likely to report being physically hurt by a family member and to have witnessed domestic violence (Nansel et al., 2001).

Protective factors

Research has also identified several protective factors that may protect youths against victimization. Within the family, positive parent–child interaction, modeling of conflict resolution, and effective communication decrease the likelihood of chronic bullying and serve as a buffer against the detrimental effects of bullying (e.g., Burkhart et al., 2013; Ledwell & King, 2013).

Research has shown that the presence of a similarly minded peer group may increase the likelihood that a bystander may intervene (Eisenberg, McMorris, Gower, & Chatterjee, 2016). Participation in special interest groups at school can also serve as a protective factor (e.g., gay–straight alliances; Earnshaw et al., 2017). Youth who have more advanced social problem-solving skills and higher social competence are less likely to be victimized (Cook, Williams, Guerra, Kim, & Sadek, 2010). A positive student–teacher relationship decreases the likelihood of being negatively affected by bullying (Cook et al., 2010; Doll, Song, Champio, & Jones, 2011) as does having at least one close supportive friendship. Having at least one positive friendship can decrease the risk of future bullying and diminish bullied youths' risk of adverse outcomes (Kendrick, Jutengren, & Stattin, 2012).

In a systematic review of metaanalyses, investigating protective factors against victimization and becoming a bully-victim, self-oriented personal competencies (e.g., good academic performance and social competencies) were the strongest protectors against victimization. Low frequency of technology use protected from involvement in cyberbullying, and positive peer interaction was the strongest protective factor against being a bully/victim (Zych, Farrington, & Ttofi, 2018). Table 7.1 lists both risk and protective factors related to bullying.

TABLE 7.1 Risk and protective factors for bullying involvement and outcomes.

Level	Risk factors	Protective factors
Individual	• Academic difficulties • Obesity • Special health-care needs (e.g., needing a wheel chair, asthma, and food allergy) • Perceived (by self or others) as minority relative to local population (e.g., race, ethnicity, religion, and gender) • LGBTQ identifying youth • Poor social skills • Poor coping/emotional self-regulation skills • Low perceived social connectedness • ACEs related to child's experiences: witnessing trauma/partner violence, experience of abuse or neglect, experience of corporal punishment • High media use (social and nonsocial media)	• Having positive friendships (e.g., one or two best/really good friends) • Advanced/positive social problem-solving skills • Positive self-esteem and self-oriented competencies/self-efficacy • Having access to a community of like individuals (e.g., hobby/interest group, religious organization, cultural group, and special needs leisure group) • Addressing a child's special health-care needs (e.g., treating ADHD, anxiety, depression) • Addressing ACEs related to the child's experiences • Low media use
Family	• Low parental support • Maltreatment/harsh parenting/corporal punishment • Problematic parenting styles: hostile/authoritarian, inconsistent/permissive, and overprotective • ACEs related to family needs. Caregiver with: mental health needs, alcohol/substance abuse, incarceration, experience of intimate partner violence	• Positive child–caregiver relationship • Authoritative parenting styles • Role modeling of healthy emotional coping skills • Role modeling of healthy social conflict resolution skills • Addressing family health needs/ACEs
School/Community	• Negative school climate • Local cultural implicit biases • High-risk sociocultural events/media coverage	• Positive student–teacher/staff relationship • Positive school climate • School responsiveness to bullying • School use of social emotional learning • Access to behavioral health professionals/supports at school

ACEs, Adverse childhood experiences.

School recommendations

School climate is a concept referring to the quality and character of school life. It is based on patterns of students', parents', and school personnels' experiences and perceptions of school life. School climate reflects the norms, goals, and values of a school. It is built upon interpersonal relationships, teaching and learning practices, and organizational structures (Thapa, Cohen, Guffey, & Higgins-D'Alessandro, 2013). While some specific, targeted bullying prevention programs have demonstrated efficacy, it appears that a continuous process of school climate improvement/reform is critical for effective bully prevention and school improvement efforts. Such whole school approaches not only prevent bullying behavior but also promote safe, supportive, responsible, engaging, and flourishing school communities (Cohen, Espelage, Twenlow, Berkowitz, & Conner, 2015). Table 7.2 provides a review of evidence-based school practices to prevent and address bullying.

TABLE 7.2 How to ask about bullying and what to say.

Approach:
1. Remember that the child or adolescent is likely reluctant to disclose their involvement in bullying. If possible, ask the caregiver to step outside of the room. Create an open environment of safety
2. Normalize the experience of bullying. Let the child know that bullying happens to other youths as well
3. State your concern. Let them know you want to understand so that you can try to help
4. Give them permission to talk and use empathic listening
5. If the child does not disclose anything specific, you can then start exploring using broader inquiries and ending with more specific questions

Broad questions to inquire about bullying:
- I'd like to hear about how school is going
- How many good friends do you have in school?
- Has there been a time when you felt afraid to go to school? Why?
- *For school age children*: Is there teasing at your school?
- *For adolescents*: Is there drama at your school?
- Do you have social media accounts?
- Are there kids that you have problems with at school? Or—are there kids at school who give you a hard time?

Specific questions to inquire about bullying:
- Have you been teased at school? Have you teased others?
- Are people ever mean to you because of ...?
- Are there kids who bully at school? Do they bully you?
- Have you been mean to another student?
- Have you gotten in trouble for something involving another student?

(Continued)

TABLE 7.2 (Continued)

Things to ask about (and document) when bullying is identified: • *What* type of bullying is occurring? (i.e., physical, social, and cyberbullying) • *Who* is involved? With which peers does the child have conflict? Who are their supports? • *When* is it happening? What time of day? How often? • *Where* is it happening? Think physical locations including "hot spots" • *Why* could this be happening? Does the child have any medical or emotional needs that are not being addressed? Are they experiencing imminent threats to their safety? • *How* are adults and peers responding at school? Have incidents been reported to the school? How is the school intervening?

The National School Climate Council (2012) defines an effective school climate improvement process as one that engages all involved in the following six essential themes in improving school climate:

1. Collaboration: The decision-making process is collaborative, democratic, and involves all stakeholders. This includes everyone from staff to students, their families, and community members. It takes into account the varied roles and perspectives of everyone involved.
2. Data-driven change: Psychometrically sound quantitative and qualitative data are used to plan and drive improvements. Data (i.e., from surveys, interviews, and focus groups) are collected regularly to evaluate progress and continue to inform the improvement process.
3. Customization: Improvement goals are personalized to the unique needs of the students and broader school community to facilitate the sustainability of the improvement process over time.
4. Adult learning: Capacity building among school teachers and staff promotes collective efficacy and skills in providing complete child education.
5. Evidence based: Curriculum, instruction, student supports, and interventions are based on scientific research and grounded in cognitive, social, and ecological theories of youth development.
6. Policy development: School policies and procedures as well as operational infrastructure are put in place to support the abovementioned themes (National School Climate Council, 2012).

The Olweus Bullying Prevention Program (1993) is the most well-researched universal, school-wide intervention program. The program has been identified as a Blueprints Promising Program by the Center for the Study and Prevention of Violence, University of Colorado at Boulder and is supported by the American Academy of Pediatrics

(AAP). Programming is offered for school staff, students (elementary, middle, and high school), parents, and the community. The program is designed to target three groups of children: Bullies and their acolytes, victims, and bystanders. Individual intervention plans are created for students who have been identified as being involved in bullying. The Olweus Bullying Prevention Program (OBPP) is based on the following components (www.clemson.edu/olweus):

1. Focusing on the whole school environment
2. Assessment of bullying at school
3. Forming a group to support bullying prevention activities, which is a representative group of individuals including an administrator, teacher from each grade, a member of the nonteaching staff, school counselor, school-based mental health professional, parent, and community representative
4. Training all staff in bullying prevention
5. Establishing and enforcing school rules and policies related to bullying
6. Involving children in regular discussions about bullying
7. Increasing adult supervision where bullying occurs
8. Intervening consistently and appropriately in bullying behaviors
9. Garnering parent support for bullying prevention
10. Providing ongoing support

The results of outcome evaluations of the program vary with the best results indicating a 50% reduction in bullying and a significant improvement in the classroom environment (University of Colorado Boulder, 2019).

In general, whole school initiatives including antibullying policies, and school-wide bullying conferences for children are associated with decreases in bullying perpetration among youth and are recommended best practice (Ttofi & Farrington, 2011). The research suggests that school-based prevention and intervention programs have significant, small to medium effects on victimization. The most effective of these programs include training in emotional control, peer counseling, and establishing school policy (Lee, Kim, & Kim, 2013). Positive and supportive bystander behaviors also have been associated with decreases in the frequency and negative impact of bullying. Programs promoting "upstanding" or a culture inviting bystanders to speak out against bullying behaviors have a positive effect on bullying reduction as well (Goodstein, 2013; Wood, Smith, Varjas, & Meyers, 2016).

A positive approach to school bullying is often recommended. Such a program consists of fostering kindness and respect, which serve as inhibitors of bullying (Lickona, 2016). These strategies are often included in social–emotional learning programs/curricula that are implemented in schools. Basic successful strategies such as cooperative/teambuilding activities and having teachers and staff praise students' demonstration of prosocial behaviors are often fundamental to these programs. Examples of current programs and curriculums being implemented (and investigated) in schools include, for example, The Olweus Bullying Prevention Program, KiVa AntiBullying Program, Positive Action, P4, Resolve It Solve It, Steps to Respect, Success in Stages, and Second Step (a social emotional learning program that has a bullying specific curriculum; Lawner, Beltz, & Moore, 2013). Research demonstrates that in general, social and emotional learning is linked to decreased bullying perpetration (Espelage, Rose, & Polanin, 2015). Lunch buddy mentoring is associated with a decline in peer victimization, with student ratings of perceived harm low and satisfaction high (Gregus, Craig, Rodriguez, Pastrana, & Cavell, 2015). Teaching adaptive coping responses is also critical. Virtual learning programs that depict animated characters in which bullying situations are presented and youth are coached on how to respond have been shown to be effective (Sapouna, Vannini, Wolke, & Aylett, 2012).

Few specific intervention strategies are found to be effective in reducing the reoccurrence of bullying. Holding a parent–teacher conference and loss of school privileges for the student bullying others were found to be effective in reducing the rate of the reoccurrence of bullying and aggressive behaviors (Ayers, Wagaman, Geiger, Bermudez-Parsai, & Hedberg, 2012). Other interventions including detention, in-school suspension, out-of-school suspension, parent phone call, and time spent in the main office were found not to be effective (Ayers et al., 2012).

Some interventions are now targeting "hot spots" in schools where bullying behaviors tend to occur (i.e., unsupervised areas, stairwells, playgrounds, and busses). Hot spot locations can be identified at each school and tend to differ with regard to gender and grade (Rapp-Paglicci, Dulmus, Sowers, & Theriot, 2004). New tools are being developed for additional mapping and study of such locations (Migliaccio, Raskauskas, & Schmidtlein, 2017), as interventions targeting hot spots have been found to be effective at reducing bullying behaviors at these specific locations (Zych, Farrington, Llorent, & Ttofi, 2017).

Zero-tolerance policies, through which the child who bullies is excluded or removed from the school, have been found to be ineffective in reducing bullying (Borgwald & Theixos, 2013; Berlowitz, Frye, & Jette, 2017). Threats of such severe punishment (i.e., suspension or expulsion) can discourage students and adults from reporting incidents of bullying. In addition, since bullying behaviors can be an early marker of other problem behaviors, the removal of the student who bullies could further complicate his/her developmental trajectory.

Group training in peer mediation does not result in significant changes in disciplinary referrals for aggressive behavior or impulsivity scores (Fast, Fanelli, & Salen, 2003). This type of intervention is strongly discouraged since it puts the targeted student at risk for revictimization (Kowalski, Limber, & Agatston, 2008).

In contrast, restorative justice (RJ) is an increasingly popular approach to responding to discipline issues including bullying and aggressive behaviors. RJ focuses on repairing harm through an inclusive process that engages all parties involved. Students come together in peer-mediated small groups to talk, ask questions, and discuss their grievances. RJ practices have the capacity to shift the focus of discipline from a lens of punishment to one of learning. They can also shift the focus from individuals to the community. While RJ approaches seem effective for addressing other rule-breaking or harm-inducing behaviors (Farrington & Ttofi, 2009), RJ does not always account for the sensitivity and complexity of school bullying (including aspects of traumatic power differential between parties) and possible resulting harmful after-effects on all those involved (i.e., a student may be further traumatized given the public nature of RJ). For these reasons, additional research on the implementation of such programs is needed (Song, & Swearer, 2016).

Recommendations for behavioral health providers

Given the high prevalence of bullying in American culture, all behavioral health providers should be assessing young patients for bullying. Signs that a child may being victimized include unexplained injuries, lost or destroyed property, frequent headaches or stomachaches (whether true or untrue), change in eating habits, difficulty in sleeping or experiencing nightmares, declining grades, avoiding school or other social situations, sudden loss of friends, decreased self-esteem, and/or self-destructive behaviors. Signs that someone may be engaging in bullying behavior include getting into physical or verbal altercations, becoming increasingly more aggressive, frequently receiving disciplinary action at school, and having unexplained new belongings.

It is recommended that aggressive behavior be identified and addressed as early as preschool. Especially during these younger years, parent training can be very effective. Parent training involves providing positive attention to prosocial behavior and modeling of social problem-solving and conflict resolution. Parent training also teaches positive discipline strategies that can be used rather than more punitive strategies, such as corporal punishment. This approach is associated with a decrease in bullying perpetration, victimization, and behavior (Burkhart, Knox, & Brockmyer, 2013; Ttofi & Farrington, 2011).

Clinicians should be educating parents on the effects of bullying and providing advocacy training in the school setting. Clinicians should be knowledgeable about their state's policies and laws and prepared to help parents to advocate for the inclusion of *evidence-based, school-wide* prevention programs in their children's schools. All US states have laws or policies about bullying prevention in schools. Information about each state's antibullying laws and policies can be found at the StopBullying.gov website (StopBullying.gov, 2019).

In addition, clinicians can assist parents with including provisions about bullying in their child's 504 Plan or Individualized Education Program (IEP). Table 7.3 provides clinician tips for guiding families in addressing bullying that occurs at school, and Table 7.4 provides tips for working with youth who bully others.

TABLE 7.3 Review of evidence-based school practices

Methods not currently supported by research:
- Zero-tolerance policies
- Conflict resolution and peer mediation
- Group treatment for children who bully
- Phone calls home
- Out-of-school suspension
- Detentions/In-school suspensions

Methods with at least some research support:
- Parent–teacher conferences (at school)
- Loss of school privileges
- Implementation of antibullying programs/social emotional learning programs that involve both a whole-school approach and parent involvement (e.g., Olweus, KiVa, and Second Step)
- Addressing a child's unmet medical needs
- Appropriate treatment of comorbid health and behavioral health conditions
- Addressing a child's disability with a 504 disability accommodation plan
- Considering if special education goals are needed to address a child's deficits

TABLE 7.4 Clinician tips for working with children involved in bullying at school.

1. Screen for bullying involvement
   a. If no concerns identified, proceed to give anticipatory guidance
   b. If concerns are identified, get more information (see Table 7.2)
2. Assess for immediate safety
   a. Is it safe for the child to return to school? (Is their safety threatened?)
   b. Does the reported information require you to act as a mandated reporter?
   c. Does the child/family require immediate crisis intervention?

(Continued)

TABLE 7.4 (Continued)

3. Ask family if they have reported their concerns to the school
   a. If not, refer them to their school district's website and bullying policy
   b. Ask them to document (see Table 7.2) incidents and report them to the school. Ask them to keep their own copy of the documentation
4. Ask them how the school has responded
   a. If needed, schedule clinical follow-up to check on resolution/outcome
5. Consider if there are any unmet needs for the child
   a. Assess for school avoidance, anxiety, depression, suicidal ideation and treat appropriately
   b. Could their medical needs be better managed? (e.g., with medical intervention or referral for other services)
   c. Could the child benefit from access to clinical support/behavioral health to address their identified emotional or behavior needs or coping skills?
   d. Could the child benefit from access to academic supports? (e.g., intervention by a school counselor, a special education plan/individualized education program)
   e. Encourage positive supports and relationships. Who is their "go to" adult at school? Can they identify friends who are supportive and helpful?
   f. Could the family use additional support? (e.g., a parent advocate through the school district)
6. If school response is inadequate and/or there is not much else to be done from the clinical setting, reach out to the school
   a. Ask family who they feel connected to/aligned with at school. Ask them if you can reach out and speak with that person (at your current visit or later)
   b. Communicate with the school to discuss evidence-based bullying prevention and intervention
7. If all else truly fails, consider these following tools of last resort
   a. Connect the family with a school advocate (available in many states for youths with suspected or identified disabilities)
   b. Consider if transferring schools could be therapeutic and advocate for a fresh start
   c. Discuss state bullying laws. Connect the family with a legal advocate if needed

Cognitive-behavioral therapy is recommended to treat internalizing symptoms and somatic complaints associated with bullying. Feelings identification, positive activity scheduling, cognitive restructuring, and development of coping strategies (i.e., stress management strategies) are needed to manage symptoms and minimize the impact of symptoms on day-to-day functioning. Problem-solving and assertiveness training have been found to be beneficial for victims of bullying (Hager & Leadbeater, 2015). Moreover, research on social skills training interventions indicates increased protective factors related to improved friendships, communication, and assertiveness skills for youth victims (Low & Van Ryzin, 2014). For youth who are engaging in bullying behavior, cognitive-behavioral therapy for anger management and social and emotional coaching is recommended.

Recommendations for the treating clinician

The AAP and the Society for Adolescent Health and Medicine recommend that health-care providers are involved in prevention and intervention efforts around bullying. Screening for peer victimization can occur during all routine medical appointments with special consideration given to those who are at greater risk (Committee on Injury, Violence, and Poison Prevention, 2009; Eisenberg & Aalsma, 2005). Table 7.5 provides information about how to talk with patients about bullying.

The AAP addresses bullying in the policy statement "Role of the pediatrician in youth violence prevention" (Committee on Injury, Violence, and Poison Prevention, 2009). This statement notes that pediatricians can collectively contribute to youth violence prevention through promotion of parenting skills. In addition, pediatricians can provide screening to recognize bullying in primary care and appropriate referral for children who are either targets of bullying or who actively bully. While there are no official practice guidelines regarding bullying, the AAP has developed curricula such as Connected Kids: Safe, Strong, and Secure (CKSSS), which it recommends pediatricians use. Among other things, the CKSSS curriculum recommends that it should be explained to children that they should seek help from an adult if they think a fight is going to begin or bullying is occurring. CKSSS recommends that anticipatory guidance regarding bullying prevention should be introduced at

TABLE 7.5 Clinician tips for working with children who bully others.

1. Figure out if the behavior is bullying (i.e., ascertain if there is a power imbalance, if it occurs repeatedly and over time)
2. Listen carefully and without judgment
3. Call the behavior bullying if it is bullying
4. Deconstruct any blaming and depersonalization of the target. Do not assign blame yourself, rather show empathy for the bully and the victim and their experiences
5. Help the parent to set clear expectations for behavior
6. Help the parent to develop a system involving natural consequences for bullying behavior
7. Provide alternative opportunities for leadership skills (if appropriate)
8. Refer to behavioral health if not already in place (especially if bully-victim). Update the existing clinician, if the family is already working with one
9. Assess for safety at home and school. (Is the child's safety threatened? Is the safety of another person threatened?) Report safety concerns immediately to parents/school personnel as appropriate. Report unsafe living circumstances/maltreatment to Children's Services if identified
10. Schedule follow up

the 6-year-old routine health-care maintenance (RHCM) visit, with reinforcement of the topic at the 8-year-old RHCM visit (AAP, 2009).

Clinicians also can use preventive measures such as encouraging patients to find enjoyable activities that promote confidence and self-esteem, model how to treat others with kindness and respect, and encourage patients to seek positive friendships (Stephens, Cook-Fasano, & Sibbaluca, 2018).

Clinicians who care for children can play a unique and important role in addressing all forms of bullying, including specific populations of children vulnerable to bullying such as children with special health-care needs and children who identify as LGBTQ. If youth are accompanied by parents, clinicians can aim to spend one-on-one time with youth to ask about issues that they may not feel comfortable discussing in front of their parents, including experiences of bullying (Hadland, Yehia, & Makadon, 2016).

They can educate parents and youth about how to recognize and respond to bullying. They may be in unique positions to identify youth who are targets of LGBTQ bullying, as many youth, including LGBTQ youth, who are bullied do not tell adults, including parents and teachers, because they worry about how these adults will react. The use of electronic psychosocial assessment tools, such as myAssessment or the Rapid Assessment for Adolescent Preventive Services, to identify high-risk behaviors may increase rates of disclosure and be a time-saving step for busy clinicians (Stephens et al., 2018).

Pediatric clinicians can ask youth about experiences of bullying and can look for symptoms indicating that youth have been bullied (such as signs of physical injury and or psychosomatic symptoms). Clinicians should refer youth experiencing clinically significant depressive, anxiety, or other psychological symptoms to appropriate mental health services (Earnshaw et al., 2017). When bullying is identified, clinicians can also reach out to school counselors and nurses to assist and advocate for their patients. They can refer families to school policies that address bullying. All US states have laws or policies about bullying prevention in schools. Information about each state's antibullying laws and policies can be found at the StopBullying.gov website. Clinicians should be knowledgeable about their states' policies and laws and prepared to help parents to advocate for the inclusion of *evidence-based, school-wide* prevention programs in their children's schools. In addition, clinicians and their health-care teams can assist parents with including provisions about bullying in their child's 504 Plan or IEP. Finally, clinicians should follow up with families to ensure that appropriate services are in place and that interventions have been successful.

Conclusion

Given that bullying is a complex social phenomenon, a systems/public health-based approach is needed to effectively address it. This should involve students, families, school personnel, health-care providers, and behavioral health clinicians. Health care and behavioral health clinicians are empowered to not only treat the individual needs of children involved in bullying but also advocate for use of evidence-based treatment methods and systems-wide policies and interventions to be implemented on individual and population-based levels. Handouts 1–4 provide a variety of resources on bullying to help clinicians, parents, and youths to understand and address this serious public health problem.

Handout 1. Resources about bullying for clinicians

Measuring bullying, victimization, perpetration, and bystander experiences: a compendium of assessment tools
CDC: National Center for Injury Prevention and Control
This compendium provides researchers, prevention specialists, and health educators with tools to measure a range of bullying experiences: bully perpetration, bully victimization, bully-victim experiences, and bystander experiences.
Available at: https://www.cdc.gov/violenceprevention/pdf/bullycompendium-a.pdf

The Resilience Project: We Can Stop Toxic Stress
The AAP
The AAP provides pediatricians and all medical home teams with the resources they need to modify practice operations to more effectively identify, treat, and refer children and youth who have been exposed to or victimized by violence.
Available at: https://www.aap.org/en-us/advocacy-and-policy/aap-health-initiatives/resilience/Pages/Resilience-Project.aspx

StopBullying.gov
The US Department of Health and Human Services
StopBullying.gov provides information from various government agencies on what bullying is, what cyberbullying is, who is at risk, and how you can prevent and respond to bullying.
Available at: stopbullying.gov

Bullying Research Network (BRNET)
College of Education and Human Services: University of Nebraska-Lincoln
Designed primarily for researchers, the purpose of this Network is to promote and assist international collaboration among bullying and peer victimization researchers. To facilitate collaboration, they we have sponsored an annual bullying research think tank and compiled research, news, and resources that are shared online with members. BRNET currently consists of *215 researchers* from 21 countries.
Available at: https://cehs.unl.edu/BRNET/

Alberti Center for Bullying Abuse Prevention
University at Buffalo
The mission of the Alberti Center is to reduce bullying abuse in schools and in the community by contributing knowledge and providing evidence-based tools to effectively change the language, attitudes, and behaviors of educators, parents, students, and

society. The center is a national resource on the prevention of bullying and other forms of school violence among school children, as well as provide research and information that address these behaviors.
Available at: http://ed.buffalo.edu/alberti.html

Violence Prevention Works!
A Foundation for Healthier Youth
Information about the OBPP. The website includes tips for addressing bullying for administrators, teachers, and parents. It also includes resources on recognizing bullying, the impact of bullying, cyberbullying, and bullying and sexual orientation.
Available at: http://www.violencepreventionworks.org/public/index.page

Bullying Resource Center
The American Academy of Child & Adolescent Psychiatry
Information about recommendations to give parents about how to ask children about bullying.
Available at: https://www.aacap.org/aacap/families_and_youth/Resource_Centers/Bullying_Resource_Center/Home.aspx#clinicalresources

Cyberbullying Research Center
This website serves as a clearinghouse of information concerning the ways adolescents use and misuse technology. It is intended to be a resource for parents, educators, mental health professionals, law enforcement officers, counselors, and others who work with youth. In addition, the site includes numerous resources to help you prevent and respond to cyberbullying incidents.
Available at: https://cyberbullying.org/

PACER's National Bullying Prevention Center
PACER's National Bullying Prevention Center actively leads social change to prevent childhood bullying, so that all youth are safe and supported in their schools, communities, and online. PACER provides innovative resources for students, parents, educators, and others and recognizes bullying as a serious community issue that impacts education, physical and emotional health, and the safety and well-being of students.
Available at: https://www.pacer.org/bullying/

Handout 2. Resources about bullying for families

StopBullying.gov
The US Department of Health and Human Services
Information to help identify the signs of bullying, prevention and intervention, and advocacy opportunities. This is a parent- and child-friendly website.
Available at: stopbullying.gov

PACER's National Bullying Prevention Center
PACER's National Bullying Prevention Center actively leads social change to prevent childhood bullying, so that all youth are safe and supported in their schools, communities and online. PACER provides innovative resources for students, parents, educators, and others, and recognizes bullying as a serious community issue that impacts education, physical and emotional health, and the safety and well-being of students.
Available at: https://www.pacer.org/bullying/

The BULLY Project
The BULLY Project is the social action campaign inspired by the award-winning film BULLY. We've sparked a national movement to stop bullying that is transforming kids' lives and changing a culture of bullying into one of empathy and action. This website contains resources for educators, students, and parents.
Available at: http://www.thebullyproject.com/

Be Strong App
Stand Strong USA
Smartphone application that provides resources, support and intervention for those affected by bullying, depression and suicide. Includes ready-access to instant phone hot line, crisis text line and trusted friends/family alert as well as free/near-free social services available within your zip code and surrounding location.
Available for: Apple iOS and Android

The Bullying Antidote: Superpower Your Kids for Life
Louise Hart and Kristen Caven
Hazelden Publishing, 2013.
Available at: Amazon.com

Bullying Hurts: Teaching Kindness Through Read Alouds And Guided Conversations
Lester L. Laminack and Reba M. Wadsworth
Heinemann Publishing, 2012
Available at: Amazon.com

Handout 3. LGBT resources about bullying

Lesbian, gay, bisexual, and transgender youth
CDC
Resources from the CDC, other government agencies, and community organizations for LGBT youth, their friends, educators, parents, and family members to support positive environments.
Available at: https://www.cdc.gov/lgbthealth/youth.htm

StopBullying.gov
the US Department of Health and Human Services
Information to help educators, families, and LGBTQ youth identify and prevent bullying toward LGBTQ youth.
Available at: https://www.stopbullying.gov/at-risk/groups/lgbt/index.html

Bullying: What Parents, Teachers Can Do to Stop It
Susan Swearer, PhD
This resource is an interview with "bullying expert" Susan Swearer about commonly asked questions about bullying.
Available at: https://www.apa.org/news/press/releases/2010/04/bullying.aspx

Be Strong App
Stand Strong USA
Smartphone application that provides resources, support and intervention for those affected by bullying, depression and suicide. Includes ready-access to instant phone hot line, crisis text line and trusted friends/family alert as well as free/near-free social services available within your zip code and surrounding location.
Available for: Apple iOS and Android

Handout 4. Resources about bullying for youth

PACER Center's Kids Against Bullying
PACER Kids Against Bullying is a creative, innovative, and educational website designed for elementary school students to learn about bullying prevention, engage in activities, and be inspired to take action.
Available at: https://www.pacerkidsagainstbullying.org/

PACER Center's Teens Against Bullying
PACER Center's Teens Against Bullying, a website created by and for teens, is a place for middle and high school students to find ways to address bullying.
Available at: https://www.pacerteensagainstbullying.org/

What Kids Can Do
The US Department of Health and Human Services
Resources targeted toward kids about bullying.
Available at: https://www.stopbullying.gov/kids/what-you-can-do/index.html

Bullying/Violence
Nemours
Resource provides teens with information about bullying, cyberbullying, and changing bullying behavior.
Available at: https://kidshealth.org/en/teens/school-jobs/?WT.ac = t-nav-school-jobs#catbullying

Be Strong App
Stand Strong USA
Smartphone application that provides resources, support, and intervention for those affected by bullying, depression, and suicide. Includes ready-access to instant phone hot line, crisis text line, and trusted friends/family alert as well as free/near-free social services available within your zip code and surrounding location.
Available for: Apple iOS and Android

Tease Monster: A Book About Teasing Vs. Bullying
Julia Cook
Boys Town Press, 2013.
Available at: Amazon.com

Weird! A Story About Dealing with Bullying in Schools
Erin Frankel
Free Spirit Publishing, 2013.
Available at: Amazon.com

Spaghetti in a Hot Dog Bun: Having the Courage to Be Who You Are
Maria Dismondy
Cardinal Rule Press, 2008
Available at: Amazon.com

Bullying Is a Pain in the Brain
Trevor Romain
Free Spirit Publishing, 1997.
Available at: Amazon.com

Important points to remember

- Approximately 20% of US children are bullied, and only 30% of these children tell an adult.
- Researchers have found links between chronic childhood peer victimization and adulthood depression, anxiety, self-criticism, fear of negative evaluation, loneliness, body dissatisfaction, eating disturbances, and suicidal behavior (Faith et al., 2008; Isaacs, Hodges, & Salmivalli, 2008).
- Positive parent–child interaction, modeling of conflict resolution, and effective communication decrease the likelihood of chronic bullying and serve as a buffer against the detrimental effects of bullying (e.g., Burkhart et al., 2013; Ledwell & King, 2013).
- Programs promoting "upstanding" or a culture inviting bystanders to speak out against bullying behaviors have a positive effect on bullying reduction.
- Peer mediation does not result in significant changes in disciplinary referrals for aggressive behavior or impulsivity scores. This type of intervention is strongly discouraged since it puts the targeted student at risk for revictimization.
- Signs that a child may being victimized include unexplained injuries, lost or destroyed property, frequent headaches or stomachaches (whether true or untrue), change in eating habits, difficulty sleeping or experiencing nightmares, declining grades, avoiding school or other social situations, sudden loss of friends, decreased self-esteem, and/or self-destructive behaviors.
- Clinicians should be knowledgeable about their state's policies and laws and prepared to help parents to advocate for the inclusion of evidence-based, school-wide prevention programs in their children's schools. All US states have laws or policies about bullying prevention in schools. Information about each state's antibullying laws and policies can be found at the StopBullying.gov website.
- Pediatricians can collectively contribute to youth violence prevention through promotion of parenting skills. In addition, pediatricians can provide screening to recognize bullying in primary care and appropriate referral for children who are either targets of bullying or who actively bully.
- Clinicians can aim to spend one-on-one time with youth to ask about issues that they may not feel comfortable discussing in front of their parents, including experiences of bullying.

References

American Academy of Pediatrics. *Bullying prevention.* (2009). <http://www.idahoaap.org/bullying.htm>.

Anderson, M., Kaufman, J., Simon, T. R., Barrios, L., Paulozzi, L., Ryan, G., et al. (2001). School-associated violent deaths in the United States, 1994-1999. *Journal of the American Medical Association, 286,* 2695–2702.

Arango, A., Opperman, K. J., Gipson, P. Y., & King, C. A. (2016). Suicidal ideation and suicide attempts among youth who report bully victimization, bully perpetration, and/or low social connectedness. *Journal of Adolescence, 51*(1), 19–29.

Ayers, S. L., Wagaman, M. A., Geiger, J. M., Bermudez-Parsai, M., & Hedberg, E. C. (2012). Examining school-based bullying interventions using multilevel discrete time hazard modeling. *Prevention Science, 13*(5), 539–550.

Bender, K. (2010). Why do some maltreated youth become juvenile offenders? A call for further investigation and adaptation of youth services. *Children and Youth Services Review, 32,* 466–473.

Beran, T. (2008). Consequences of being bullied at school. In D. Pepler, & W. Craig (Eds.), *Understanding and addressing bullying: An international perspective* (pp. 44–66). Bloomington, ID: Authorhouse.

Berlowitz, M. J., Frye, R., & Jette, K. M. (2017). Bullying and zero-tolerance policies: The school to prison pipeline. *Multicultural Learning and Teaching, 12*(1), 7–25.

Borgwald, K., & Theixos, H. (2013). Bullying the bully: Why zero-tolerance policies get a failing grade. *Social Influence, 8*(2-3), 149–160.

Burkhart, K., Knox, M., & Brockmyer. (2013). Pilot evaluation of the ACT raising safe kids program on children's bullying behavior. *Journal of child and family studies, 22*(7), 942–951.

Centers for Disease Control and Prevention. (2017). *WISQARS. Ten leading causes of death, United States.* Atlanta, GA: Centers for Disease Control and Prevention. Retrieved from <https://webappa.cdc.gov/sasweb/ncipc/leadcause.html>.

Cohen, J., Espelage, D., Twenlow, S. W., Berkowitz, M. W., & Conner, J. P. (2015). Rethinking effective bully and violence prevention effects: Promoting healthy school climates, positive youth development, and preventing bully-victim-bystander behavior. *International Journal of Violence and Schools, 15,* 2–40.

Committee on Injury, Violence, and Poison Prevention. (2009). Role of the pediatrician in youth violence prevention. *Pediatrics, 124*(1), 393–402.

Compas, B. E., Jaser, S. S., Dunn, M. J., & Rodriguez, E. M. (2012). Coping with chronic illness in childhood and adolescence. *Annual Reviews of Clinical Psychology, 8,* 455–480.

Connolly, I., & O'Moore, M. (2003). Personality and family relations of children who bully. *Personality and Individual Differences, 35*(3), 559–567.

Cook, C. R., Williams, K. R., Guerra, N. G., Kim, T. E., & Sadek, S. (2010). Predictors of bullying and victimization in childhood and adolescence: A meta-analytic investigation. *School Psychology Quarterly, 25*(2), 65–83.

Copeland, W. E., Wolke, D., Angold, A., & Costello, E. J. (2013). Adult psychiatric outcomes of bullying and being bullied by peers in childhood and adolescence. *The Journal of the American Medical Association, 70*(4), 419–426.

Craig, W., Harel-Fisch, Y., Fogel-Grinvald, H., HBCSC Violence & Injuries Prevention Focus Group; HBSC Bullying Writing Group., et al. (2009). A cross-national profile of bullying and victimization among adolescents in 40 countries. *International journal of public health, 54*(Suppl 2), 216–224.

Davis, S., & Nixon, C. *The youth voice project. Preliminary Results from the Youth Voice Project: Victimization and Strategies.* (2010). Retrieved from: <http://njbullying.org/documents/YVPMarch2010.pdf>.

Doll, B., Song, S., Champio, A., & Jones, K. (2011). Classroom ecologies that support or Discourage bullying. In D. L. Espelage, & S. M. Swearer (Eds.), *Bullying in North American schools* (2nd ed., pp. 147–158). Philadelphia, PA: Routledge.

Duncan, R. D. (2011). Family relationships of bullies and victims. *Bullying in North American schools, 2*, 191–204.

Earnshaw, V. A., Reisner, S. L., Juvonen, J., Hatzenbuehler, M. L., Perrotti, J., & Schuster, M. A. (2017). LGBTQ bullying: translating research to action in pediatrics. *Pediatrics, 140*, e20170432.

Eisenberg, M. E., & Aalsma, M. C. (2005). Bullying and peer victimization: Position paper of the Society of Adolescent Medicine. *Journal of Adolescent Medicine, 36*, 88–91.

Eisenberg, M. E., McMorris, B. J., Gower, A. L., & Chatterjee, D. (2016). Bullying victimization and emotional distress: Is there strength in numbers for vulnerable youth? *Pediatrics—Adolescent Health and Medicine, 86*, 13–19.

Espelage, D. L., & Holt, M. K. (2013). Suicidal ideation and school bullying experiences after Controlling for depression and delinquency. *Adolescent Health, 53*, 527–531.

Espelage, D. L., Rose, C. A., & Polanin, J. R. (2015). Social-emotional learning program to reduce bullying, fighting, and victimization among middle school students with disabilities. *Remedial and Special Education, 36*(5), 263–274.

Faith, M. A., Malcolm, K. T., & Newgent, R. A. (2008). Reducing potential mental health issues and alcohol abuse through an early prevention model for victims of peer harassment. *Work, 31*(3), 327–335.

Faith, M. A., Reed, G., Heppner, C. E., Hamill, L. C., Tarkenton, T. R., & Donewar, C. W. (2015). Bullying in medically fragile youth: A review of risks, protective factors, and recommendations for medical providers. *Journal of Developmental and Behavioral Pediatrics, 36*, 285–301.

Farrington, D. P., & Ttofi, M. M. (2009). How to reduce school bullying. *Victims and Offenders, 4*, 321–326.

Fast, J., Fanelli, F., & Salen, L. (2003). How becoming mediators affects aggressive students. *Children & Schools, 25*(3), 161–171.

Fekkes, M., Pijpers, F. I. M., & Verloove-Vanhorick, S. P. (2004). Bullying: Who does what, when, and where? Involvement of children, teachers, and parents in bullying behavior. *Health Education Research, 20*(1), 81–91.

Frisén, A., Lunde, C., & Hwang, P. (2009). Peer victimisation and its relationships with perceptions of body composition. *Educational Studies, 35*(3), 337–348.

Gini, G., & Pozzoli, T. (2013). Bullied children and psychosomatic problems: A meta-analysis. *Pediatrics, 132*(4), 720–729.

Gladden, R. M., Vivolo-Kanto, A. M., Hamburger, M. E., & Lumpkin, C. D. (2014). *Bullying surveillance among youths: Uniform definitions for public health and recommended data elements, Version 1.0.* Atlanta, GA: National Center for Injury Prevention and Control, Centers for Disease Control and Prevention, and US Department of Education.

Goodstein, Phyllis Kaufman (2013). *How to stop bullying in classrooms and schools: Using Social Architecture to Prevent, Lessen, and End Bullying* (pp. 110–141). Philadelphia, PA: Routledge.

Gregus, S. J., Craig, J. T., Rodriguez, J. H., Pastrana, F. A., & Cavell, T. A. (2015). Lunch buddy Mentoring for children victimized by peers: Two pilot studies. *Journal of Applied School Psychology, 31*(2), 167–197.

Hadland, S. E., Yehia, B. R., & Makadon, H. J. (2016). Caring for lesbian, gay, bisexual, transgender, and questioning youth in inclusive and affirmative environments. *Pediatric Clinics, 63*(6), 955–969.

Hager, A. D., & Leadbeater, B. J. (2015). The longitudinal effects of peer victimization on physical Health from adolescence to young adulthood. *Journal of Adolescent Health, 58*(31).

Heerde, J. A., & Hemphill, S. A. (2018). Are bullying perpetration and victimization associated with adolescent deliberate self-harm? A meta-analysis. *Archives of Suicide Research*, 1–42.

Hertz, M. F., Donato, I., & Wright, J. (2013). Bullying and suicide: A public health approach. *Journal of Adolescent Health*, *53*(1 Suppl), S1–S3.

Holt, M. K., Matjasko, J. L., Espelage, D., Reid, G., & Koenig, B. (2013). Sexual risk taking and bullying among adolescents. *Pediatrics*, *132*(6), e1481–e1487.

Ilola, A. M., Lempinen, L., Huttunen, J., & Sourando, A. (2016). Bullying and victimization are common in four-year-old children and are associated with somatic symptoms and conduct and peer problems. *Acta Paediatrica*, *105*(5), 522–528.

Isaacs, J., Hodges, E. V., & Salmivalli, C. (2008). Long-term consequences of victimization by peers: A follow-up from adolescence to young adulthood. *International Journal of Developmental Science*, 2(4), 387–397.

Kendrick, K., Jutengren, G., & Stattin, H. (2012). The protective role of supportive friends Against bullying perpetration and victimization. *Journal of Adolescence*, *35*(4), 1069–1080.

Klomek, A. B., Marrocco, F., Kleinman, M., Schonfeld, I. S., & Gould, M. S. (2007). Bullying, depression, and suicidality in adolescents. *Journal of the American Academy of Child & Adolescent Psychiatry*, *46*(1), 40–49.

Kowalski, R. M., Limber, S. P., & Agatston, P. W. (2008). *Cyber bullying: Bullying in the digital world*. Malden, MA: Blackwell Publishing.

Lawner, E., Beltz, M., & Moore, A.K. (2013). What works for mentoring programs: Lessons from experimental evaluations of programs and interventions. Child Trends.

Lawson, M. A., Lawson, T., Downder, J., & Anderson, E. (2013). Analyzing sub-population Profiles and risk factors for school bullying. *Children and Youth Services*, *35*(6), 973–983.

Leary, M. R., Kowalski, R. M., Smith, L., & Phillips, S. (2003). Teasing, rejection, and violence: Case studies of the school shootings. *Aggressive Behavior*, *29*, 202–214.

Ledwell, M., & King, V. (2013). Bullying and internalizing problems: Gender differences and the buffering role of parental communication. *Journal of Family Issues*, *36*(5), 543–566.

Lee, S., Kim, C., & Kim, D. H. (2013). A meta-analysis of the effect of school-based anti-bullying programs. *Journal of Child Health Care*, *19*(2), 136–153.

Lickona, T. (2016). *Tolerance, Diversity, and Respect for Conscience: The Neglected Issue*. State University of New York at Cortland. Available from http://www2.cortland.edu/centers/character/images/sex_character/Tolerance%20Diversity%20and%20Respect%20for%20Conscience%20april%2006.pdf.

Loukas, A., & Pasch, K. E. (2012). Does school connectedness buffer the impact of peer Victimization on early adolescents' subsequent adjustment problems? *The Journal of Early Adolescence*, *33*, 245–266.

Low, S., & Van Ryzin, M. (2014). The moderating effects of school climate on bullying prevention efforts. *School Psychology Quarterly*, *29*(3), 306.

Lucas, S., Jernbro, C., Tindberg, Y., & Janson, S. (2016). Bully, bullied, and abused. Associations between violence at home and bullying in childhood. *Scandinavian Journal of Public Health*, *44*(1), 27–35.

McKenna, M., Hawk, E., Mullen, J., & Hertz, M. (2011). Bullying among middle school and high school students – Massachusetts, 2009. *Morbidity and Mortality Weekly Report*, *60*(15), 465–471.

Migliaccio, T., Raskauskas, J., & Schmidtlein, M. (2017). Mapping the landscapes of bullying. *Learning Environments Research*, *20*(3), 365–382.

Modecki, K. L., Minchin, J., Harbaugh, A. G., Guerra, H. G., & Runions, K. C. (2014). Bullying prevalence across contexts: A meta-analysis measuring cyber and traditional bullying. *Journal of Adolescent Health*, *55*, 602–611.

Molcho, M., Craig, W., Due, P., Pickett, W., Harel-Fisch., Overpeck, M., & HBSC Bullying Writing Group. (2009). Cross-national time trends in bullying behavior 1994-2006: Findings from Europe and North America. *International Journal of Public Health, 54*, 1–10.

Moore, S. E., Norman, R. E., Suetani, S., Thomas, H. J., Sly, P. D., & Scott, J. G. (2017). Consequences of bullying victimization in childhood and adolescence: A systematic review and meta-analysis. *World Journal of Psychiatry, 7*(1), 60.

Nansel., et al. (2001). Bullying behaviors among U.S. youth: Prevalence and association with psychosocial adjustment. *The Journal of the American Medical Association, 285*(16), 2094–2100.

Nansel, T. R., Craig, W., Overpeck, M. D., Saluja, G., & Ruan, W. J. (2004). Cross-national consistency in the relationship between bullying behaviors and psychosocial adjustment. *Archives of Pediatric and Adolescent Medicine, 158*, 730–736.

National Academies of Science, Engineering, and Medicine. (2016). *Bullying as an adverse childhood experience*. <www.cdc.gov/violenceprevention.org>.

National Autistic Society (2017). *Bullying: A guide for parents*. Retrieved from <http://researchautism.net>.

National Center for Educational Statistics (2016). *Bullying prevalence*. Retrieved from <https://nces.ed.gov>.

National School Climate Council (2012). *The school climate improvement process: Essential elements. school climate brief, no. 4*. Available online at <https://files.eric.ed.gov/fulltext/ED573705.pdf>.

Rapp-Paglicci, L., Dulmus, C. N., Sowers, K. M., & Theriot, M. T. (2004). "Hotspots" for bullying: Exploring the role of environment in school violence. *Journal of Evidence-Based Social Work, 1*(2–3), 131–141.

Sansen, L. M., Iffland, B., & Neuner, F. (2014). The trauma of peer victimization: Psychophysiological and emotional characteristics of memory imagery in subjects with social anxiety disorder. *Psychophysiology, 52*(1), 107–116.

Sapouna, M., Vannini, N., Wolke, D., & Aylett, R. (2012). Individual and social network Predictors of the short-term stability of bullying victimization in the United Kingdom and Germany. *British Journal of Educational Psychology, 82*(2), 225–240.

Shetgiri, R., Lin, H., Auila, R. M., & Flores, G. (2012). Parental characteristics associated with bullying perpetration in US children aged 10 to 17 years. *American Journal of Public Health, 102*(12), 2280–2286.

Shetgiri, R., Lin, H., & Flores, G. (2015). Suboptimal maternal and paternal mental health are associated with child bullying perpetration. *Child Psychiatry & Human Development, 46*(3), 455–465.

Shields, A., & Cicchetti, D. (2001). Parental maltreatment and emotion dysregulation as risk factors for bullying and victimization in middle childhood. *Journal of Clinical Child Psychology, 30*(3), 349–363.

Song, S. Y., & Swearer, S. M. (2016). The cart before the horse: The challenge and promise of restorative justice consultation in schools. *Journal of Educational and Psychological Consultation, 26*(4), 313–324. Available from https://doi.org/10.1080/10474412.2016.1246972.

Stephens, M. M., Cook-Fasano, H. T., & Sibbaluca, K. (2018). Childhood bullying: Implications for physicians. *American Family Physician, 97*(3), 187–192.

StopBullying.gov. (2019). *Laws, policies & regulations*. Retrieved from <https://www.stopbullying.gov/laws/index.html#skip>.

Swearer, S. M., Espelage, D. L., Koening, B., Barry, B., et al. (2012). A social-ecological model of bullying prevention and intervention in early adolescence. In S. R. Jimerson, A. B. Nickerson, M. J. Mayer, & M. J. Furlong (Eds.), *Handbook of school violence and school safety* (pp. 333–355). New York: Routledge.

Takizawa, R., Maughan, B., & Arseneault, L. (2014). Adult health outcomes of childhood bullying victimization: evidence from a five-decade longitudinal British birth cohort. *American Journal of Psychiatry, 171*(7), 777–784.

Thapa, A., Cohen, J., Guffey, S., & Higgins-D'Alessandro, A. (2013). A review of school climate research. *Review of Educational Research, 83*(3), 357–385.

Ttofi, M. M., & Farrington, D. P. (2011). Effectiveness of school-based programs to reduce bullying: A systematic and meta-analytic review. *Journal of Experimental Criminology, 7* (1), 27–56.

University of Colorado Boulder. (2019). *Blueprints for healthy youth development*. Retrieved from <https://www.blueprintsprograms.org/factsheet/olweus-bullying-prevention-program>.

Van Cleave, J., & Davis, M. M. (2006). Bullying and peer victimization among children with Special health care needs. *Pediatrics, 118*(4), 2112–2119.

Van Geel, M., Vedder, P., & Tanilon, J. (2014). Relationship between peer victimization, cyberbullying, and suicide in children and adolescents. *JAMA Pediatrics, 168*(5), 435–442.

Vaughn, M. G., Fu, Q., Beaver, K. M., DeLisi, M., Perron, B. E., & Howard, M. O. (2011). Effects of childhood adversity on bullying and cruelty to animals in the United States: Findings from a national sample. *Journal of Interpersonal Violence, 26*(17), 3509–3525.

Waasdorp, T. E., Pas, E. T., Zablotsky, B., & Bradshaw, C. P. (2017). Ten-year trends in bullying and related attitudes among 4th- to 12th-graders. *Pediatrics, 139*(6), e20162615.

Wolfe, T. (2013). Loneliness Updated: An Introduction. Loneliness Updated: Recent research on loneliness and how it affects our lives, 1.

Wolke, D., Copeland, W. E., Angold, A., & Costello, E. J. (2013). Impact of bullying in childhood on adult health, wealth, crime, and social outcomes. *Psychological Science, 24* (10), 1958–1970.

Wood, L., Smith, J., Varjas, K., & Meyers, J. (2016). Engaging upstanders: Class-wide approach to promoting positive bystander behavior. *School Psychology Forum, 10*(1), 66–77.

Zych, I., Farrington, D. P., Llorent, V. J., & Ttofi, M. M. (2017). *Protecting children through anti-bullying interventions. Protecting children against bullying and its consequences* (pp. 57–68). Cham: Springer.

Zych, I., Farrington, D. P., & Ttofi, M. M. (2018). Protective factors against bullying and cyberbullying: A systematic review of meta-analyses. *Aggression and Violent Behavior, 45*, 4–19.

Further reading

Olweus, D. Olweus Bullying Prevention Program. *Blueprints for healthy youth development*. <https://www.blueprintsprograms.org/factsheet/olweus-bullying-prevention-program>.

Clemson University, Institute on Family and Neighborhood Life. Olweus Bullying Prevention Program, 2019. <http://olweus.sites.clemson.edu/>.

Klomek, A. B., Marrocco, F., Kleinman, M., Schonfeld, I. S., & Gould, M. S. (2010). Peer victimization, depression, and suicidality in adolescents. *Suicide and Life Threatening Behavior*. Available from https://doi.org/http://doi.org.10.1521/suli.2008.38.2.166.

Maiano, C., Aime, A., Salvas, M. C., Morin, A. J. S., & Normand, C. L. (2016). Prevalence and correlates of bullying perpetration and victimization among school-aged youth with intellectual disabilities: A systematic review. *Research in Developmental Disabilities, 49-50*, 181–195.

Olweus, D. (1993). *Bullying at school: What we know and what we can do*. Malden, MA: Blackwell Publishing.

Rigby, K. (2005). Why do some children bully at school? The contributions of negative attitudes towards victims and the perceived expectations of friends, parents and teachers. *School Psychology International*, *26*(2), 147–161.

Sterzing, P., Shattuck, P., Narendorf, S., Wagner, M., & Cooper, B. (2012). Bullying involvement and autism spectrum disorders: Prevalence and correlates of bullying involvement among adolescents with an autism spectrum disorder. *Archives of Adolescent and Pediatric Medicine*. Available from https://doi.org/10.1001/archpediatrics.2012.790.

Twyman, K. A., Saylor, C. F., Saia, D., Macias, M. M., Taylor, L. A., & Spratt, E. (2010). Bullying and ostracism experiences in children with special health care needs. *Journal of Developmental Behavioral Pediatrics*, *31*, 1–8.

CHAPTER

8

Problematic use of screen media and mobile devices

Sarah E. Domoff[1], *Aubrey L. Borgen*[1] *and Chelsea Robinson*[2]

[1]Department of Psychology, Central Michigan University, Mount Pleasant, MI, United States, [2]Department of Health Sciences, Central Michigan University, Mount Pleasant, MI, United States

Screen media and mobile device use during childhood and adolescence: rates of mobile device ownership and amount of screen time

Screen media [e.g., television (TV), video games, and computers/laptops] and mobile devices (e.g., smartphones and tablets) play an important role in everyday life, and they are used for a substantial amount of each day by individuals of all ages. Research suggests that 95% of the Americans now own a cellphone (phone that has a capacity to make calls and texts), with 77% owning a smartphone (i.e., phone that has the capacity to access the Internet; Pew Research Center, 2018). Recently, there has been a sharp increase in smartphone ownership among young adults, with 92% of young adults 18–29 years old now owning a smartphone (Pew Research Center, 2018). Ownership of other electronic devices has also substantially increased; about half of the Americans own tablets and the majority own laptops (Pew Research Center, 2018). Research conducted with the parents of teenagers and pre-teenagers found that parents, *themselves*, spend more than 9 hours each day with screen media (Lauricella et al., 2016).

Given the ubiquity of screens in today's society, there is concern about how the use of mobile devices and other screen media affects

Clinician's Toolkit for Children's Behavioral Health
DOI: https://doi.org/10.1016/B978-0-12-816024-4.00008-5

children and adolescents. Approximately 98% of children 8 years old or younger live in a household with a TV, with the same percentage living in households where a mobile device is present (Rideout, 2017). Forty-two percent of children in this age range now own their own tablet device (Rideout, 2017). Children 8 years old or younger spend an average of about 2 hours of screen media use per day (Rideout, 2017), youth ages 8–12 years average about 6 hours, and adolescents 12–18 years average about 9 hours of entertainment media use (not for school purposes) per day (Rideout, 2015).

For young children, the most common format of media consumption is TV (Rideout, 2017). The second most commonly used media platform for children up to age 8 years is mobile device. In 2015 this trend was similar for tweens (i.e., 8–12 year old children), in which the majority of their screen time was primarily TV or tablet use (Rideout, 2015). Media use is somewhat different for teenagers, with smartphones and computers being their most used media platforms. Among children ages 8 years and older, the primary use of these devices is watching TV, DVDs, or other videos. Both teens and tweens use their screen devices as a format for listening to music, along with playing video-, computer-, or mobile games at high rates. While not their most common use of screens, teenagers use social media at higher rates than tweens. In 2015 the most commonly used social media site by teenagers was Facebook (Pew Research Center, 2015). About half of the teenagers reported that they used Instagram, and about 40% reported use of Snapchat. The majority of teenagers (71%) reported that they use more than one social media site.

Given the growth in mobile device ownership and amount of screen time children have each day, it is critical that clinicians assess children's media consumption and mobile device and application (app) use. Popular social media apps of youth change frequently, and the sources of preferred media content (i.e., via smartphone vs tablet vs TV) also change (and often differs based on child and family demographics). Thus clinicians working with children and adolescents will need to regularly ask children about the varieties of screen media they use/consume and their preferred content and apps.

Simply asking about how much a child uses screen media (e.g., how many hours of screen time does your child have?) provides limited useful information to the clinician. Also vital to development and behavioral health outcomes is *what* the child is exposed to (i.e., the content), *when* the child consumes screen media or uses his/her mobile device (i.e., the context), and *how* the child's screen media use is impacting his or her life (i.e., problematic use). The next section illustrates why careful assessment and intervention regarding media use should be a routine part of clinical treatment. The next section also describes how to distinguish between problematic versus normative media use. Handout 1 is a guide for screen media assessment with parents, older children, and adolescents.

Developmental, health, and mental health outcomes related to screen time and problematic media use: content and context matters

Content of screen media impacts a child's development and behavioral health

Advertisements

A 2016 estimate indicates that children ages 2–17 years old were exposed to between 40,000 and 45,000 TV food advertisements during the year (Frazier & Harris, 2017). Because advertisements have only recently begun to reach children through new media platforms (i.e., websites, smart phones, applications, etc.), researchers struggle to monitor the advertisements viewed by children today. Although it was previously relatively easy to measure children's television advertisement exposure via observational studies, evaluating advertisement content online proves to be difficult due to how quickly websites change their content. The research that does exist to date has shown that advertisements may encourage unhealthy lifestyles and high-risk behavior among youth (Lapierre, Fleming-Milici, Rozendaal, McAlister, & Castonguay, 2017).

According to a study by Harris (2014), food marketing increases children's food consumption, both immediately and in the future (Lapierre et al., 2017). Thus, reducing exposure to TV advertisements is increasingly considered an important focus of childhood obesity prevention initiatives. In addition, children's preferences for certain food brands are impacted by advertisements in video games, as well as product placements (Lapierre et al., 2017). As most food advertisements tend to be for high-calorie and processed foods, and few commercials tend to focus on healthy foods such as fruits and vegetables, food advertisements can lead to unhealthy preferences among children (Harris, 2014).

Alcohol and tobacco advertisements also have been linked to maladaptive childhood outcomes. Exposure to alcohol advertising increases the likelihood that adolescents will start drinking and increase the amount that adolescents who already consume drink (Anderson, de Bruijn, Angus, Gordon, & Hastings, 2009). As early onset of alcohol drinking increases one's risk of becoming alcohol dependent later in life, these outcomes are particularly concerning (Hingson, Heeren, & Winter, 2006). Recent research also suggests that alcohol brands have a strong presence on Facebook, Twitter, and YouTube, increasing children's exposure to alcohol advertisement further (Chassiakos, Radesky, Christakis, Moreno, & Cross, 2016). Research suggests that e-cigarette use, and subsequent conventional cigarette use, may also increase as a result of increased TV advertisements (Duke et al., 2014; Dutra & Glantz, 2014).

The overwhelming exposure to all marketing advertisements in general may cause additional harm to children. Advertisements and other media depicting idealized bodies of women are associated with negative body image among female viewers (Grabe, Ward, & Hyde, 2008). Consistent research has also found significant relationships between advertisement exposure, materialism and parent–child conflict (Buijzen & Valkenburg, 2003). Newer media advertisements actively engage children, as opposed to passive engagement involved in watching TV, through "advergames" (games that advertise products and are marketing tools). Children may not recognize that they are being marketed to in these newer online formats, potentially increasing the negative outcomes of advertisements on children. In addition, because social media allow targeted advertisements that reflect content that the user has posted, it will be critical to understand how targeted advertisements may influence youth (Lapierre et al., 2017).

Social media and websites

Similar to how advertisements for high-risk behaviors negatively influence children and adolescents, evidence suggests that high-risk behavior is frequently portrayed on social media by youth themselves. Several studies have shown that adolescents post about alcohol use, alcohol overuse, illicit drug use, high-risk sexual behavior, self-injury, and disordered eating. According to a recent review on the subject, peer viewers of this content are more likely to think of the behavior as normal or even desirable, thus increasing the likelihood of additional high-risk behaviors (Chassiakos et al., 2016).

A study by Livingstone, Kirwil, Ponte, and Staksrud (2014) showed that children are concerned about many types of content they view on the Internet. The study evaluated about 10,000 child reports (ages 9–16 years) of risks that concerned them on the Internet via an open-ended survey question. Of the children who mentioned risks, 22% mentioned pornography, 18% mentioned cyberbullying, and 18% mentioned violent content (Livingstone et al., 2014). These results demonstrate how far reaching this potentially harmful content is, thus confirming the need for clinicians working with children and adolescents to ask about concerning content that youth are exposed to in both traditional (commercial TV) and new formats (e.g., via social media, gaming apps, and other Internet-based entertainment sources).

Video games

Playing video game (gaming) influences youths' social outcomes, and the impact of gaming depends on the *content* of these games. A meta-analysis conducted in 2014 concluded that playing violent video games relates to increased aggressive behavior and decreased prosocial outcomes, whereas playing prosocial video games has the opposite effects (Greitemeyer & Mügge, 2014). For both types of games, small-to-medium effect sizes for social outcomes were found in experimental, longitudinal, and correlational studies. These effects appear to be similar across cultures and across different modalities of aggression (Anderson et al., 2010). Across different types of studies, exposure to violence in video games was found to be positively associated not just with aggressive behavior, but also lack of empathy and desensitization.

Because the content of the majority of top-selling video games contains violence, there is great concern regarding which types of games should be played by children (Dill, Gentile, Richter, & Dill, 2005). Longitudinal research examining the links between playing competitive video games and aggression validates this concern. For example, one study surveyed young adults and adolescents over 4 years about their video game habits and aggression. The results indicated that playing competitive video games predicted higher levels of aggressive behavior over time, with aggressive affect as mechanistic link (Adachi & Willoughby, 2016). A recent meta-analysis confirmed this finding: studies with a duration of more than 1 year had the largest effect size, in comparison to those that were conducted within 1 year or less (Prescott, Sargent, & Hull, 2018). This indicates that long-term effects of prolonged video game use may be more significant than short-term use.

Additional research demonstrates how playing violent video game elicits physiological indicators of the fight-or-flight response in children as well. Gentile, Bender, and Anderson (2017) randomly assigned children to play violent or nonviolent video games and measured the associated cortisol levels and cardiovascular changes, both of which are characteristics of the fight-or-flight response. The results indicated that children who played violent video games had increased cortisol levels for boys and girls and increased cardiovascular activity for boys only when compared to children who played equally exciting nonviolent games. Playing violent video games also increased aggressive thoughts. These findings suggest that playing violent video games may activate the sympathetic nervous system and fight-or-flight response, leading to an increase in the cortisol stress hormone (Gentile et al., 2017). Taken together, understanding the content of video games that are preferred by children seeking services in our clinics is crucial to deciphering whether and how screen time may be impacting a child's physical health, mental health, and social functioning.

Screen media use in different contexts

In addition to assessing the content of screen media a child consumes, similarly important is understanding the contexts in which a child uses mobile devices and other screen media. This section details how the different contexts of screen media use can impact health and development.

Displaced interactions and activities

Viewing screen media may displace other activities integral to a child's development. For example, one possible mechanism by which viewing TV influences children is through the displacement of interactive playtime with caregivers (Radesky, Schumacher, & Zuckerman, 2015). Even background TV during infant and toddler play has been shown to decrease parent–child interactions (Courage, 2017). Although parents may feel increasingly comfortable with allowing children to use apps marketed as "educational," research shows that young children need to interact with their natural environments to learn important skills such as empathy, self-regulation, social skills, and problem-solving skills (Radesky et al., 2015).

In addition, children under the age of two have minimal abilities to relate video content to the real world, and adult interaction may be necessary to help children apply lessons learned. Interactive media use by children may also displace activities such as climbing and building that help build the sensorimotor and visual motor skills used in science and math (Radesky et al., 2015). These findings indicate that clinicians should stress the importance of screen-free play during childhood.

Academic performance

Media multitasking, which can either occur when two types of media are being used simultaneously or when a type of screen media is being used while doing another task (i.e., completing homework and eating dinner), can pose many difficulties to children's everyday lives (Wallis, 2010). One study investigated three components of children's executive function (i.e., working memory, shifting, and inhibition) in relationship to media multitasking (Baumgartner, Weeda, van der Heijden, & Huizinga, 2014). These researchers studied 523 early adolescents via self-report and standardized performance-based tasks and concluded that adolescents who frequently media multitask reported more problems in all three domains of executive functioning. These adolescents also reported more behavioral problems, including problems with task switching, focus, and inappropriate behavior inhibition, thus potentially leading to school and social problems as well.

Additional research demonstrates how technological distractions directly influence students' studying habits. For example, Rosen, Carrier, and Cheever (2013) observed 263 middle school, high school, and university students, while they were studying for 15 minutes in their homes. Observers noted the technology present in the room and coded minute-by-minute on-task behavior and off-task technology use. They found that students studied for an average of 6 minutes before being distracted, most often by technology (i.e., social media and texting).

In addition, students who preferred task-switching behaviors tended to have more technology devices available and spent more time off-task than others. The students who checked Facebook were also more likely to have lower GPAs than those who did not (Rosen et al., 2013). Therefore the context of using screen media, especially during school work, may negatively influence children's and adolescents' academic performance.

Sleep health

The use of technology during different times of the day, especially at bedtime, can have negative outcomes on children's and adolescents' sleep quality and quantity. With about 75% of school-aged children not getting the recommended amount of sleep, it is important to understand technology's influence on youths' sleep patterns (National Sleep Foundation, 2006). Lack of sleep and poor sleep quality can interfere with various aspects of daily life and relate to poor school performance, obesity risk, and various psychological problems (LeBourgeois et al., 2017). Because 60% of adolescents report using a device within the hour before bedtime, concerns have been raised about the potentially negative effects of screen media exposure before bedtime (Hysing et al., 2015). In keeping, research suggests that nighttime technology use decreases adolescents' sleep quality and sleep quantity, resulting in increased daytime sleepiness (LeBourgeois et al., 2017).

There are three mechanisms often cited for how screen time influences children's sleep: time displacement, psychological stimulation, and light (LeBourgeois et al., 2017).

In the vast majority (over 90%) of studies examining associations between screen time and sleep, it was found that increased screen time was associated with delayed bedtime and shorter sleep duration. These results show that the use of technology at night may directly displace time that the child should be asleep (Hale & Guan, 2015). Another study showed that even the presence of technology that was left on overnight in children's bedrooms significantly predicted insufficient sleep duration (Buxton et al., 2015). Similarly, another study that assessed the relationship between adolescent media use and sleep efficiency found that media use after bed, awakenings by phone notifications at night, and sleep offset were all associated with sleep efficiency (Fobian, Avis, & Schwebel, 2016). The effects of nighttime media use may be exacerbated in children because they are not able to compensate for lost sleep by sleeping later (Basner, Spaeth, & Dinges, 2014). Cumulatively, these studies demonstrate the need for an integrated approach to minimize youths' screen use at bedtime and during sleep hours.

Evening screen media use may further inhibit child and adolescent sleep quality due to its emotional stimulation. A recent study of 467 Scottish adolescents assessed the specific effects of social media on sleep quality. The researchers concluded that nighttime social media use and reported emotional investment in the content were both associated with poor sleep. These results suggest that adolescents who feel more emotionally connected to their social media may have a more difficult time disconnecting at night, because they may fear missing out on new content (Woods & Scott, 2016).

The light emitted by screen media devices further contributes to children's and adolescents' difficulty falling asleep. A study on young adults found that reading on a screen device before bedtime reduced rapid eye movement sleep and delayed sleep onset (Chang, Aeschbach, Duffy, & Czeisler, 2015). Exposure to light-emitting screen devices also has been shown to result in suppressed melatonin release, which is normally released in the evening to promote sleep (LeBourgeois et al., 2017). Blue light, the short-wavelength light that is commonly emitted from screen devices, has been associated with increasing alertness, altering sleep, and shifting the circadian clock. In addition, these effects seem to affect children more drastically than adults due to children's increased sensitivity to the light (LeBourgeois et al., 2017). Because of the effects of screen media on children, parents must be educated about the negative outcomes of child evening screen media usage, and they should be asked to reduce the presence of screens in the bedroom.

Problematic use of screen media

In addition to the content of media and the contexts in which they use screen media, *how* children use screen media is related to their behavioral health. For example, a child's screen media use becomes problematic when he or she excessively uses screen media and *the use interferes with the child's functioning*. Most research on problematic media use has focused on video game addiction, also known as pathological gaming and Internet gaming disorder (IGD). The American Psychiatric Association's *Diagnostic and Statistical Manual of Mental Disorders*, 5th edition (DSM-5; American Psychiatric Association, 2013) has listed IGD as a potential mental health diagnosis in Section III (Conditions for Further Study). There are nine symptoms of IGD, including (1) withdrawal when unable to game, (2) tolerance (needing to game longer or spend increasing amounts of time on gaming), (3) preoccupation with games, (4) unsuccessful attempts to control game play, (5) loss of interest in activities that the child previously found enjoyable, (6) continued use despite psychosocial consequences of use, (7) deceiving others about amount of gaming, (8) gaming to relieve negative effect, and (9) losing a significant relationship or educational/career opportunities due to gaming (American Psychiatric Association, 2013). Although not an official diagnosis in the DSM-5, the International Classification of Diseases (11th edition) has included gaming disorder in its most recent edition (World Health Organization, 2018). Research is ongoing to further understand IGD (e.g., etiology, prevalence, and comorbid conditions) to inform whether this condition will be an official diagnosis in the next edition of the DSM.

Recently, a parent report measure of problematic media use in children has been developed, utilizing the nine symptoms of IGD as indicators of problematic use of gaming and other types of screen media (Domoff et al., 2017). This measure, the Problematic Media Use Measure (PMUM), consists of 27 items (3 items per symptom) in its full-scale version, and nine items in its shortened screener (PMUM-short form). Example items include "My child becomes frustrated when he or she cannot use screen media," "My child's screen media use causes problems for the family," and "My child uses screen media to feel better." The PMUM has excellent psychometric properties and was acceptable for use with both boys and girls as a measure of screen media "addiction." Study authors found that a child's problematic (addictive) use of screen media was a better predictor of a variety of psychosocial outcomes, such as hyperactivity and inattention, peer relationship problems, and emotional symptoms than a child's overall screen time (Domoff et al., 2017). In other words, *how* children use screen media and whether it disrupts their functioning matter more than simply the amount of screen time. Study authors are currently validating a self-report version of the PMUM for administration to older children and adolescents, as well as identifying clinical cutoff scores to aid in diagnostic assessments by behavioral health and pediatric care providers.

Examples of specific health and mental health conditions impacted by screen media use

In addition to considering the potential impact of screen media on children in the general population, it is important for clinicians working with clinically referred youths to be aware of how screen media use may contribute to, exacerbate, or coincide with presenting concerns. Conditions that have been linked with aspects of screen media use are outlined next. It should be noted that although there are associations between screen media use and a variety of symptoms, it cannot be assumed that one causes the other (i.e., correlation does not equal causation). When there is strong evidence to suggest a potential causal mechanism, it is made explicit in the following sections.

Childhood obesity

Both the content and context of childhood screen media use have been associated with childhood obesity risk. According to data from Wen, Baur, Rissel, Xu, and Simpson (2014), at a young age, children who watch more hours of TV (on average) are likely to have a higher body mass index (BMI). In a related study of 5- to 10-year-old children, researchers concluded that the odds of being overweight were 4.6 times greater for children that were exposed to greater than 5 hours of TV on average per day, compared to those who were exposed to less than 2 hours each day (Gortmaker et al., 1996). In fact, there seems to be a causal relationship between screen media exposure and obesity risk, as has been shown through intervention studies, reduction of child screen time associates with slowed BMI gains (Robinson et al., 2017).

Mealtime television viewing

Although many mechanisms of effect have been hypothesized, a growing body of evidence suggests that screen media's effect on dietary intake may be the mechanism linking screen media exposure to childhood obesity risk. According to a study by Matheson et al. (2004) up to one-third of daily caloric intake and half of children's meals are consumed in the presence of a screen. The presence of such media may prompt the child to eat, extend the total eating duration, or distract from the sense of satiety (Robinson & Matheson, 2015). In addition, children tend to eat high-energy foods and beverages and less fruits and vegetables when they are in front of a TV (Coon, Goldberg, Rogers, & Tucker, 2001). This tendency is particularly unhealthy given that screen media exposure can lead to increased energy consumption in the absence of hunger (Chaput et al., 2011).

Evidence also suggests that the growing prevalence of screen media during mealtime may negatively influence child–caregiver interactions. A study by Radesky et al. (2014) used nonparticipant observational methods to describe mobile device use by caregivers at a fast food restaurant. Of the 55 caregivers observed, 40 used smartphones at some point during the meal. Researchers noted that device absorption, or the extent to which the caregiver engages with the device instead of the child, was a common theme; a majority of the caregivers observed in this study were rated as highly absorbed with their devices. Additional research supports that screen media exposure during mealtime prompts children to request advertised foods more from their parents (Coon et al., 2001). Although more research needs to be done to fully understand the influence of screen media on the mealtime environment, these findings suggest that screen media use may displace conversations between children and caregivers and interfere with children's ability to recognize feelings of fullness, thus contributing to childhood obesity risk.

Food advertisements

Food advertisements are another possible mechanism linking screen media exposure to poor dietary quality. As previously reported, children are exposed to 40,000–45,000 TV food advertisements each year (Frazier & Harris, 2017). A recent literature review on the subject suggested that food advertisements do influence children's preferences and intake, which can be particularly damaging given that advertisements tend to be for calorie-dense foods. Additional experimental studies have concluded that commercials during animated content increase children's automatic eating of foods not being advertised, and fast food branding can change children's actual perception of taste (Robinson et al., 2017).

Sleep

As screen time associates with poor sleep, inadequate sleep is also cited as a likely mechanism linking screen time to obesity and poor dietary quality. According to Miller, Lumeng, and LeBourgeois (2015), sleep deprivation can cause specific appetite-regulating hormones to increase feelings of hunger and decrease satiety. In addition, sleep deprivation may influence children's food choices, making them less likely to choose nutritionally dense foods. The shortened total sleep time may itself be an obesity risk factor because it may lead the child to eat outside of the normal mealtimes (Miller et al., 2015).

Displaced physical activity

Although displaced physical activity is often thought of as a mechanism linking screen time to childhood obesity, a recent literature review on the subject has found conflicting data. However, intervention studies that reduced screen time only resulted in minor, if any, increases in physical activity (Robinson et al., 2017). Thus displaced physical activity may not be a strong mechanistic link between screen time and obesity (Robinson et al., 2017). However, more research is needed to address this question.

Major depressive disorder

In 2017 about 11% of youth aged 12–17 reported that they had experienced at least one major depressive episode (Mental Health America, 2018). Research has begun to investigate the relations between screen time and media use with depression in youth, and many studies suggest that there is a connection. One study investigating the media use of Canadian youth suggested that substantial amounts of screen time may be a risk factor for developing depression symptoms (Maras et al., 2015). After controlling for multiple covariates, the results indicated that increased time with screen-based activities was related to severity of depression. This study also investigated the relations between different types of media use, finding that playing video games and using a computer were significantly associated with depressive symptoms. Other studies suggested similar findings in the United States (e.g., Cao et al, 2011; Kremer et al., 2014).

A meta-analysis was recently conducted to integrate the various findings about media use and depression among youths (Liu, Wu, & Yao, 2016). The results from 16 studies suggested that children and young adolescents with more daily screen time had a 12.3% increase in risk for depression. Computer use was associated with a 27.6% increase in risk of depression compared to TV watching or video gaming. This study also conducted dose-response analysis, finding that use of screens in moderation may actually be associated with lower depression. It is important to note that it is not yet clear whether youths who are more depressed seek more screen time or whether too much screen time is associated with an increased risk of depression. Regardless of which came first, clinicians working with youths who are at risk for depression should consider the content of media exposure (e.g., is the social media the child is consuming exacerbating or worsening depressive symptoms?), as well as the context of their media consumption (e.g., are they using mobile devices or watching TV after bedtime and is their sleep impacted by such use?).

Attention-deficit hyperactivity disorder

Another common psychological diagnosis among children and adolescents is attention-deficit hyperactivity disorder (ADHD). One study investigated the impact of video games and TV on a young person's capacity for sustained attention (Swing, Gentile, Anderson, & Walsh, 2010). The study included child and parent reports of video game time and TV time, along with teacher ratings of attention problems. They found that for children in middle childhood (third to fifth grade students), the association between attention problems and video games was more consistent than that between TV and attention. In addition, the study helped further the evidence suggesting that increased screen time may exacerbate ADHD symptoms. When earlier attention problems and gender were controlled for, increased exposure to screen media (TV and video games) was associated with later attention problems.

A recent meta-analysis was conducted to integrate analyses of 45 studies examining ADHD symptoms and media use among youths (Nikkelen, Valkenburg, Huizinga, & Bushman, 2014). The focus of the analysis was on the three major behaviors identified as criteria in the DSM-5: attention problems, hyperactivity, impulsivity, as well as an ADHD composite of the three criteria. The meta-analysis first investigated attention problems specifically, finding a moderate correlation with combined measures of media use. For impulsivity the analysis revealed a small, but significant, correlation with media use. Composite ADHD symptoms were positively correlated with various measures of media use. Unlike the previous study, the meta-analysis did not find any difference in the strength of the correlation between attention problems and playing video game or watching TV. In addition, the results suggest that boys may be more susceptible to the impact of screen time on ADHD-related behaviors, compared to girls.

Eating disorders

Eating disorders often develop during adolescence, yet the age of diagnosis has been decreasing. Lifetime prevalence of anorexia nervosa is between 0.5% and 2%, with diagnosis typically occurring between the ages of 13 and 18 years (Campbell & Peebles, 2014). Anorexia nervosa is also one of the most dangerous disorders, with a mortality rate of 5%–6% (Franko et al., 2013). Prevalence for bulimia nervosa is somewhat higher, possibly up to 3% of the population. Although many past studies have investigated the impact of the "skinny ideal" in advertising and TV on disordered eating and body image, many research studies are now looking into the effect of social media use on body image and disordered eating.

One study specifically examined the association between Facebook use and body image disturbance among adolescent females (Meier & Gray, 2014). The results suggested that it was not the amount of time spent using Facebook or the Internet that was impactful, but the amount of time used for photo activity. That is, time spent adding new photos or editing photos on the social networking site was associated with greater thin ideal internalization, self-objectification, weight dissatisfaction, and drive for thinness (Meier & Gray, 2014). The authors suggest that there may be a bidirectional relationship between the photo interaction and body image. That is, adolescents with an elevated thin ideal internalization and body dissatisfaction are driven to interact more heavily with the photo features while engaging in heavily appearance-focused activities reinforces those ideals. While there was not an association between overall Facebook use and self-objectification or appearance comparison, there was a significant difference when comparing groups of social networking users and nonusers. When examining that group relationship, girls who use Facebook were more likely to be dissatisfied with their bodies, compared to girls who did not use Facebook.

Taken together, it is important for clinicians to be aware of symptom- or disorder-specific correlates of screen media use. That is, investigating how screen media use, including social media use, may coincide with presenting concerns is an important part of both assessment and treatment planning phases in today's digital age.

Assessment of screen media use

Heretofore, we have outlined the immense role that screen media play in today's society, as well as key components of screen media use that may impact youths receiving clinical services. Although not exhaustive, the review of how screen media use correlates with common presenting concerns further illustrates the importance of incorporating assessment of screen media use into one's practice. Next, we provide short assessment protocols that clinicians can use to integrate screening for media use and overuse in their intake appointments.

Clinicians should emphasize assessing (1) content of media, (2) settings and time of day that child views/consumes screen media (i.e., context), and (3) problematic media use. Asking parents only to report on the number of hours of screen media use per day is unreliable and lacking in information that could help tailor treatment. Clinicians should not rely solely on parental estimates of a child's daily screen time. To assist with this, we provide two assessment guides at the end of this chapter: (1) one that clinicians could follow with parents (of children up to age 11 years) and (2) another focused on interviewing older children and adolescents. The second guide may be particularly useful if parents are not aware of the child's favorite apps or the extent of their media and mobile phone use. We recommend using these guides at intake assessments.

Addressing problematic screen media use

Research on how to best intervene on problematic media use is growing, but there are limited treatment studies. One intervention that specifically seeks to address problematic use of social media is currently being piloted. The Development of Healthy Social Media Practices (DHSMP) intervention was originally developed for inpatient adolescents and at-risk youth receiving mental health treatment. This group intervention is led by a clinician and comprises six 1-hour sessions (a shorter two-session version is available for adolescents receiving psychiatric inpatient treatment). It is intended to teach participants about healthy media practices with the goal of preventing negative outcomes associated with screen media. During the intervention, participants learn to distinguish between positive and negative content while recognizing how diverse types of content may impact them. In addition, the intervention encourages participants to become aware of their own social media habits by completing self-monitoring and reflection activities. Importantly, adolescents learn coping skills to adjust to conflict on social media. Adolescents are guided through using an online problem-solving model to resolve problematic social media practices. For intervention groups conducted in outpatient settings, there are coinciding sessions for parents, which are designed to help them model healthy media use and scaffold their adolescents' DHSMP and responsible technology use.

Media use is an important part of the daily lives of adolescents and children, and it is crucial for clinicians and other professionals to recognize this and understand the impact of media and mobile device use on youth development. A part of this involves acknowledging that different types of media can have positive or negative influences on youth. Clinicians can assess the content that youths are exposed to and the times and locations in which they are viewing screen media and using mobile devices. Utilizing measures such as the PMUM (Domoff et al., 2017) to screen for problematic use is also recommended. It is important for clinicians to assess these three domains in order to identify whether media use is impacting a child's physical or mental health, and how treatment can target the specific type of problematic use.

Handout 1. Screen media assessment guide: interview questions for parents

Assess content the child is exposed to

- Sample questions: What does your child watch or play? What are your child's favorite TV shows? What websites or apps does your child visit/use?

____

____

- Determine if the content is not developmentally appropriate (contains aggressive and/or sexual content). Also, ensure that the content does not elicit strong negative reactions in the child, such as fear.
- Intervene: help the parent set restrictions on content and choose content that is appropriate. Recommend using www.commonsensemedia.org to peruse reviews of a variety of screen media (e.g., apps, websites, TV shows). Recommend preventing or replacing use of violent media.
- Intervene: encourage online safety procedures, such as blocking content, restricting access, and turning off WiFi after bed.

Assess when the child uses screen media:

- Sample questions: Does your child have access to media or screens after bedtime? Are media/devices viewed/used during family interactions? Does your child watch use mobile device during school or while doing homework?

____

____

- Determine if there are times when no screen media are used. Determine if there are "screen-free" zones in the home (e.g., during meals or in the bedroom).
- Intervene: recommend limit setting at bedtime (no use of screen media approximately 1 hour before bedtime). Also recommend setting aside times where no screens are present (particularly during family activities).
- Intervene: encourage parental modeling of healthy device use during social interactions

Screen for problematic media use

- Use PMUM-short form to screen for excessive media use that interferes with child functioning.
- Ask if the child communicates with others online or via mobile device (e.g., texting, social media). Ask if the child has experienced conflict online or through messaging friends.
- Intervene: if child has excessive media use, work with parents to reduce child's screen time and increase nonscreen media activities (that the child finds enjoyable).
- Intervene: enhance coping skills around negative social interactions online; suggest receiving offline support from friends.

Handout 2. Screen media assessment guide: interview questions for older children and adolescents

Assess content the youth is exposed to

- Sample questions: What are your favorite TV shows? What websites or apps do you visit/use most? What types of social media do you use? Do you play video games (which ones)?

____

____

- Determine if the content is not developmentally appropriate (contains aggressive and/or sexual content). Also, ensure that the content is not "triggering" to the client or potentially exacerbating symptoms underlying reason for referral.
- Intervene (for children and young adolescents): help the parent set restrictions on content and choose content that is appropriate. Recommend using www.commonsensemedia.org to peruse reviews of a variety of screen media (e.g., apps, websites, and TV shows).
- Intervene (for children and young adolescents): encourage online safety procedures, such as blocking content, restricting access, and turning off WiFi after bed.
- Intervene (for adolescents): provide psychoeducation on how social media impacts users (see the "Addressing problematic screen media use" section for additional information).

Assess when the youth uses screen media:

- Sample questions: Do you bring your phone with you to bed? Do you have a TV in your bedroom? Do notifications wake you up at night? How often do you check your phone during school or while doing homework?

____

____

- Determine if there are times when no screen media are used. Determine if there are "screen-free" zones in the home (e.g., during meals or in the bedroom).
- Intervene: recommend limit setting at bedtime (no use of screen media approximately 1 hour before bedtime). Also recommend setting aside times where no screens are present (particularly during family activities).
- Intervene: encourage parental modeling of healthy device use during social interactions.

- Intervene (for adolescents): Use psychoeducation and motivational interviewing to help adolescent identify media use/mobile device practices that they may want to change.

Screen for problematic media use:

- Use PMUM-Short Form to screen for excessive media use that interferes with child functioning.
- Ask if the child communicates with others online or via mobile device (e.g., texting, social media). Ask if the child has experienced conflict online or through messaging friends. Sample questions: Have there been times when you sent a text or posted something online that you regret? Have you been hurt by something posted online?

____

____

- Intervene: if child has problematic or excessive media use, work with parents to reduce child's screen time and increase nonscreen media activities (that the child finds enjoyable).
- Intervene: enhance coping skills around negative social interactions online (see the "Addressing problematic screen media use" section for additional information). Suggest receiving offline support from friends.

Tools for controlling media use

Need to put technology restrictions on your adolescent's device? Many companies provide information on their websites about built-in parental control options for their devices (e.g., support.apple.com; https://m.windowscentral.com/how-set-kid-friendly-windows-10-pc-child-account). Make sure to keep up to date on these free options on specific devices, as these types of parental controls are still being developed and continue to evolve. For up-to-date resources on tips for using controls or apps to manage media use, please reference www.commonsensemedia.org. The list next contains the descriptions of applications (inclusion on this list does not indicate endorsement of these products). Please note that apps and features change frequently, developed by Rachel Gerrie.

- Circle: Comprehensive monitoring, tracking, and filtering of content on devices that range from general to very specific such as enabling/disabling certain websites/apps after a certain amount of time.
- Moment and moment family: Tracks usage and allows you to set time limits as well as turnoff devices with "Family Dinner Time" mode.
- NetSanity: Allows you to block apps/sites, add content filters and time restrictions and provides location of the device.
- OurPact: Blocks content/apps on your adolescent's phone, uses geolocation to locate, and enables you to set scheduled device time.
- Pocketpoints: Earn points by locking phone while on school grounds. Points can be exchanged for deals at participating local businesses.
- unGlue: Sets a schedule for different kinds of media activity (e.g., 30 minutes for social media).

Important points to remember

- Children 8 years old or younger spend an average of about 2 hours of screen media use per day (Rideout, 2017), youth 8–12 years average about 6 hours, and adolescents 12–18 years average about 9 hours of entertainment media use per day (Rideout, 2015).
- Several studies have shown that adolescents post about alcohol use, alcohol overuse, illicit drug use, high-risk sexual behavior, self-injury, and disordered eating. According to a recent review on the subject, peer viewers of this content are more likely to think of the behavior as normal or even desirable, thus increasing the likelihood of additional high-risk behaviors (Chassiakos et al., 2016).
- Playing violent video game relates to increased aggressive behavior and decreased prosocial outcomes (Greitemeyer & Mügge, 2014).

- Although parents may feel increasingly comfortable with allowing children to use apps marketed as "educational," research shows that young children need to interact with their natural environments to learn important skills such as empathy, self-regulation, social skills, and problem-solving skills (Radesky et al., 2015).
- Students studied for an average of 6 minutes before being distracted, most often by technology (i.e., social media, texting; Rosen et al., 2013).
- There are three mechanisms often cited for how screen time influences children's sleep: time displacement, psychological stimulation, and light (LeBourgeois et al., 2017).
- There seems to be a causal relationship between screen media exposure and obesity risk, as has been shown through intervention studies, reduction of child screen time associates with slowed BMI gains (Robinson et al., 2017).

References

Adachi, P. J., & Willoughby, T. (2016). The longitudinal association between competitive video game play and aggression among adolescents and young adults. *Child Development, 87*, 1877–1892. Available from https://doi.org/10.1111/cdev.12556.

American Psychiatric Association. (2013). *Diagnostic and statistical manual of mental disorders* (5th ed.). Arlington, VA: American Psychiatric Publishing.

Anderson, C. A., Shibuya, A., Ihori, N., Swing, E. L., Bushman, B. J., Sakamoto, A., ... Saleem, M. (2010). Violent video game effects on aggression, empathy, and prosocial behavior in Eastern and Western countries: A meta-analytic review. *Psychological Bulletin, 136*, 151–173. Available from https://doi.org/10.1037/a0018251.

Anderson, P., de Bruijn, A., Angus, K., Gordon, R., & Hastings, G. (2009). Impact of alcohol advertising and media exposure on adolescent alcohol use: A systematic review of longitudinal studies. *Alcohol and Alcoholism, 44*, 229–243. Available from https://doi.org/10.1093/alcalc/agn115.

Basner, M., Spaeth, A. M., & Dinges, D. F. (2014). Sociodemographic characteristics and waking activities and their role in the timing and duration of sleep. *Sleep, 37*, 1889–1906. Available from https://doi.org/10.5665/sleep.4238.

Baumgartner, S. E., Weeda, W. D., van der Heijden, L. L., & Huizinga, M. (2014). The relationship between media multitasking and executive function in early adolescents. *The Journal of Early Adolescence, 34*, 1120–1144. Available from https://doi.org/10.1177/0272431614523133.

Buijzen, M., & Valkenburg, P. M. (2003). The effects of television advertising on materialism, parent–child conflict, and unhappiness: A review of research. *Journal of Applied Developmental Psychology, 24*, 437–456. Available from https://doi.org/10.1016/S0193-3973(03)00072-8.

Buxton, O. M., Chang, A. M., Spilsbury, J. C., Bos, T., Emsellem, H., & Knutson, K. L. (2015). Sleep in the modern family: Protective family routines for child and adolescent sleep. *Sleep Health, 1*, 15–27. Available from https://doi.org/10.1016/j.sleh.2014.12.002.

Campbell, K., & Peebles, R. (2014). Eating disorders in children and adolescents: State of the art review. *Pediatrics, 134*, 582–592. Available from https://doi.org/10.1542/peds.2014-0194.

Cao, H., Qian, Q., Weng, T., Yuan, C., Sun, Y., Wang, H., & Tao, F. (2011). Screen time, physical activity and mental health among urban adolescents in China. *Preventive Medicine*, *53*, 316–320. Available from https://doi.org/10.1016/j.ypmed.2011.09.002.

Chang, A. M., Aeschbach, D., Duffy, J. F., & Czeisler, C. A. (2015). Evening use of light-emitting eReaders negatively affects sleep, circadian timing, and next-morning alertness. *Proceedings of the National Academy of Sciences of the United States of America*, *112*, 1232–1237. Available from https://doi.org/10.1073/pnas.1418490112.

Chaput, J. P., Visby, T., Nyby, S., Klingenberg, L., Gregersen, N. T., Tremblay, A., … Sjödin, A. (2011). Video game playing increases food intake in adolescents: A randomized crossover study. *The American Journal of Clinical Nutrition*, *93*, 1196–1203. Available from https://doi.org/10.3945/ajcn.110.008680.

Chassiakos, Y. R., Radesky, J., Christakis, D., Moreno, M. A., & Cross, C. (2016). Children and adolescents and digital media. *Pediatrics*, *138*, e1–e18. Available from https://doi.org/10.1542/peds.2016-2593.

Coon, K. A., Goldberg, J., Rogers, B. L., & Tucker, K. L. (2001). Relationships between use of television during meals and children's food consumption patterns. *Pediatrics*, *107*, 1–9. Available from https://doi.org/10.1542/peds.107.1.e7.

Courage, M. L. (2017). Screen media and the youngest viewers: Implications for attention and learning. In F. C. Blumberg, & P. J. Brooks (Eds.), *Cognitive development in digital contexts* (pp. 3–28). San Diego, CA: Elsevier Academic Press. Available from https://doi.org/10.1016/C2015-0-06250-5.

Dill, K. E., Gentile, D. A., Richter, W. A., & Dill, J. C. (2005). Violence, sex, race, and age in popular video games: A content analysis. In E. Cole, & J. H. Daniel (Eds.), Psychology of women book series. Featuring females: Feminist analyses of the media (pp. 115–130). Washington, DC: American Psychological Association. Available from http://dx.doi.org/10.1037/11213-008.

Domoff, S. E., Harrison, K., Gearhardt, A. N., Gentile, D. A., Lumeng, J. C., & Miller, A. L. (2017). Development and validation of the problematic media use measure: A parent report measure of screen media "addiction" in children. *Psychology of Popular Media Culture*. Available from https://doi.org/10.1037/ppm0000163, Advance online publication.

Duke, J. C., Lee, Y. O., Kim, A. E., Watson, K. A., Arnold, K. Y., Nonnemaker, J. M., & Porter, L. (2014). Exposure to electronic cigarette television advertisements among youth and young adults. *Pediatrics*, *134*, 1–8. Available from https://doi.org/10.1542/peds.2014-0269.

Dutra, L. M., & Glantz, S. A. (2014). Electronic cigarettes and conventional cigarette use among US adolescents: A cross-sectional study. *Journal of American Medical Association Pediatrics*, *168*, 610–617. Available from https://doi.org/10.1001/jamapediatrics.2013.5488.

Fobian, A. D., Avis, K., & Schwebel, D. C. (2016). The impact of media use on adolescent sleep efficiency. *Journal of Developmental and Behavioral Pediatrics*, *37*, 9–14. Available from https://doi.org/10.1097/DBP.0000000000000239.

Franko, D. L., Keshaviah, A., Eddy, K. T., Krishna, M., Davis, M. C., Keel, P. K., & Herzog, D. B. (2013). A longitudinal investigation of mortality in anorexia nervosa and bulimia nervosa. *American Journal of Psychiatry*, *170*, 917–925. Available from https://doi.org/10.1176/appi.ajp.2013.12070868.

Frazier, W. C., & Harris, J. L. (2017). *Trends in television food advertising to young people: 2016 Update*. Retrieved from <http://uconnruddcenter.org/files/TVAdTrends2017.pdf>.

Gentile, D. A., Bender, P. K., & Anderson, C. A. (2017). Violent video game effects on salivary cortisol, arousal, and aggressive thoughts in children. *Computers in Human Behavior*, *70*, 39–43. Available from https://doi.org/10.1016/j.chb.2016.12.045.

Gortmaker, S. L., Must, A., Sobol, A. M., Peterson, K., Colditz, G. A., & Dietz, W. H. (1996). Television viewing as a cause of increasing obesity among children in the

United States, 1986-1990. *Archives of Pediatrics & Adolescent Medicine, 150,* 356–362. Available from https://doi.org/10.1001/archpedi.1996.02170290022003.

Grabe, S., Ward, L. M., & Hyde, J. S. (2008). The role of the media in body image concerns among women: A meta-analysis of experimental and correlational studies. *Psychological Bulletin, 134,* 460–476. Available from https://doi.org/10.1037/0033-2909.134.3.460.

Greitemeyer, T., & Mügge, D. O. (2014). Video games do affect social outcomes: A meta-analytic review of the effects of violent and prosocial video game play. *Personality and Social Psychology Bulletin, 40,* 578–589. Available from https://doi.org/10.1177/0146167213520459.

Hale, L., & Guan, S. (2015). Screen time and sleep among school-aged children and adolescents: A systematic literature review. *Sleep Medicine Reviews, 21,* 50–58. Available from https://doi.org/10.1016/j.smrv.2014.07.007.

Harris, J. L. (2014). Demonstrating the harmful effects of food advertising on children and adolescents. In A. B. Jordan, & D. Romer (Eds.), *Media and the well-being of children and adolescents* (pp. 44–51). New York: Oxford University Press.

Hingson, R. W., Heeren, T., & Winter, M. R. (2006). Age at drinking onset and alcohol dependence: Age at onset, duration, and severity. *Archives of Pediatrics & Adolescent Medicine, 160,* 739–746. Available from https://doi.org/10.1001/archpedi.160.7.739.

Hysing, M., Pallesen, S., Stormark, K. M., Jakobsen, R., Lundervold, A. J., & Sivertsen, B. (2015). Sleep and use of electronic devices in adolescence: Results from a large population-based study. *British Medical Journal Open, 5,* 1–7. Available from https://doi.org/10.1136/bmjopen-2014-006748.

Kremer, P., Elshaug, C., Leslie, E., Toumbourou, J. W., Patton, G. C., & Williams, J. (2014). Physical activity, leisure-time screen use and depression among children and young adolescents. *Journal of Science and Medicine in Sport, 17,* 183–187. Available from https://doi.org/10.1016/j.jsams.2013.03.012.

Lapierre, M. A., Fleming-Milici, F., Rozendaal, E., McAlister, A. R., & Castonguay, J. (2017). The effect of advertising on children and adolescents. *Pediatrics, 140,* S152–S156. Available from https://doi.org/10.1542/peds.2016-1758V.

Lauricella, A. R., Cingel, D. P., Beaudoin-Ryan, L., Robb, M. B., Saphir, M., & Wartella, E. A. (2016). *The Common Sense census: Plugged-in parents of tweens and teens.* San Francisco, CA: Common Sense Media.

LeBourgeois, M. K., Hale, L., Chang, A. M., Akacem, L. D., Montgomery-Downs, H. E., & Buxton, O. M. (2017). Digital media and sleep in childhood and adolescence. *Pediatrics, 140,* S92–S96. Available from https://doi.org/10.1542/peds.2016-1758J.

Liu, M., Wu, L., & Yao, S. (2016). Dose–response association of screen time-based sedentary behaviour in children and adolescents and depression: A meta-analysis of observational studies. *British Journal of Sports Medicine, 50,* 1252–1258. Available from https://doi.org/10.1136/bjsports-2015-095084.

Livingstone, S., Kirwil, L., Ponte, C., & Staksrud, E. (2014). In their own words: What bothers children online? *European Journal of Communication, 29,* 271–288. Available from https://doi.org/10.1177/0267323114521045.

Maras, D., Flamant, M. F., Murray, M., Buckholz, A., Henderson, K. A., Obeid, N., & Goldfield, G. (2015). Screen time is associated with depression and anxiety in Canadian youth. *Preventive Medicine, 73,* 133–138. Available from https://doi.org/10.1016/j.ypmed.2015.01.029.

Matheson, D. M., Wang, Y., Klesges, L. M., Beech, B. M., Kraemer, H. C., & Robinson, T. N. (2004). African-American girls' dietary intake while watching television. *Obesity Research, 12,* 32S–37S. Available from https://doi.org/10.1038/oby.2004.266.

Meier, E. P., & Gray, J. (2014). Facebook photo activity associated with body image disturbance in adolescent girls. *Cyberpsychology, Behavior and Social Networking, 17*(4), 199–206. Available from https://doi.org/10.1089/cyber.2013.0305.

Mental Health America. (2018). *2017 State of mental health in America - Youth data*. Retrieved from <http://www.mentalhealthamerica.net/issues/2017-state-mental-health-america-youth-data>.

Miller, A. L., Lumeng, J. C., & LeBourgeois, M. K. (2015). Sleep patterns and obesity in childhood. *Current Opinion in Endocrinology, Diabetes, and Obesity, 22*, 41–47. Available from https://doi.org/10.1097/MED.0000000000000125.

National Sleep Foundation. (2006). *Sleep in America poll*. Retrieved from <https://sleepfoundation.org/sites/default/files/2006_summary_of_findings.pdf>.

Nikkelen, S., Valkenburg, P., Huizinga, M., & Bushman, B. (2014). Media use and ADHD-related behaviors in children and adolescents: A meta-analysis. *Developmental Psychology, 50*(9), 2228–2241. Available from https://doi.org/10.1037/a0037318.

Pew Research Center. (2015). *Teens, social media & technology overview 2015*. Retrieved from <http://www.pewinternet.org/2015/04/09/teens-social-media-technology-2015/>.

Pew Research Center. (2018). *Mobile fact sheet*. Retrieved from <http://www.pewinternet.org/fact-sheet/mobile/>.

Prescott, A. T., Sargent, J. D., & Hull, J. G. (2018). Meta-analysis of the relationship between violent video game play and physical aggression over time. *Proceedings of the National Academy of Sciences of the United States of America, 115*, 9882–9888. Available from https://doi.org/10.1073/pnas.1611617114.

Radesky, J. S., Kistin, C. J., Zuckerman, B., Nitzberg, K., Gross, J., Kaplan-Sanoff, M., ... Silverstein, M. (2014). Patterns of mobile device use by caregivers and children during meals in fast food restaurants. *Pediatrics, 133*, e843–e849. Available from https://doi.org/10.1542/peds.2013-3703.

Radesky, J. S., Schumacher, J., & Zuckerman, B. (2015). Mobile and interactive media use by young children: The good, the bad, and the unknown. *Pediatrics, 135*, 1–3. Available from https://doi.org/10.1542/peds.2014-2251.

Rideout, V. (2015). *The Common sense census: Media use by tweens and teens*. San Francisco, CA: Common Sense Media.

Rideout, V. (2017). *The Common sense census: Media use by kids age zero to eight*. San Francisco, CA: Common Sense Media.

Robinson, T. N., & Matheson, D. M. (2015). Environmental strategies for portion control in children. *Appetite, 88*, 33–38. Available from https://doi.org/10.1016/j.appet.2014.12.001.

Robinson, T. N., Banda, J. A., Hale, L., Lu, A. S., Fleming-Milici, F., Calvert, S. L., & Wartella, E. (2017). Screen media exposure and obesity in children and adolescents. *Pediatrics, 140*, S97–S101. Available from https://doi.org/10.1542/peds.2016-1758K.

Rosen, L. D., Carrier, L. M., & Cheever, N. A. (2013). Facebook and texting made me do it: Media-induced task-switching while studying. *Computers in Human Behavior, 29*, 948–958. Available from https://doi.org/10.1016/j.chb.2012.12.001.

Swing, E. L., Gentile, D. A., Anderson, C. A., & Walsh, D. A. (2010). Television and video game exposure and the development of attention problems. *Pediatrics, 126*, 214–221. Available from https://doi.org/10.1542/peds.2009-1508.

Wallis, C. (2010). *The impacts of media multitasking on children's learning and development: Report from a research seminar*. New York: The Joan Ganz Cooney Center at Sesame Workshop.

Wen, L. M., Baur, L. A., Rissel, C., Xu, H., & Simpson, J. M. (2014). Correlates of body mass index and overweight and obesity of children aged 2 years: Findings from the healthy beginnings trial. *Obesity, 22*, 1723–1730. Available from https://doi.org/10.1002/oby.20700.

Woods, H. C., & Scott, H. (2016). #Sleepyteens: Social media use in adolescence is associated with poor sleep quality, depression and low self-esteem. *Journal of Adolescence, 51*, 41–49. Available from https://doi.org/10.1016/j.adolescence.2016.05.008.

World Health Organization. (2018). Gaming disorder. In *International statistical classification of diseases and related health problems* (11th ed.). Retrieved from <http://www.who.int/classifications/icd/en/>.

CHAPTER

9

Physical punishment and child maltreatment

Michele Knox

Department of Psychiatry, University of Toledo College of Medicine and Life Sciences, Toledo, OH, United States

Bella's older sister, Quinn, aged 6, grabbed the TV remote out of her hand and changed the channel. Angry, 4-year-old Bella began to yell at her sister. Then both pushed each other. Their mother, being frustrated with their fighting, grabbed Bella and spanked her repeatedly, while yelling, "Never, ever hit your sister again. We do NOT hit people in this house!"

While the irony of this situation is not lost on most people, this type of situation plays out in households across the nation on a regular basis. In fact, research shows that physical punishment occurs from infancy through the teen years in many families, and children around Bella's age are the people in our nation who are most likely to be hit by another person (Straus & Donnelly, 2001). Ironically, the hitter is typically the person in charge of keeping the child safe and promoting his or her well-being—the child's parent. Often, the act of hitting is done in the name of discipline and also called something such as "spanking" or "whupping."

Physical punishment (also called corporal punishment) is defined as "any punishment in which physical force is used and intended to cause some degree of pain or discomfort, however, light. Most involves hitting ("smacking," "slapping," "spanking") children, with the hand or with an implement—a whip, stick, belt, shoe, wooden spoon, etc. But it can also involve, for example, kicking, shaking or throwing children, scratching, pinching, biting, pulling hair or boxing ears, forcing children to stay in uncomfortable positions, burning, scalding or forced ingestion" (United Nations Committee on the Rights of the Child, 2018, para 11).

Clinician's Toolkit for Children's Behavioral Health
DOI: https://doi.org/10.1016/B978-0-12-816024-4.00009-7

One of the problematic issues with Bella's situation involves the modeling of aggressive behavior. In fact, most human behaviors are learned through modeling, and young children are especially prone to learn in this manner. Furthermore, aggressive behavior, in particular, is readily acquired through this mechanism (Bandura, 1973). So, while Bella's mother's intention seems to be to teach her to NOT hit, her behavior makes it more likely that she *will* hit. This may be part of the reason that physical punishment repeatedly is found to be associated with a significantly increased likelihood of aggressive behavior in children who are hit by their parents (Gershoff & Grogan-Kaylor, 2016).

Another concerning feature of Bella's situation is that her mother is trying to teach her a lesson when Bella is in a mental state that is not conducive to learning. When a person is threatened or being attacked, the stress response system changes brain activity such that the areas of the brain responsible for learning new information are in states less conducive to learning. In this situation the child's brain is focused largely on escaping pain and preventing injury, and new learning is not likely to happen. In fact, caregiver use of physical punishment is associated with "low moral internalization" (Gershoff & Grogan-Kaylor, 2016). This means, the more the parents rely on physical punishment the *less likely* children are to internalize those parents' values and behave morally in the absence of authority figures.

Perhaps the most problematic aspect of Bella's situation, though, is that spanking places her at heightened risk for a host of negative outcomes. These include (from Gershoff & Grogan-Kaylor, 2016)

- child aggression,
- child antisocial behavior,
- child externalizing behavior problems (e.g., rule breaking and defiance),
- child internalizing behavior problems (e.g., anxiety and depression),
- child mental health problems,
- negative parent–child relationship,
- impaired cognitive ability,
- low self-esteem,
- low moral internalization,
- being a victim of physical abuse,
- adult antisocial behavior, and
- adult mental health problems.

These associations were identified through meta-analyses on more than 100 studies on physical punishment (not abuse) representing research on more than 160,000 individuals. Why these relationships exist is not entirely clear, but professionals are increasingly recognizing that spanking children is a risky and potentially harmful endeavor.

At minimum, it is now evident that physical punishment, such as physical abuse, activates the body's stress response system and may negatively affect the growing brain at a very critical period in brain development (Gershoff, 2016).

Unfortunately, despite its association with several negative developmental, behavioral, and mental health outcomes, physical punishment remains commonplace in the United States. About two-thirds of the young children in the United States are spanked by their parents (Regalado, Sareen, Inkelas, Wissow, & Halfon, 2004), and most teens (85%) report that they were spanked or slapped by their mothers at some point in their development (Bender et al., 2007).

The high rate of use of physical punishment in the United States is out of step with many other parts of the world. The United Nations Convention on the Rights of the Child (UNCRC; UN General Assembly, 1989), a comprehensive description of children's rights, is the most widely ratified international human rights treaty. The UNCRC calls for the prohibition and eradication of corporal punishment in the home, out-of-home placements, child care organizations, penal systems, and schools. The United States is the sole nation of all of the UN nations, which has not ratified the convention. Furthermore, as of the writing of this chapter, 58 nations, not including the United States, have prohibited corporal punishment of children in all settings, including the home (Global Initiative to End All Corporal Punishment of Children, 2018).

Several organizations charged with tracking and promoting the health and well-being of youths have come out against physical punishment of children. The Centers for Disease Control and Prevention, for example, lists physical punishment as a health risk and calls for legislative action to promote societal norms about nonviolent, effective discipline and to prevent the harms related to physical punishment (Fortson, Klevens, Merrick, Gilbert, & Alexander, 2016).

Furthermore, a variety of professional organizations have developed statements to advise professionals and caregivers against physical punishment of children. For example, the American Academy of Pediatrics (AAP) "recommends that adults caring for children use healthy forms of discipline, such as positive reinforcement of appropriate behaviors, setting limits, redirecting, and setting future expectations. The AAP recommends that parents do not use spanking, hitting, slapping, threatening, insulting, humiliating, or shaming" (Sege, Siegel, AAP Council on Child Abuse, and Neglect, & AAP Committee on Psychosocial Aspects of Child and Family Health, 2018, p. 6). The National Association of Pediatric Nurse Practitioners directs its professionals to educate parents about the harmful effects of corporal punishment and to instruct them about alternative forms of discipline (National Association of Pediatric Nurse Practitioners,

2006). The American Academy of Child and Adolescent Psychiatry (2012) states, "When assessing and treating children and families, child and adolescent psychiatrists should provide information to families about the hazards associated with corporal punishment and encourage and assist parents to modify their child's behavior by other methods." In addition, many other professional organizations have made similar statements.

How to advise parents about physical punishment

As many US parents still use physical punishment, routine anticipatory guidance may be the best method for prevention (Sege et al., 2018). There is some evidence indicating that delivering anticipatory guidance in a supportive manner may be effective in fostering positive, nonviolent parenting practices (Sege, Hatmaker-Flanigan, De Vos, Levin-Goodman, & Spivak, 2006). However, this guidance needs to be provided very early because, by 12 months, roughly a quarter to a half of parents is already spanking their children (Straus & Stewart, 1999). Health-care providers can broach the topic at infant well visits. A statement as simple as "We have learned that spanking is not good for children, so we are asking all of our families not to use it" may be an effective way to start. In addition to anticipatory guidance, clinicians should regularly ask about discipline, as in the scenario next.

> At a well visit, Dr. Smith asks 6-year-old Alex's mother what type of discipline the family uses. She admits that she gives Alex "whuppings," and states, "I don't like to have to whup him, but he just doesn't listen. Sometimes, it's the only thing that works."

Parents often make statements like this when explaining their use of physical punishment. Although our professional organizations have statements about physical punishment, many of us are never taught exactly how to respond to such statements. For this reason, the following guidance is provided. Some points may be useful for some families, while others may not. It will be important to get to know your families well and choose the responses that will be most helpful and effective on a case-by-case basis.

Most parents don't want to hit. Many parents will express reservations like Alex's mother did. When this occurs, it can be useful to simply reflect the parents' apprehension about physical punishment. That is, the clinician can state something like, "my sense is that you really don't like to whup him," or "it sounds like you would rather use other methods if you found some that were effective." For some parents, it may be helpful to point out, "Some parents start hitting and can't stop. Their child gets hurt, and that parent feels terrible. Let's not put you in that position." Especially through early anticipatory guidance, we can make the point that, "If we make a commitment to never hit our children, we won't get ourselves into this bind." In fact, instinctual processes such as behaving aggressively when angry are very hard to stop once started. Perhaps in part for this reason, most parents who physically abuse their children start with physical punishment that escalates into physical abuse. Warning parents about this can sometimes get them to reconsider physical punishment.

Professionals can use motivational-interviewing (MI) techniques to address this issue as well. For example, one can ask something like "On a scale of 1–10, with 10 being very, very helpful, how helpful do you think hitting is for your child?" or "On a scale of 1–10, with 10 being very, very much, how much do you like hitting your child?" If parents use a number less than 10, they can be asked why they did not choose a higher number. For example, if the parent says "5," one can ask, "Why did you say 5 and not 9 or 10?" This method elicits "change talk" that allows the parent to use his or her own reasoning to process and discuss reasons NOT to hit. [For details on how to use MI in medical settings, see Douaihy, Kelly, and Gold (2015).] The practitioner also can ask the parent to tell about a time when hitting was not helpful, describe how they feel after hitting or what it was like when they hit the hardest. In these conversations, many parents will express guilt or remorse, and evidence of motivation for change that can be reflected by the practitioner.

It doesn't work. Although Alex's mother feels that spanking works, research suggests that for most kids, it does not improve behavior in the short and long term. In one study that tracked parent–child interactions in real time, children who were hit or slapped by parents tended to misbehave again within 10 minutes (Holden, Williamson, & Holland, 2014). A meta-analysis on the issue concluded that children who are spanked are equally likely to be defiant as compliant after physical punishment (Gershoff & Grogan-Kaylor, 2016). Clinicians addressing this may simply ask parents, "Has your child had similar behavior problems since you starting spanking?" and then help the parents to consider whether the technique is actually helping. It may then be helpful to point out that children whose parents rely on spanking are less likely to adopt their parents' values and morals than those who are not spanked. Lastly, the clinician can state that a parenting technique "works" when the child learns or becomes a better person because of it. The clinician can make the point that children learn by watching and imitating adults, especially parents, then ask, "If we hit when we are angry, what do they learn?"

You suggest alternatives to spanking, but a parent says, "I want him to be prepared for the real world. I want him to be tough, not soft."

Statements like this reflect sincere, caring concern about the child's future well-being, and the clinician should reflect that, as in, "I hear you. As his parent, you want to make sure he is ready for the world and all it can bring. That's a parent's job!" The clinician can then help the parent to think through their goals and wishes for the child, asking questions, such as "If your child were prepared for the real world, what would that look like? How would they treat others? How would they handle themselves?" In most cases the clinician can accurately point out that certain parenting approaches are more likely to lead to those outcomes, but harsh parenting is not one of them. If the parent's goals suggest a desire to avoid outcomes such as antisocial behavior, the clinician can cite the research summarized above and suggest that spanking will not help with those goals.

In addition, it may be useful to help the parent to consider what lesson the child is really learning. One could ask, "Spanking involves one person intentionally inflicting pain on the persons/he loves; what does this teach your child about love and relationships? Spanking requires the child to submit to violence without retaliation or response; is that what we want for him to do in the future? Is this teaching him to 'just take it' when hurt by others?" The clinician can suggest that lessons in self-defense, assertiveness, or the like may be better to meet the parent's goal of preparing the child for the real world.

It makes things worse. Clinicians can summarize the associations between spanking and the host of negative outcomes (listed earlier), such as childhood aggression and antisocial behavior that have been identified in the research.

You make suggestions about nonviolent discipline and suggest that a parent not hit, spank, or whup his children, and he replies, "But I was spanked and I turned out fine!"

The best response to this question *does not* involve convincing the parent he is actually "not fine," or could be "finer!" This type of response may leave the parent feeling insulted. In turn the parent may become defensive and unlikely to learn or take advice. It is when parents feel heard, respected, and understood that they are in mental states conducive to learning. Therefore it is best to use reflective, empathic listening and reply with something like, "You were spanked and things turned out well for you, so why would it be different for your child?" Clinicians can then help the parent to apply the concept of "risk" to this topic. Smoking is a good analogy. Not everyone who smokes will die from smoking. However, smoking increases the risk of cancer and mortality. Health-care providers advise against it because of this risk.

Similarly, while not every single child who is spanked will experience these effects, spanking increases the *risk* of several negative outcomes, including poor moral internalization, aggressive and antisocial behavior, externalizing behavior problems (e.g., rule breaking and defiance), internalizing behavior problems (e.g., anxiety and depression), mental health problems, negative parent–child relationships, impaired cognitive ability, low self-esteem, becoming a victim of physical abuse, adult antisocial behavior, and adult mental health problems. No caring parent would do anything to increase risks like those! For example, a parent would not even consider giving a medication to their child that had a list of such side effects. When parents consider spanking in this light, they often decide against it.

In keeping, it can be very helpful to remind parents of all the things that they do to reduce the "risk" of negative outcomes and suffering for their children. For example, you may note that they read with them, dress them warmly in the cold weather, feed them healthy food, and/or make them wear seat belts or sit in car seats. You can point out that they do these things to reduce the risk of negative outcomes—poor academic performance, illness, injury, etc. Why would they spank and potentially undo so much of the hard work they do every day to decrease the risk of negative outcomes? The statement, "Let's not take chances with our kids" can be fitting here.

In some cases, another good response to the "I turned out fine..." statement is to suggest that the parent probably turned out fine DESPITE physical punishment, not BECAUSE OF it. Especially for families you know well, you may be able to point out that the individual's parents monitored their activities, set firm limits, and helped them in various other ways—all of which may have reduced the risk of negative outcomes and tampered the negative effects of physical punishment. It is important to take care to avoid sounding critical of the individual's parents. Something as simple as "Back then, when your parents used physical punishment, we didn't know what we know now. They did not have the research results we do, or the other tools that we have now. They did what they thought was best. But we know more now..." can make this point. One can add, for example, that infants and children did not have to be in car seats or use seat belts many years ago. Once we learned that this was potentially very dangerous for children, we changed our behaviors. Similar analogies can be made with smoking, tanning without sunscreen, and other behaviors that are now known to pose health risks.

In addition to these methods, many parents will need to be educated about alternatives to physical punishment. Handout 1 provides a brief explanation of the negative outcomes of physical punishment as well as information about alternatives and resources with detailed parenting guidance. The website StopSpanking.org provides tips for pediatricians that may be used by other professionals as well (StopSpanking.org, 2019). Further, the Gundersen Center for effective discipline provides "a guide for responding to tough questions about corporal punishment" (Gundersen Lutheran Medical Center, 2016).

In collaborative care settings, providers can link parents to a professional with expertise in parenting and behavior management who works in the practice, agency, or organization. In other cases, parents may need to be referred to as an outside expert, such as a clinical child psychologist or social worker, for more comprehensive guidance.

Best practices in interviewing about child maltreatment

Clinicians also play key roles in the identification, prevention, reporting and treatment of child abuse, and neglect. Although definitions vary somewhat according to state laws, child maltreatment is typically understood to include physical abuse, sexual abuse, neglect, psychological abuse, and, in some areas, witnessing domestic violence. National surveys indicate that 15% of all youth in the United States experience some form of child maltreatment in a given year, and 25% of youth will experience some child maltreatment by age 18 (Finkelhor, Turner, Shattuck, & Hamby, 2015).

Child maltreatment rarely stops without intervention, and the first step in intervention is usually correctly identifying and reporting child maltreatment to police or child protective services (CPS). Most of these reports are made by professionals. In fact, research consistently indicates that about two-thirds of child maltreatment reports are made by teachers, police officers, attorneys, medical and social services professionals, and the like (U.S. Department of Health and Human Services, 2018).

Assessing child maltreatment is a delicate matter for many reasons. For one, maltreatment very often occurs within the context of the family, family friends, or acquaintances. In fact in 2016 over three-quarters (78.0%) of the substantiated child maltreatment fatalities in the United States involved at least one parent (U.S. Department of Health and Human Services, 2018). Although sexual abuse was once thought to be most commonly perpetrated by strangers, it is now widely understood that the perpetrator of child sexual abuse is typically a family member, family friend, or someone known to the family. These and other facts make it difficult for the clinician to assess maltreatment, particularly when the youth presents for services with family members. Related factors, such as the clinician's familiarity with the family, concerns about the benefits of reporting, limited time and reimbursement, and insufficient training, are also issues that impede proper reporting (Flaherty & Sege, 2005; Gunn, Hickson, & Cooper, 2005; Jones et al., 2008).

For these and other reasons, compliance with mandated reporting is far from ideal. In a study of 327 primary care physicians, for example, only 24% of the cases in which children were considered possibly abused were reported, and only 73% of the children considered to be likely or very likely abused were reported (Flaherty et al., 2008). These finding suggest that there is much work to do in helping professionals to fulfill their reporting duties.

Fortunately, there are several methods and opportunities to overcome these obstacles and improve mandated reporting. Clinicians with limited time can give screening measures for patients and parents to complete while waiting. The Child Welfare Information Gateway (n.d.a) provides screening tools and other resources that may be useful to a variety of professionals. For practitioners who struggle with reimbursement issues, the American Academy of Pediatrics (2019) publishes a guide on how to code and bill for preventive interventions.

Several points can be made to help professionals overcome obstacles to reporting maltreatment. First, clinicians concerned about time constraints should be aware that CPS in most states do not require paperwork. Reporting typically can be done anonymously, by phone, and phone calls can take very little time, as CPS intake workers ask for limited information. Furthermore, mandated reporters typically are not obligated to tell families that they are reporting. Clinicians following mandated reporting laws are often protected by the law in that they are immune from any civil or criminal liability related to mandated reports. It is critical that clinicians not assume that the families in their practice would not engage in maltreatment. Indeed, professionals must remain vigilant and recognize that research suggests that child maltreatment occurs across ethnic, socioeconomic, religious, and other backgrounds.

Clinicians concerned about outcomes of reporting should be informed that a child's removal from the home is a rare outcome. Lastly, several resources exist (e.g., Christian & Committee on Child Abuse and Neglect, 2015; Kellogg, 2005) that provide clinicians with detailed descriptions of signs and indicators of maltreatment. These resources take some of the "guess work" out of maltreatment-related decision-making.

With obstacles overcome, professionals can appreciate the significant benefits to mandated reporting. Perhaps, most importantly, the likelihood of continued abuse is high when it is not reported and addressed. Furthermore, adverse outcomes such as health and mental health problems such as posttraumatic stress disorder, suicide, aggressive behavior, delinquency, criminal behavior, and substance abuse have all been linked to child maltreatment and may be prevented or reduced if abuse is reported and eventually stopped.

In some cases, there are suspicious injuries and histories that raise concerns about maltreatment (for a summary, see Christian & Committee on Child Abuse and Neglect, 2015; Kellogg, 2005). In many cases, however, obvious physical indicators of child maltreatment are not evident. Thus one of the most effective ways to assess for maltreatment is to ask focused and thoughtful questions. The maltreatment assessment should address all types of child maltreatment including emotional/psychological abuse, witnessing violence in the home, sexual abuse, physical abuse, and neglect. The following sample questions and tips for doing this effectively are listed:

- How did your nose/finger/arm, etc. get broken? (if injury is evident)
- What happens when you get in trouble at home?
- Do you get punished? How do you get punished?
- What happens at home (or care setting) when people get angry?
- Has there been a time when a person hit you? Has there been a time when someone hurt you some other way?
- Has someone been mean to you or called you names?
- Have you seen or heard people fighting at home?
- Has someone made you feel scared?
- Have you been told to keep secrets?
- Have you been at home alone for a long time?
- Has there been a time when you were hungry for a long time but didn't have something to eat?
- Has there been a time when you didn't have a safe place to sleep?
- Are there times when you are alone with no one to take care of you?
- Do you know what I mean when I say "privates?" Has someone touched your privates, or put their body on your privates? Has someone made you touch or put your body on their privates?
- Has someone shown you naked people or private parts on something such as a computer, TV, or tablet?

Ask follow-up questions if needed. A good follow-up statement following a positive response to these questions is simply "Tell me about that." Many of the responses to the abovementioned questions will not indicate maltreatment. Reports of minor incidents are common, especially among young children who do not understand the intent of these questions. For example, a child might tell about seeing people fighting on the television. The clinician should acknowledge these and should

NOT say something like, "no that's not what I mean." Instead, the clinician can ask the question again, or be somewhat more specific, asking, for instance, "Have you seen your family members fighting?"

Interview the youth without the parent present, if possible. As mentioned above, psychological and physical abuses often are perpetrated by a caregiver, and sexual abuse perpetrators are usually family or someone known to the family. Further, witnessing violence in the home frequently involves family members. Thus to promote open and honest responding, it is best to interview the youth alone.

Use simple, common, everyday words. Use language you are sure that the child understands, and use questions that keep the number of ideas to a minimum. Keep questions open-ended whenever possible. If you have to be specific, such as "when you said 'he' punched you, do you mean your dad or your brother," provide an "or someone else" option. However, be aware that you do not need to gather many details. If you learn enough to suspect maltreatment and report it, the child is then likely to be interviewed by a trained forensic interviewer who is trained to gather details.

Use reflections where possible. For example, "so you said you saw your mom and Mark hitting each other, is that right?" This lets the youth know that you have heard and understood them and clarifies that you heard them correctly.

Do not ask leading questions. Questions such as "What happened to your nose—did your parents hit you?" and "You said someone touched your pee-pee. Was it your uncle?" are obviously leading questions to be avoided. Keep in mind, though, that even questions, such as "Who else was in the kitchen with you?," can be leading as well.

Observe nonverbal behaviors. For example, note if the child covers her eyes and shakes her head when disclosing an incident, or if the child gets tearful.

Be empathic, but not aghast. The most potent single interviewing technique is empathy. Use language that expresses an appreciation of what the patient is going through. For example, "it seems like these things are hard to talk about," or "you look sad" (if you see tears). Do not engage in verbal or nonverbal communication that expresses disgust, shock, anger, or value judgments (e.g., that was wrong.).

Mandated reporting of suspected maltreatment

Each US state, as well as American Samoa, the District of Columbia, Guam, the Northern Mariana Islands, Puerto Rico, and the US Virgin Islands, has its own set of laws outlining who must report child maltreatment and what must be reported. Who is mandated to report and under what circumstances mandated reporters must report, both vary from state to state and territory to territory. Summaries of state laws are available at the Child Welfare Information Gateway (2016). An interactive map providing the details of state's reporting laws is also available from the American Professional Society on the Abuse of Children (2017). Because of these wide variations in state and territory laws, it is imperative that professionals and the public have detailed understanding of their laws, and that they update their knowledge whenever they relocate.

Who reports. Although most states mandate reporting by child educators, mental health and health-care providers, law enforcement officers, and child care workers, it is important to note that other professions—such as employees at camps, photograph processors, and animal control officers—are mandated in certain states. In contrast, clergy are expressly not compelled to report suspected maltreatment in certain states.

Some reporting issues relevant to mandated reporting in medical settings are worth noting. First, a mandated reporter cannot delegate or assign their duty to report to others. If a mandated reporter knows or suspects abuse, then he or she must make a report. This is the case regardless of whether an attending or other authority instructs otherwise, or whether others on a treatment team were also aware of the abuse. It is also important to note that some individuals who are still in training, such as interns or residents, are mandated reporters in some states.

When to report. Usually, mandated reporters are obligated to report when they suspect or have reason to believe that child maltreatment is occurring or has occurred. In some cases, reporting must take place if maltreatment is thought to be likely to occur, or if the child faces a threat of maltreatment in the future. Members of the public in certain jurisdictions must report known maltreatment, but the public in other areas have the option to report it.

Who is considered a victim. Although most laws require reporting for maltreated individuals under the age of 18, there are some laws mandating reporting for somewhat older people with impairments or disabilities. Prenatal drug exposure, human trafficking, involvement in child pornography, and other contexts are reasons for mandated reporting in some, but not all, locations as well.

Where to report. Reporting is typically made to a CPS or child welfare agency, but various laws state that reporting may be made to sherriff, police, Tribal social services or law enforcement agencies. Toll-free reporting hotlines also are available in many areas. A list of them by state is available at the Child Welfare Information Gateway (n.d.b) webpage.

How to report. When calling, the reporter should state that he/she would like to make a report of suspected or known child maltreatment. CPS will typically then ask for the following information (however, it is important to note that a report should be made even if the reporter does not have all, or even most, of these details):

- The name and address of the maltreated child.
- The child's age.
- The name, contact information, and address of the parent/caregiver.
- The reason you know or suspect the child has been or is at risk of being maltreated.
- Any other details that may be helpful to the investigation. This may include other indicators of the child's risk or vulnerability, such as impairments, mental health or medical illnesses, or disabilities.

Whether the reporter's name must be in the written report also varies by state. Many, but not all, states require that the reporter's identity be kept confidential and not released to the public. In some cases the reporter may not be certain that an incident would be considered maltreatment. In this case the individual may choose to call CPS and describe the incident without revealing identifying information. CPS staff will sometimes provide feedback as to whether the information is reportable.

Conclusion

In summary, research has clearly identified many negative outcomes associated with physical punishment of children. In keeping, many professional organizations have made statements suggesting that care providers advise parents not to use physical punishment and recommend the use of other techniques. There are several ways that clinicians can have respectful conversations with parents to help them to choose methods other than physical punishment. Clinicians also have important roles in identifying and reporting suspected child maltreatment. Reporting laws vary by state/territory, so clinicians are advised to read the laws in their area. There are many methods that clinicians can use to screen for maltreatment, and reporting, in most cases, can be quick and uncomplicated. Guiding parents away from physical punishment and reporting suspected maltreatment are critical child protection tasks, and clinicians who regularly engage in these practices are effective leaders in the prevention of child maltreatment and related suffering.

Handout 1. Why and how to not hit, spank, slap, or whup your child

Physical punishment of children is related to many negative outcomes (Gershoff & Grogan-Kaylor, 2016), including higher chances of

- child aggression,
- child antisocial behavior,
- child externalizing behavior problems (e.g., rule breaking, defiance),
- child internalizing behavior problems (e.g., anxiety, depression),
- child mental health problems,
- negative parent–child relationships,
- impaired cognitive ability,
- low self-esteem,
- victim of physical abuse,
- low moral internalization (less likely to take on parents' values and morals),
- adult antisocial behavior, and
- adult mental health problems.

Sometimes parents say spanking "works" because the child stops misbehavior after the spanking. However, research shows that spanked children are as likely to behave well as to misbehave in the minutes following a spanking. Also, spanking and other techniques have similar short-term results, but spanking carries the "costs" listed earlier.

Knowing this, many parents ask, "If I can't spank, what CAN I Do?"

Here are strategies that work (excerpts taken with permission from Knox & Lentini, 2010):

- *Make not hitting a family rule.* Make a vow to yourself that you will not hit, no matter what happens. That way, when you are angry, you will not resort to hurting your child. Share the vow with your partner and/or other caregivers so that they will do the same. Teach your children that hitting is not ok. Tell them that you will not hurt them and they are not to hurt others. Through your calm, "grown-up" response to anger, show your children that solving problems with words is better than with force.
- *Set firm, consistent limits.* Consistency is the key. Once a consequence is set, stick to it. Ensure that every caretaker agrees on the rules as well as the response or consequence to use if your child does not comply with the rules. When for the first time a rule is broken, immediately explain to your child what he did wrong

and give one warning (e.g., not to do it again or there will be a specific consequence). If the misbehavior is major, such as aggression, do not give a warning. If the rule is again broken, then give a consequence (e.g., a time out, can't play with a specific toy, can't watch TV, use the computer, or play video game for a specified period of time) The time out should be brief, and end when the child is calm. Long time outs are not recommended, and parents should try to limit them to a maximum of 1 minute per year of age (e.g., 3 minutes for a 3-year old). Time out should be in a place that is free of fun things and activities (e.g., not near a TV, computer, phone or toys, and no talking during time out). If you have tried time out and it has not worked, or your child will not stay in time out, please see the following video: https://www.coursera.org/lecture/everyday-parenting/time-out-from-reinforcement-y3gUi.

- *Reward good behavior*. Help your child practice doing what you ask by giving him something simple that you know he will do (e.g., Please hand me a tissue.). Do this when your child is in a good mood and the likelihood of compliance is highest. Then reward him with praise (Good job! I like how you help me). Do this often, at least a few times daily. Identify the opposite of the problem behavior (e.g., sharing toys for a child who has trouble sharing; not yelling when told "no") and praise or reward it every single time it happens. If you plan to give your child a toy or privilege, give it as a reward immediately following good behavior. These efforts will pay off.
- *Stay one step ahead.* Tantrums are most likely when a child is sleepy or hungry. Set an early bedtime and regular nap schedule. Feed young children frequently. Recognize your child's cues; whining, clenched fists, angry facial expressions and the like often suggest it is time to prevent problems before they occur (e.g., remove the child from the situation and provide a structured activity). Always there have several different things on hand to occupy young children on trips away from home.
- *Use distraction.* Distract toddlers who are on the verge of problem behaviors. Point out something nearby that may interest them. Keep their hands occupied by having them stack, carry or move favorite or novel items. Dance with them, play act, or otherwise engage them to distract them from their problem behavior. Never give them a privilege or reward during or right after a tantrum.
- *Take breaks*. Take a break from a crying baby or child who is in the midst of a tantrum. Make sure the child is safe, and then take time to cool off and regain composure, if possible going outside or sitting in a car or another room for a period of time until anger subsides.

Say to yourself something like "It's okay," or "I can handle this," etc. Call a friend or family member who is a good listener for support.

Some parents say, "I need more help!"

Here are some resources that may help:

- Eunice Kennedy Shriver National Institute of Child Health and Human Development, NIH, DHHS. Adventures in parenting (free download). (2001). <https://www.nichd.nih.gov/sites/default/files/publications/pubs/documents/adventures_in_parenting_rev.pdf>.
- Vieth, V. (2014). From sticks to flowers: Guidelines for child protection professional working with parents using scripture to justify corporal punishment. *William Mitchell Law Review*, *40*(3), 1–36.
- Durrant, J. Positive discipline in everyday parenting, 4th ed. (free download). (2016). <https://resourcecentre.savethechildren.net/library/positive-discipline-everyday-parenting-pdep-fourth-edition>.
- Alternatives to Spanking. <http://stopspanking.org/resources/>.
- How to use Time Out effectively. <https://www.coursera.org/lecture/everyday-parenting/time-out-from-reinforcement-y3gUi>.

Important points to remember

- About two-thirds of the young children in the United States are spanked by their parents (Regalado et al., 2004), and most teens (85%) report that they were spanked or slapped by their mothers at some point in their development (Bender et al., 2007).
- As of the writing of this chapter, 58 nations, not including the United States, have prohibited corporal punishment of children in all settings, including the home (Global Initiative to End All Corporal Punishment of Children, 2018).
- The Centers for Disease Control and Prevention lists physical punishment as a health risk and calls for legislative action to promote societal norms about nonviolent, effective discipline and to prevent the harms related to physical punishment (Fortson et al., 2016).
- National surveys indicate that 15% of all youth in the United States experience some form of child maltreatment in a given year, and 25% of youth will experience some child maltreatment by age 18 (Finkelhor et al., 2015).
- It is critical that clinicians not assume that the families in their practice would not engage in maltreatment. Indeed, professionals must remain vigilant and recognize that research suggests that child maltreatment occurs across ethnic, socioeconomic, religious, and other backgrounds.

References

American Academy of Child and Adolescent Psychiatry. *Corporal punishment*. (2012). From <https://www.aacap.org/aacap/Policy_Statements/2012/Policy_Statement_on_Corporal_Punishment.aspx> Retrieved 05.03.19.

American Academy of Pediatrics. *Coding for pediatric preventive care, 2019 [PDF file]*. (2019). From <https://www.aap.org/en-us/Documents/coding_preventive_care.pdf> Retrieved 05.03.19.

American Professional Society on the Abuse of Children. *Child maltreatment reporting laws*. (2017). From <http://centerforchildpolicy.org/reportinglaws.html> Retrieved 13.03.19.

Bandura, A. (1973). *Aggression: A social learning analysis*. Prentice-Hall.

Bender, H. L., Allen, J. P., McElhaney, K. B., Antonishak, J., Moore, C. M., Kelly, H. O., & Davis, S. M. (2007). Use of harsh physical discipline and developmental outcomes in adolescence. *Development and Psychopathology, 19*, 227–242.

Child Welfare Information Gateway. *Identification, screening, and assessment of child abuse & neglect*. (n.d.a). From <https://www.childwelfare.gov/topics/systemwide/assessment/family-assess/id-can/> Retrieved 05.03.19.

Child Welfare Information Gateway. *State child abuse and neglect reporting numbers*. (n.d.b). From <https://www.childwelfare.gov/topics/systemwide/assessment/family-assess/id-can/https://www.childwelfare.gov/organizations/?CWIGFunctionsaction = rols:main.dspList&rolType = Custom&RS_ID = 5> Retrieved 05.03.19.

Child Welfare Information Gateway. *Mandatory reporters of child abuse and neglect.* (2016). From <https://www.childwelfare.gov/pubPDFs/manda.pdf> Retrieved 05.03.19.

Christian, C. W., & Committee on Child Abuse and Neglect. (2015). The evaluation of suspected child physical abuse. *Pediatrics, 135*, e1337–e1354.

Douaihy, A., Kelly, T. M., & Gold, M. A. (Eds.), (2015). *Motivational interviewing: A guide for medical trainees.* Oxford University Press.

Finkelhor, D., Turner, H. A., Shattuck, A., & Hamby, S. L. (2015). Prevalence of childhood exposure to violence, crime, and abuse: Results from the national survey of children's exposure to violence. *JAMA Pediatrics, 169*(8), 746–754.

Flaherty, E. G., & Sege, R. (2005). Barriers to physician identification and reporting of child abuse. *Pediatric Annals, 34*(5), 349–356.

Flaherty, E. G., Sege, R. D., Griffith, J., Price, L. L., Wasserman, R., Slora, E., ... Abney, D. (2008). From suspicion of physical child abuse to reporting: primary care clinician decision-making. *Pediatrics, 122*(3), 611–619.

Fortson, B. L., Klevens, J., Merrick, M. T., Gilbert, L. K., & Alexander, S. P. (2016). *Preventing child abuse and neglect: A technical package for policy, norm, and programmatic activities.* Atlanta, GA: National Center for Injury Prevention and Control, Centers for Disease Control and Prevention.

Gershoff, E. T. (2016). Should parents' physical punishment of children be considered a source of toxic stress that affects brain development? *Family Relations, 65*(1), 151–162.

Gershoff, E. T., & Grogan-Kaylor, A. (2016). Spanking and child outcomes: Old controversies and new meta-analyses. *Journal of Family Psychology, 30*(4), 453.

Global Initiative to End All Corporal Punishment of Children. (2018). From <https://endcorporalpunishment.org/countdown/> Retrieved 05.11.19.

Gundersen Lutheran Medical Center. *A guide for responding to tough questions about corporal punishment [PDF file].* (2016). From <http://www.gundersenhealth.org/app/files/public/4769/CED-Guide-for-responding-to-corporal-punishment-questions.pdf> Retrieved 05.03.19.

Gunn, V. L., Hickson, G. B., & Cooper, W. O. (2005). Factors affecting pediatricians' reporting of suspected child maltreatment. *Ambulatory Pediatrics, 5*(2), 96–101. Available from https://doi.org/10.1367/AO4-094R.1.

Holden, G. W., Williamson, P. A., & Holland, G. W. O. (2014). Eavesdropping on the family: A pilot investigation of corporal punishment in the home. *Journal of Family Psychology, 28*(3), 401–406. Available from https://doi.org/10.1037/a0036370.

Jones, R., Flaherty, E. G., Binns, H. J., Price, L. L., Slora, E., Abney, D., ... Sege, R. D. (2008). Clinicians' description of factors influencing their reporting of suspected child abuse: report of the Child Abuse Reporting Experience Study Research Group. *Pediatrics, 122*(2), 259–266.

Kellogg, N. (2005). The evaluation of sexual abuse in children. *Pediatrics, 116*(2), 506–512.

Knox, M., & Lentini, J. (2010). On spanking. *Pediatrics for Parents, 26*(5–6), 25. (3).

National Association of Pediatric Nurse Practitioners. (2006). NAPNAP position statement on corporal punishment. *Journal of Pediatric Health Care, 20*, 43A–44A.

Regalado, M., Sareen, H., Inkelas, M., Wissow, L. S., & Halfon, N. (2004). Parents' discipline of young children: Results from the National Survey of Early Childhood Health. *Pediatrics, 113*, 1952–1958, 2004.

Sege, R. D., Hatmaker-Flanigan, E., De Vos, E., Levin-Goodman, R., & Spivak, H. (2006). Anticipatory guidance and violence prevention: results from family and pediatrician focus groups. *Pediatrics, 117*(2), 455–463.

Sege, R. D., Siegel, B. S., & AAP Council on Child Abuse and Neglect &AAP Committee on Psychosocial Aspects of Child and Family Health. (2018). Effective discipline to raise healthy children. *Pediatrics, 142*(6), 1–10.

StopSpanking.org. (2019). *Help for pediatricians*. A Pediatrician's Peaceful Parenting Resource. From <https://stopspanking.org/resources/pediatricians/> Retrieved 05.03.19.

Straus, M., & Donnelly, D. (2001). *Beating the devil out of them*. New Brunswick, New Jersey: Transaction Publishers.

Straus, M. A., & Stewart, J. H. (1999). *Corporal punishment by American parents: national data on prevalence, chronicity, severity, and duration, in relation to child and family characteristics, Clinical Child and Family Psychology Review* (2, pp. 55–70).

United Nations Committee on the Rights of the Child. (2018). *General comment no. 8*, para. 11.

U.S. Department of Health & Human Services, Administration for Children and Families, Administration on Children, Youth and Families, Children's Bureau. *Child maltreatment 2016*. (2018). From <https://www.acf.hhs.gov/cb/research-data-technology/statistics-research/child-maltreatment> Retrieved 05.03.19.

UN General Assembly, Convention on the Rights of the Child. (1989). United Nations, Treaty Series, Vol. 1577 (p. 3). Available from <http://www.refworld.org/docid/3ae6b38f0.html> Accessed 06.08.18.

CHAPTER

10

Bedtime and sleep problems in children

Kimberly Hunter

Department of Psychiatry, University of Toledo College of Medicine and Life Sciences, Toledo, OH, United States

Sleep disturbances in infancy, childhood, and adolescence are common problems impacting between 25% and 40% of youth (Bhargava, 2011; Meltzer, Plaufcan, Thomas, & Mindell, 2014; Waters, Suresh, & Nixon, 2013). Sleep problems can include more behaviorally based issues, such as bedtime tantrums/refusal, frequent night wakings, sleep onset delays, and insomnia, and more medically based sleep disorders, such as parasomnias (night terrors and sleepwalking) and sleep-disordered breathing (SDB) [obstructive sleep apnea (OSA) and snoring]. Certain sleep issues are more common during certain developmental periods. For example, in infancy and early childhood, frequent night wakings and settling problems/delays are most prevalent, while insomnia and delayed bedtimes are more common in older children and adolescents and lead to sleep deprivation (Gruber, Cassoff, & Knauper, 2011; Meltzer, Johnson, Crosette, Ramos, & Mindell, 2010; Moturi & Avis, 2010).

Sleep problems can lead to significant sleep deficits in youth leading to a variety of negative consequences, such as behavior issues, inattention, hyperactivity, academic and learning issues, neurocognitive deficits, deficits in daytime functioning, anxiety, depression, parental/family stress, and health issues including obesity, growth deficits, hypertension, cardiovascular problems, and increased accidents/injuries (Bhargava, 2011; Gruber et al., 2011; Maski & Kothare, 2013; Meltzer et al., 2010; Owens, 2008; Paruthi et al., 2016).

The consequences of sleep deficits frequently lead to changes in a child's mood, behavior, and daytime functioning, and these behaviors

Clinician's Toolkit for Children's Behavioral Health
DOI: https://doi.org/10.1016/B978-0-12-816024-4.00010-3

may be more noticeable to parents than sleep deficits themselves (Bhargava, 2011). Sleep deprivation in children often manifests differently than in adults. For example, hyperactivity, inattention, irritability, poor frustration tolerance, noncompliance, and impulsivity are frequently seen in children with sleep issues (Gruber et al., 2011). On the contrary, excessive daytime sleepiness and psychomotor slowing are manifested more in sleep-deprived older teens and adults (Bhargava, 2011; Gruber et al., 2011; Maski & Kothare, 2013). Consequently, parents may not connect behavior issues to sleep problems/deficits, leading to missed opportunities to correct the problem (Maski & Kothare, 2013).

In fact, numerous studies have shown that many parents do not bring up sleep issues with their child's pediatrician as they may not recognize their child's sleep as problematic or they may not know what constitutes a sleep problem. This leads to many sleep problems going unrecognized, thereby further delaying treatment (Byars, Yolton, Rausch, Lanphear, & Beebe, 2012; Meltzer et al., 2010, 2014; Waters et al., 2013). In addition, studies have found that pediatricians often do not ask about children's sleep issues especially after infancy and toddlerhood due to lack of physician training on sleep, insufficient time, lack of understanding about the seriousness of insufficient sleep on children's functioning, and the belief that parents will bring it up on their own if there is a problem (Bhargava, 2011; Meltzer et al., 2010, 2014). Documentation on sleep recommendations/referrals in the medical record also is rare, and many standardized assessments at well-child visits do not have standardized questions on sleep (Meltzer et al., 2010). This is particularly concerning as research has found that sleep problems tend to persist or even worsen over time without the necessary intervention, and many children with sleep problems may be prone to having more sick visits (Byars et al., 2012; Meltzer et al., 2014; Owens & Mindell, 2011).

Research has documented that improvements in quality and duration of sleep lead to better mental health and physical health outcomes overall (Gruber et al., 2011; Paruthi et al., 2016). Thus timely assessment and appropriate treatment of sleep problems in youth are advised. Consequently, it is important for providers in pediatric settings to become well-equipped at screening and treating these sleep issues. It is also advised that clinicians offer education on healthy sleep habits preventatively to improve the chances of children developing healthy sleep habits in the first place (Gruber et al., 2011). While sleep issues can have many undesirable and potentially harmful effects, the good news is that there are many effective strategies to prevent and/or treat these issues. The purpose of this chapter is to better educate providers in pediatric settings about common sleep issues facing children in their practices and to provide developmentally appropriate and evidence-based recommendations and strategies to treat them.

Recommended amounts of sleep

To assess whether children are getting enough sleep, it is important to understand the sleep needs across the different developmental periods. In 2016 the American Academy of Pediatrics (AAP) endorsed the following consensus sleep guidelines, titled "Recommended Amount of Sleep for Pediatric Populations," based on recommendations made by the American Academy of Sleep Medicine for sleep duration for infants to adolescents [American Academy of Pediatrics (AAP), 2016; Paruthi et al., 2016]. See Table 10.1 for their recommended sleep durations. The AAP also recommended that these guidelines be shared with parents and youth during clinical visits.

TABLE 10.1 Recommended sleep durations for children.

Ages	Recommended sleep durations
Infants 4–12 months	12–16 h/day, including naps
Children 1–2 years of age	11–14 h/day, including naps
Preschool children 3–5 years of age	10–13 h/day, including naps
School-aged children 6–12 years of age	9–12 h/day
Adolescents 13–18 years of age	8–10 h/day

Assessment

To formally assess sleep, routine well visits should include questions about bedtimes, duration of sleep, and sleep problems that a child may be experiencing so that recommendations for interventions and/or referral to a sleep specialist can be made to address these issues (Waters et al., 2013). Obtaining a thorough family history of sleep disorders is also recommended as many disorders, such as OSA, narcolepsy, and restless legs syndrome, can be inherited (Moturi & Avis, 2010). It is also important that older children and adolescents be asked directly about their sleep, as parents may not know about sleep delays since they may be less involved at bedtime (Meltzer et al., 2014). Due to findings that link sleep deficits with behavior problems, parents should be asked about problematic behaviors such as hyperactivity, concentration problems, aggression, irritability, noncompliance, and impulsivity as these behaviors may be indicators of sleep problems.

Furthermore, educating parents on these symptoms may help them to better identify their child's sleep cues, leading to timelier bedtimes (Gruber et al., 2011).

TABLE 10.2 BEARS screening questions[a] (Mindell & Owens, 2015).

B = Bedtime problems	
E = Excessive daytime sleepiness	
A = Awakenings during the night	
R = Regularity and duration of sleep	
S = Sleep-disordered breathing	

[a]*Used with permission from Wolters Kluwer.*

Sleep diaries completed by parents or older children/teens for a 2-week period prior to their clinic visit also are recommended to guide the assessment process. These can detect variability in sleep patterns that otherwise may be missed during the history-taking process (Moturi & Avis, 2010). Sleep diaries should include time in bed, sleep-onset time, night wakings, total sleep time at night, nap time/duration, and final wake time (Honaker & Meltzer, 2014). The BEARS (Mindell & Owens, 2015) is a brief, free, five-item screening tool recommended for use in the primary care setting (see Table 10.2). The BEARS acronym has been used to help clinicians remember the different areas of sleep to assess during their appointments (Bhargava, 2011; Waters et al., 2013). If parent or child answers yes to any of the questions, clinicians should ask for additional information. Use of the BEARS has been shown to better detect sleep problems in the pediatric setting (Bhargava, 2011; Mindell & Owens, 2015). Handout 1 is a brief clinician reference with the BEARS, a list of screening questions, and recommended sleep hours.

Pediatric insomnia

Pediatric insomnia is the most common sleep disorder in childhood. It impacts approximately 20%–30% of infants and toddlers and up to 5% of school-aged children. It is most common in children aged 0–5 but also can impact older children and adolescents (Meltzer et al., 2010; Owens & Mindell, 2011; Owens, 2018; Vriend & Corkum, 2011). The primary symptoms include difficulty falling asleep, settling problems, and/or problems maintaining sleep leading to insufficient sleep for the child (Meltzer & Mindell, 2014). Pediatric insomnia also may also lead to significant impairment in a parent's life, including reduced sleep, deficits in daytime functioning, parenting stress, and marital conflict (Bhargava, 2011).

Behavioral insomnia of childhood is pediatric insomnia with a behavioral component such as an inappropriate sleep association (i.e., not being able to fall asleep without a parent's presence, being rocked to sleep, needing the television on, and falling asleep with a bottle) or poor limit-setting by the caregiver (Bhargava, 2011; Owens & Mindell, 2011). Behavioral insomnia includes bedtime refusal or resistance, delayed sleep onset, and prolonged and/or frequent night wakings and often is a combination of the above, all of which require parental intervention (Honaker & Meltzer, 2014; Meltzer, 2010). It is diagnosed after the age of 6 months since parental intervention and frequent wakings are considered normal prior to 6 months of age (Meltzer, 2010).

Numerous studies have demonstrated the effectiveness of behavioral interventions (such as graduated extinction, bedtime routines, and sleep education) for pediatric insomnia with large effect sizes (Honaker & Meltzer, 2014; Meltzer & Mindell, 2014; Mindell, Telofski, Wiegand, & Kurtz, 2009).

For instance, a meta-analysis of 16 controlled trials and 12 within-subjects studies of behavioral interventions for insomnia in young children 0–17.9 years of age found a moderate level of evidence supporting the use of behavioral interventions. The meta-analysis specifically found significant positive effects for sleep-onset latency, number of night wakings, duration of night wakings, and sleep efficiency outcomes in typical children. As a result, the implementation of these behavioral interventions in clinical practice was highly recommended (Meltzer & Mindell, 2014).

Additional literature reviews and numerous studies also have examined the effectiveness of specific behavioral interventions for infants, toddlers, and young children. Behavioral interventions should be the first line of treatment recommended to parents, as these interventions help children fall asleep and stay asleep without their parent's assistance leading to longer sleep duration and improved sleep quality (Moturi & Avis, 2010; Owens & Mindell, 2011).

Prior to implementing specific interventions for insomnia, it is recommended that medical providers screen for and rule out any medical, psychiatric, or developmental disorders that may be contributing to insomnia. Providers should also assess children's nap schedules, as inappropriately timed or inconsistent napping can lead to symptoms of insomnia (Moturi & Avis, 2010). The next section will include information on the most commonly studied and recommended behavioral interventions for specific bedtime problems.

Interventions for sleep-onset association insomnia

Sleep-onset associated insomnia is very common among infants, toddlers, and even older children and involves children needing a certain activity, place, or someone (e.g., parent) to help them fall asleep at bedtime or during the night. Common presentations include needing to fall asleep during activities such as breastfeeding, cosleeping, and being rocked, held, or comforted (Bhargava, 2011; Honaker & Meltzer, 2014). These associations frequently lead to reduced sleep duration as they prolong time to sleep, and children do not learn how to soothe themselves to sleep without intervention at bedtime or after awaking. The interventions most recommended and found to be empirically supported for these issues are geared towards infants and young children and involve sleep hygiene/parent education regarding use of developmentally appropriate and consistent bedtimes (usually between 7:00 and 8:30 p.m.), as well as the use of a bedtime routine (Bhargava, 2011; Honaker & Meltzer, 2014; Meltzer, 2010; Mindell, Li, Sadeh, Kwon, & Goh, 2015; Moturi & Avis, 2010; Waters et al., 2013). Education is highly cost-effective and efficacious and can be preventative when parents are provided information about good sleep habits early in the child's development (Honaker & Meltzer, 2014). Preventative education methods also include teaching parents to observe their child/infant's cues for sleepiness and then placing them sleepy but awake in their crib or bed so that they learn to fall asleep on their own and "self-soothe." An important benefit to this is that when they wake up in the night, they can get themselves to sleep without parents' intervention (Bhargava, 2011). This is especially important as night wakings or brief arousals are normal, and most people learn to fall back asleep quickly and on their own (Owens & Mindell, 2011). Additional interventions for infants include directing parents to differentiate nighttime from daytime by keeping night wakings calm in a dark and quiet room and refraining from stimulating interactions or play in contrast to more stimulating daytime activities.

Use of bedtime routines is empirically supported and leads to increased total sleep duration, shorter sleep-onset latency, fewer number and duration of night wakings, earlier bedtimes, and less parental reports of sleep problems in young children (Meltzer, 2010; Mindell et al., 2009, 2015). Bedtime routines typically involve soothing, prebedtime activities lasting no longer than 30 minutes that are implemented at the same time and in the same order every night. They typically involve a few activities that end in the bedroom, which are highly reinforcing to children such as reading and singing. Positive bedtime routines are a variation on bedtime routines that add the use of praise and positive reinforcement after each step in the routine to increase compliance. The routine is ended if a child has a tantrum or is noncompliant and the child is put to bed at that point (Moturi & Avis, 2010). For example, one recommended routine could be a short bath, put on pajamas, brush teeth, use the potty, and parents read a book in a child's bed before lights out. Parents would praise them after each step and would prompt them for the next activity to keep the momentum going. Parents are also educated on the concept of the extinction burst in that a child's behaviors often get worse before they get better when a new intervention is initiated (Mindell & Owens, 2015). Parents are instructed on being consistent with their approach, not giving in, and eventually, a child's negative behaviors will decrease.

Extinction procedures are also highly recommended, and both unmodified extinction and graduated extinction have been found to be highly effective in the literature (Gradisar et al., 2016; Honaker & Meltzer, 2014; Meltzer, 2010). Unmodified extinction procedures, also known as "crying it out," involve the parent putting the child to bed awake, monitoring for safety, and ignoring any crying and/or calling out until the next morning (Honaker & Meltzer, 2014). Although extinction is highly successful when implemented properly, it can be highly stressful for both children and parents and can lead to parents not implementing the procedures consistently or abandoning these methods altogether. "Crying it out" is not recommended for newborns and young infants because they are unable to soothe themselves yet and they require support from their parents. The predictable, repeated, holding, soothing, swaddling, rocking, and parent–child interactions in the context of a low-stress home environment during infancy set the stage for self-soothing skills.

Graduated extinction, also known as progressive delay responding, may be more acceptable to many parents. It is considered highly effective even though it may take longer to achieve results (Gradisar et al., 2016; Honaker & Meltzer, 2014; Meltzer, 2010; Moturi & Avis, 2010). This approach involves parents putting the child to bed awake and then ignoring any crying and/or calling out for progressively longer periods of time before a brief response like "go to sleep" is given. Each night the length of time is increased (i.e., 3, 5, and 10 minutes) until the child is falling asleep on their own and/or through the night (Honaker & Meltzer, 2014). This can be used at bedtime and/or during night wakings. Providers help parents decide on how long to wait based on their child's temperament and parent's tolerance to crying (Bhargava, 2011; Honaker & Meltzer, 2014).

Bedtime fading has also been highly recommended in the literature for children over the age of 3 who have late or delayed bedtimes. This involves initially putting children to bed to match the time a child normally falls asleep and then gradually fading the bedtime backward (earlier) every night until the desired bedtime is achieved (Gradisar et al., 2016; Honaker & Meltzer, 2014). Consistent wake times also are used to facilitate an earlier bedtime. Consistency is the key to all of the above behavioral interventions.

Case example

Billy is a 3-year-old boy who cries every night after his parents tuck him in. His parents have started staying in his room and will rub his back until he falls asleep. When they try to leave before he falls asleep, he will cry and they will resume rubbing his back. His parents tell his pediatrician, Dr. Smith, that they are frustrated by how long it takes to get Billy to sleep. Dr. Smith recommends graduated extinction/progressive delay responding. He recommends Billy's parents tuck him in at his usual bedtime of 8:00 p.m. after all of his needs have been met. Parents are then directed to tell Billy that it is time to go to bed and that they will see him in the morning. Dr. Smith explains that Billy will definitely call out for his parents or cry for them since he is used to their attention. He recommends that the parents wait for 5 minutes before going into Billy's room even though he is crying for them. He tells the parents that after 5 minutes, to go into his room and tell Billy calmly "time to go to sleep." He tells the parents that they should follow this procedure for the remainder of the night, waiting 5 minutes before going into his room. He recommended doing this for the first two nights, and at the third night, wait 8 minutes before responding. Dr. Smith tells them to increase the time that they wait to respond every two to three nights until he is falling asleep on his own. He tells them they are to ignore his crying, they are not to rub his back, and they are not to talk to him until the brief check-in time when they simply say "time to go to sleep." Dr. Smith educates them about the extinction burst phenomena that predicts that his crying will get worse before it gets better, and as long as they stick to the program, his crying will eventually disappear.

Interventions for limit-setting association insomnia

Some bedtime delays are considered to be due to insufficient limit setting on the parent's part and involve children delaying their bedtime by repeatedly getting out of bed, stalling, throwing tantrums, and/or refusing to go to sleep. In these cases, parents do not set consistent limits with their child's noncompliant behavior and frequently give in to their child's demands, which further reinforce negative behaviors and maintain the sleep delay. This form of insomnia typically occurs after the age of 2 when children are mobile, and it may cooccur with night wakings (Bhargava, 2011).

Behavioral interventions for Limit-Setting Association Insomnia include the use of sleep hygiene education methods described above but also include teaching parents to have bedtime rules and to put the child consistently back in bed each time with minimal interactions (Bhargava, 2011; Meltzer, 2010). Use of positive reinforcement is recommended for appropriate behaviors. For example, parents can praise children for following the bedtime routine and staying in bed and provide a reinforcer or reward immediately the next morning. In Billy's case, for example, the parents can rub his back on mornings after he successfully stays in bed without calling out. For any of the above interventions, parents are again instructed about the "extinction burst" phenomenon where behaviors get worse before they get better especially by day 2 (Bhargava, 2011).

Case example

Jessica is a 4-year-old girl who refuses to stay in bed after her parents put her to bed at 9:00 p.m. She reportedly gets out of her bed, demands water or a snack, asks for another book, says she has to use the bathroom, or says she is scared. Her parents will sometimes get her a snack or read her another book but she still gets out of bed and throws herself down on the ground screaming and refusing to go to bed. Sometimes it takes an hour to get her to lie down before eventually falling asleep. Her parents ask her pediatrician, Dr. Brown, for help. Dr. Brown educates them on appropriate sleep times for preschoolers and recommends that parents start her bedtime at 8:00 p.m. She instructs them on using a consistent bedtime routine every night and suggests a snack, pajamas, brushing her teeth, and having parents read her one to two short books once the rest of the routine is complete. She recommends that parents make sure all of her needs have been met before her routine begins, because once they put her in bed, they are not to give into any of her demands. She tells them that, giving into her demands, even one time, will be enough for her to keep testing their limits and her tantrums will continue. She recommends that each time she gets out of bed, they pick her up and put her into bed without giving into any of her demands and they should not even talk to her except to say, "see you in the morning." Dr. Brown instructs them that her tantrums may worsen once they start this new plan. She tells them that as long as they are consistent, her behavior will getter better over time.

Psychophysiologic or primary insomnia

Older children and adolescents can also struggle with insomnia involving sleep-onset or sleep maintenance issues. Unlike insomnia in younger children, the contributing factors are more likely to be related to physiological arousal and anxiety about sleep rather than parental behaviors, which is why it is frequently called psychophysiologic or primary insomnia (Owens & Mindell, 2011). Few studies have looked at treatments for insomnia in adolescents. However, the most recommended strategies involve reducing prebedtime arousal and include sleep hygiene education, use of set bed and wake times, eliminating naps, using beds for sleeping only, use of a variety of cognitive-behavioral therapy strategies to reduce anxiety, reducing stimulating activities at bedtime (screen time), and removing electronics from bedrooms (Moturi & Avis, 2010; Owens & Mindell, 2011).

Case example

Jake is a 13-year-old who has difficulty falling asleep each night. He tries to go to bed at 11:00 p.m. but often takes 2 hours to fall asleep each night. He often complains that his mind is always thinking about things like what he needs to do the next day. He usually plays on his phone or watches Netflix until he falls asleep. He has a hard time waking up at 6:00 am for school and often misses the bus because he cannot get ready in time. When he gets home from school, he usually falls asleep on his bed doing homework. When he wakes up, he drinks a soda to help him get through his homework. Jake's mother brings him to his pediatrician, Dr. Gomez, for help. Dr. Gomez recommends that Jake eliminate caffeine in the afternoon. He tells him to start doing his homework in the kitchen in order to avoid napping, which is most likely contributing to his insomnia. He also recommends unplugging from his electronic devices by 8.00 p.m. to help with winding down and that he should charge his phone in the kitchen to avoid the temptation of using it at night. He recommends that Jake only get into his bed when wanting to fall asleep and recommends a 10:00 p.m. bedtime. Dr. Gomez tells Jake that if he is still awake after 15 minutes, he should get out of bed and read in the living room until getting sleepy and that he should repeat this procedure until he is able to fall asleep. He also recommends listening to a relaxation CD once he is lying in bed, along with writing down his thoughts/worries in a journal at bedtime so they do not keep him awake.

Sleep-disordered breathing

SDB is another common sleep issue which consists of nocturnal breathing abnormalities and includes both habitual/primary snoring and OSA. Habitual snoring is considered snoring without any obstructive events, while OSA consists of sleep fragmentation and intermittent hypoxia (Bhargava, 2011; O'Brien, 2015). It tends to peak in the preschool years/early childhood due to the ratio of tonsils and adenoids compared to airway size (Bhargava, 2011; O'Brien, 2015). Symptoms of SDB impacts approximately 4%–20% of children, whereas habitual snoring occurs in 1.5% – 6% of children (O'Brien, 2015). OSA verified via polysomnography occurs in 1%–4% of children (O'Brien, 2015).

OSA is associated with numerous negative consequences including pulmonary hypertension, cardiovascular problems, poor growth, learning deficits, and behavioral problems if left untreated (Waters et al., 2013). Unlike the behavioral sleep disturbances, OSA is more likely to go unnoticed, as most parents do not observe apnea events. Consequently, researchers believe that OSA is underdiagnosed and that the prevalence rate is most likely much higher. Thus assessing for risk factors is important. The most common risk factors for OSA include snoring and adenotonsillar hypertrophy (Bhargava, 2011). In 2012 the AAP revised their previous 2002 evidenced-based clinical practice guidelines to provide updated recommendations for diagnosis and treatment of OSA in the pediatric population. In that guideline the AAP mandates that all children/adolescents should be assessed for snoring at every well visit (AAP, 2012).

Because some children have OSA and do not snore, providers should screen for additional risk factors, such as obesity, daytime fatigue, daytime mouth breathing, reactive airway disease, chronic sinus problems, restless sleep, sweating while sleeping, parasomnias, African-American race, family history of OSA, and presence of craniofacial abnormalities at birth (AAP, 2012; Bhargava, 2011; Durmer & Chervin, 2007; Moturi & Avis, 2010). Providers also should be aware of other associated features of OSA including chronic morning headaches, dry mouth/throat, nocturnal enuresis, history of chronic ear infections, early morning thirst, chronic nasal congestion, and feelings of grogginess after waking up (Moturi & Avis, 2010). Numerous studies have found that children with OSA are more likely to exhibit symptoms of inattention, hyperactivity and impulsivity that mimic attention deficit hyperactivity disorder (ADHD) (Herman, 2015; Moturi & Avis, 2010). This is likely due to OSA's significant negative impact on sleep duration and quality producing fragmented sleep.

Thus screening for OSA in children with ADHD symptoms is of utmost importance to prevent misdiagnosing children with ADHD and providing appropriate treatment for OSA (Herman, 2015; Moturi & Avis, 2010).

Polysomnography (PSG) is the gold standard in the assessment of OSA. The thresholds for OSA in youth are lower than adults, with OSA being defined as one or more obstructive events per hour of sleep on a PSG (Waters et al., 2013). AAP (2012) recommends that an overnight PSG should be performed for children who snore and have symptoms OSA, and if a PSG is not accessible, then other diagnostic tests or referrals to specialists should be considered. Because OSA tends to persist and even worsen over time, adenotonsillectomy (AT) is the primary treatment of choice and has a high success rate (Moturi & Avis, 2010; Waters et al., 2013). A meta-analysis found that symptoms of OSA are alleviated in up to 83% cases after AT in healthy children (Brietzke & Gallagher, 2006; Moturi & Avis, 2010). Older age, obesity, and severe initial disease are factors that may reduce the success rates, although AT does reduce the severity of OSA in obese children (Waters et al., 2013). AAP (2012) recommends that AT be the first line of therapy for children with adenotonsillar hypertrophy and that high-risk patients should be monitored as inpatients postoperatively. It also recommends that patients should be reevaluated after the operation to assess whether further treatment is needed, that objective assessment should be performed in patients who are considered high risk or have lasting symptoms of OSA after treatment and that continuous positive airway pressure should be used if an AT is not performed or if OSA continues. Furthermore, AAP (2012) recommends weight loss in patients who are overweight or obese in addition to other treatment and that intranasal corticosteroids may be considered for children with mild OSA if AT is not indicated or for mild postoperative OSA.

Parasomnias

Parasomnias are also common in children and involve unwelcome physical events that occur during sleep (Bhargava, 2011). The most common parasomnias include bruxism (grinding teeth), sleep talking, nightmares, night terrors, and sleepwalking. Parasomnias are usually benign and can be inherited. Children frequently outgrow them as they age, and are typically absent by adolescence (Waters et al., 2013). Parasomnias affect between 5% and 35% of children depending on the disorder and age group (Meltzer et al., 2010). They can be very upsetting to parents, especially as children usually have no recollection of these occurrences aside from nightmares. Parents are more likely to report on parasomnias than OSA if asked, since they are more noticeable and frequently require parental intervention.

The most common evidence-based interventions for any parasomnia is education including increasing duration of sleep and use of good sleep hygiene prior to bedtime, as sleep deprivation and/or sleep fragmentation are leading causal factors. Even an extra 30 minutes of sleep can significantly reduce parasomnias (Waters et al., 2013). Assessing reasons for chronic inadequate sleep, and screening for possible OSA or other sleep-related disorders are also recommended, as parasomnias (especially night terrors) frequently cooccur with OSA (Bhargava, 2011; Moturi & Avis, 2010). This may necessitate a referral to a sleep specialist. Aspects of illness such as a fever can also lead to parasomnias and may be acute in nature. Relaxation techniques can also be used to help children feel less anxious before bed (Waters et al., 2013). For sleepwalking, safety proofing a child's room, placing a child's mattress on the floor, and putting extra locks on doors to prevent children from leaving the home are all strategies to increase child safety (Waters et al., 2013).

Media recommendations

Most children today have access and significant exposure to various forms of media whether it be from televisions, computers, smartphones, gaming systems, or tablets. Many studies have found that frequent use of media and screen time before bedtime and increased access to devices in bedrooms is a major contributing factor to sleep deprivation and bedtime delays in youth. Hale and Guan (2015) found that in 90% of the studies reviewed, all types of screen time were negatively associated with sleep outcomes including reduced sleep duration and sleep onset delays (Hale & Guan, 2015). Furthermore, Falbe et al. (2014) found that children who sleep near a screen, sleep with a TV in the bedroom and/or have high amounts of total screen time had less sleep in general. Since media usage is not likely going away anytime soon, it is important for providers to ask about media use/screen time at bedtime. In order to improve sleep outcome and reduce the negative impact of media use on sleep, the AAP recommends that all screens be turned off 30 minutes before bedtime and that no screens be allowed in children's bedrooms (AAP, 2016).

Summary

- Sleep problems are common among children, and providers should screen for sleep problems at every well visit.
- The BEARS is a quick and efficient screening tool and is highly recommended.
- Parents should be educated on sleep needs and provided with education on good sleep hygiene.
- Behavioral strategies are empirically supported to help with pediatric insomnia which is the most common sleep problem in children.
- All children should be screened for snoring, along with other risk factors of OSA at well-visits.
- Polysomnography (PSG) is the gold standard for ruling out SDB/OSA from snoring.
- AT is the treatment of choice for OSA in most children.
- Parents should be educated to enforce rules including no screens in bedroom and screens should be turned off at least 30 minutes before bed.

Handout 1. Quick reference guide for clinicians on children's sleep

Recommended sleep duration for children

Ages	Recommended sleep duration
Infants 4–12 months	12–16 h/day, including naps*
Children 1–2 years of age	11–14 h/day, including naps*
Preschool children 3–5 years of age	10–13 h/day, including naps*
School-aged children 6–12 years of age	9–12 h/day*
Adolescents 13–18 years of age	8–10 h/day*

*As cited by AAP (2016) and Paruthi et al.(2016).

BEARS screening questions (Mindell & Owens, 2015)

B = Bedtime problems
E = Excessive daytime sleepiness
A = Awakenings during the night
R = Regularity and duration of sleep
S = Sleep-disordered breathing/Snoring

Questions to ask parents

- Time in bed
- Time to sleep
- Wake up time in the morning
- Naptimes and length of naps
- Does child appear overly tired or sleepy during the day/Have difficulty waking up in the morning
- Access to electronics/media/screens/TV in bedroom
- Behavioral difficulties (hyperactivity, inattention, impulsivity, aggression, noncompliance)
- Parasomnias (sleepwalking, night terrors, sleep talking, nightmares, teeth grinding)

Important points to remember

- Sleep problems can lead to significant sleep deficits in youth leading to a variety of negative consequences such as behavior issues, inattention, hyperactivity, academic and learning issues, neurocognitive deficits, deficits in daytime functioning, anxiety, depression, parental/family stress, and health issues including obesity, growth deficits, hypertension, cardiovascular problems, and increased accidents/injuries.
- Parents should be asked about problematic behaviors such as hyperactivity, concentration problems, aggression, irritability, noncompliance, and impulsivity as these behaviors may be indicators of sleep problems.
- Numerous studies have demonstrated the effectiveness of behavioral interventions (such as graduated extinction, bedtime routines, and sleep education) for pediatric insomnia with large effect sizes.
- Behavioral interventions should be the first line of treatment recommended to parents as these interventions help children fall asleep and stay asleep without their parents' assistance leading to longer sleep duration and improved sleep quality.
- The American Academy of Pediatrics mandates that all children/ adolescents should be assessed for snoring at every well visit.
- Numerous studies have found that children with OSA are more likely to exhibit symptoms of ADHD including inattention and, hyperactivity and impulsivity that mimic ADHD. This is likely due to OSA's significant negative impact on sleep duration and quality.

References

American Academy of Pediatrics. (2012). Clinical practice guideline: Diagnosis and management of childhood obstructive sleep apnea syndrome. *Pediatrics, 130*(3), 576–584.

American Academy of Pediatrics (AAP). *American Academy of Pediatrics supports childhood sleep guidelines*. (2016). Retrieved from American Academy of Pediatrics website <https://www.aap.org/en-us/about-the-aap/aap-press-room/Pages/American-Academy-of-Pediatrics-Supports-Childhood-Sleep-Guidelines.aspx>.

Bhargava, S. (2011). Diagnosis and management of common sleep problems in children. *Pediatrics in Review, 32*(3), 91–99. Available from https://doi.org/10.1542/pir.32-3-91.

Brietzke, S. E., & Gallagher, D. (2006). The effectiveness of tonsillectomy and adenoidectomy in the treatment of pediatric obstructive sleep apnea/hypopnea syndrome: A meta-analysis. *Otolaryngology—Head and Neck Surgery, 134*(6), 979–984.

Byars, K. C., Yolton, K., Rausch, J., Lanphear, B., & Beebe, D. W. (2012). Prevalence, patterns, and persistence of sleep problems in the first 3 years of life. *Pediatrics, 129*(2), e276–e284.

Durmer, J. S., & Chervin, R. D. (2007). Pediatric sleep medicine. *CONTINUUM: Lifelong Learning in Neurology, 13*(3), 153–200.

Falbe, J., Davison, K. K., Franckle, R. L., Ganter, C., Gortmaker, S. L., Smith, L., ... Taveras, E. M. (2014). Sleep duration, restfulness, and screens in the sleep environment. *Pediatrics, 135*(2), e367–e375.

Gradisar, M., Jackson, K., Spurrier, N. J., Gibson, J., Whitham, J., Williams, A. S., ... Kennaway, D. J. (2016). Behavioral interventions for infant sleep problems: A randomized control trial. *Pediatrics, 137*(6), e20151486.

Gruber, R., Cassoff, J., & Knauper, B. (2011). Sleep health education in pediatric community settings: Rationale and practical suggestions for incorporating healthy sleep education into pediatric practice. *Pediatric Clinics of North America, 58*, 735–754.

Hale, L., & Guan, S. (2015). Screen time and sleep among school-aged children and adolescents: A systematic literature review. *Sleep Medicine Reviews, 21*, 50–58.

Herman, D. (2015). Attention deficit/hyperactivity disorder and sleep in children. *Sleep Medicine Clinic, 10*, 143–149. Available from https://doi.org/10.1016/j.jsmc.2015.02.003.

Honaker, S. M., & Meltzer, L. J. (2014). Bedtime problems and night wakings in young children: An update of the evidence. *Paediatric Respiratory Reviews, 15*, 333–339.

Maski, K., & Kothare, S. V. (2013). Sleep deprivation and neurobehavioral functioning in children. *International Journal of Psychophysiology, 89*, 259–264.

Meltzer, L. J. (2010). Clinical management of behavioral insomnia of childhood: Treatment of bedtime problems and night wakings in young children. *Behavioral Sleep Medicine, 8* (3), 172–189.

Meltzer, L. J., Johnson, C., Crosette, J., Ramos, M., & Mindell, J. A. (2010). Prevalence of diagnosed sleep disorders in pediatric primary care practices. *Pediatrics, 125*(6), e1410–e1418.

Meltzer, L. J., & Mindell, J. A. (2014). Systematic review and meta-analysis of behavioral interventions for pediatric insomnia. *Journal of Pediatric Psychology, 39*(8), 932–948.

Meltzer, L. J., Plaufcan, M. R., Thomas, J. H., & Mindell, J. A. (2014). Sleep problems and sleep disorders in pediatric primary care: Treatment recommendations, persistence, and health care utilization. *Journal of Clinical Sleep Medicine, 10*(4), 421–426.

Mindell, J., & Owens, J. (2015). *A clinical guide to pediatric sleep: Diagnosis and management of sleep problems* (3rd ed.). Philadelphia, PA: Wolters Kluwer.

Mindell, J. A., Li, A. M., Sadeh, A., Kwon, R., & Goh, D. (2015). Bedtime routines for young children: A dose-dependent association with sleep outcomes. *Sleep, 38*(5), 717–722.

Mindell, J. A., Telofski, L. S., Wiegand, B., & Kurtz, E. S. (2009). A nightly bedtime routine: Impact on sleep in young children and maternal mood. *Sleep, 32*(5), 599–606.

Moturi, S., & Avis, K. A. (2010). Assessment and treatment of common pediatric sleep disorders. *Psychiatry, 7*(6), 24–37.

O'Brien, L. M. (2015). Sleep-related breathing disorder, cognitive functioning, and behavioral-psychiatric syndromes in children. *Sleep Medicine Clinic, 10*, 169–179.

Owens, J. A. (2008). Sleep disorders and attention-deficit/hyperactivity disorder. *Current Psychiatry Reports, 10*, 439.

Owens, J. A. (2018). Behavioral sleep problems in children. In R. D. Chervin, & A. G. Hoppin (Eds.), *UpToDate*. Waltham, MA: UpToDate Inc. <https://www.uptodate.com/contents/behavioral-sleep-problems-in-children>. Accessed 28.06.18.

Owens, J. A., & Mindell, J. A. (2011). Pediatric insomnia. *Pediatric Clinics of North America, 58*, 555–569.

Paruthi, S., Brooks, L. J., D'Ambrosio, C., Hall, W. A., Kotagal, S., Lloyd, R. M., ... Wise, M. S. (2016). Concensus statement of the American Academy of Sleep Medicine on the recommended amount of sleep for healthy children: Methodology and discussion. *Journal of Clinical Sleep Medicine, 12*(11), 1549–1561.

Vriend, J., & Corkum, P. (2011). Clinical management of behavioral insomnia of childhood. *Psychology Research and Behavior Management, 4*, 69–79.

Waters, K. A., Suresh, S., & Nixon, G. M. (2013). Sleep disorders in children. *Medical Journal of Australia, 199*(8), S31–S35.

CHAPTER

11

Sexual development: it's not just for teens*

Amy Russell

Russell Consulting Specialists, LLC, Vancouver, WA, United States

Talk to her about sex, and start early. It will probably be a bit awkward, but it is necessary. ***Chimamanda Ngozi Adichie, Dear Ijeawele, or a Feminist Manifesto in Fifteen Suggestions (2017).***

Introduction

Understanding sexual development in children and youth of all ages is as helpful as understanding cognitive, social, and physical development (South Australian Government, Department for Education and Child Development, Catholic Education SA, & Association of Independent Schools of SA, 2013). When caregivers are able to recognize typical, healthy sexual development as well as concerning, maladaptive, or problematic sexual development, attitudes, and behaviors in children, they can do better at establishing appropriate boundaries, helping shape healthy sexual relationships, and ensuring safety for their children and others around them. Caregivers, and the professionals who support them should be familiar with what is expected from children and youth throughout their sexual development, so they can better seek out assistance when sexually inappropriate or concerning behaviors and emotions are identified (South Australian Government, Department for Education and Child Development et al., 2013). Unfortunately,

* Portions of this paper were originally published in the William Mitchell Law Review, Vol. 40(3), 2014. Reprinted with permission of the author.

Clinician's Toolkit for Children's Behavioral Health
DOI: https://doi.org/10.1016/B978-0-12-816024-4.00011-5

caregivers may be less likely to accurately identify concerning and problematic sexual behaviors than normative sexual behaviors in children and youth, especially for children ages 4 years and younger (Marriage et al., 2017). Similarly, caregivers may struggle with how to appropriately intervene when they are able to identify concerning and problematic behaviors; this is especially true when young children exhibit maladaptive sexual behaviors (Marriage et al., 2017).

When caregivers lack understanding of normative sexual development, they may become overly punitive with children or become disengaged and not respond with appropriate boundary-setting for healthy development, leading to sexual fears or inhibitions as youth age (Kurtuncu, Akhan, Tanir, & Yildiz, 2015). Furthermore, this lack of understanding can result in inappropriate referrals to the child welfare, mental health, and juvenile justice systems, potentially resulting in inappropriate determinations and classifications, and subsequent stigmatization of youth who are not sexually inappropriate or aggressive. When youth display sexualized behaviors as a result of their own sexual development, family norms, cultural practices, or their own victimization, this normative sexual play or sexual reactivity is often mislabeled and may lead to inappropriate diagnoses and treatment (Thigpen & Fortenberry, 2009). A lack of understanding of normal sexual development may also lead to the premature dismissal of inappropriate sexual behaviors as cases of "children being children."

Professionals such as medical and mental health-care providers can be instrumental in preventing these negative outcomes by providing education on children's sexual development for caregivers. Therefore it is vitally important for medical and mental health-care providers to be able to recognize concerning sexualized or sexually reactive behaviors in children and youth, and to accurately provide information, support, and referrals to caregivers when appropriate (Breuner, Mattson, AAP Committee on Adolescence, & AAP Committee on Psychosocial Aspects of Child and Family Health, 2016; Kurtuncu et al., 2015). While it is critical for children to receive appropriate referrals and treatment for inappropriate behaviors, it is also important not to "overrespond" to them.

Understanding normative sexual development in children and youth

It is not uncommon for adults to attach "adult" meanings and motivations to children's behaviors (Vosmer, Hackett, & Callanan, 2009). Youth advocates express frustration that, as a result of this type of misattribution, a "7-year-old child could never return home again after two incidents of genital fondling of a 5-year-old sibling"; that a 12-year-old is perceived as a "predatory pedophile for life" after experimental, consensual sexual contact with another same-age child; and 10-year-old children are being forced to register as sex offenders across the country (Chaffin & Bonner, 1998).

Research tells us that between 40% and 85% of the children will engage in some sexualized behaviors with other children before they turn 18 (Johnson, 1996). When assessing these behaviors, caregivers and professionals should pay attention to the context of the behaviors. When the interaction is between children or youth, it is particularly important to determine whether the children who engage in the behaviors are of similar age, size, and developmental levels (Chaffin et al., 2008; Johnson, 1996). If there are no power differentials between the children, and if the participation of the children is mutual and voluntary, it may be considered normative developmental behavior (Kenny, Dinehart, & Wurtele, 2015; South Australian Government, Department for Education and Child Development et al., 2013). When limited in type and frequency, when the activities are spontaneous, and when the children participate for information-gathering and exploration purposes, it may be normative play (Chaffin et al., 2008; Johnson, 1996; Kenny et al., 2015; South Australian Government, Department for Education and Child Development et al., 2013). The ages and the culture of the children involved also impact the behaviors in which children may engage (Chaffin et al., 2008; Friedrich, Fisher, Broughton, Houston, & Shafran, 1998; South Australian Government, Department for Education and Child Development et al., 2013).

Sexual behaviors exhibited by children change as they mature (Friedrich et al., 1998; Miragoli, Camisasca, & Di Blasio, 2017). Some examples of normative sexual behaviors in children ages 2–6 years include masturbation or self-touching, showing their genitals to and looking at the genitals of their peers, as well as attempts to view adults in the nude (American Academy of Pediatrics, 2014; Kenny et al., 2015).

Children of this age may engage in games such as "doctor" and demonstrate an interest in body parts and their functions; these young children may also enjoy taking off their clothes and being nude (South Australian Government, Department for Education and Child Development et al., 2013). Normative sexualized behaviors may be exhibited more frequently in children up to 6 years of age than in the later years. This may be explained as a natural expression of their curiosity about their bodies when young, as well as an impact of social norms and prohibitions regarding public expressions of sexuality and sexual behaviors as they age (Miragoli et al., 2017).

Nonaggressive kissing between similar-aged children and self-stimulation that occurs in private are generally typical and natural sexual behaviors for children between 6 and 9 years of age (South Australian Government, Department for Education and Child Development et al., 2013; Vosmer et al., 2009). During this time of development, children may masturbate to self-sooth and begin to demonstrate an increased sense of privacy about their bodies (South Australian Government, Department for Education and Child Development et al., 2013).

They may also talk about genitalia and sex acts using profanity, demonstrate an increased interest in gender differences, seek out others of the same age to look at or touch their genitals, and express more interest in more "adult" sexuality (South Australian Government, Department for Education and Child Development et al., 2013). These normative behaviors are brief in nature, occur occasionally, and are easily redirected (American Academy of Pediatrics, 2014; Johnson, 2002; South Australian Government, Department for Education and Child Development et al., 2013).

Youth ages 10–12 years begin to formulate their associations with sex and girlfriends and/or boyfriends. When children are approaching early adolescence, masturbation becomes more common, as does a youth's interest in sex. They begin to more frequently utilize sexual language and engage in consensual kissing with their peers (South Australian Government, Department for Education and Child Development et al., 2013). While they demonstrate an increased desire for privacy, they also begin to find humor and thrill in fleeting exhibitionism with same-age peers (South Australian Government, Department for Education and Child Development et al., 2013).

Sexual development is arguably most significant during adolescence. It is a time when youth begin to more formally establish their sexual identity, and a time during which multiple factors impact their own sexuality and sexual relationships with others, either positively or negatively (McNeely & Blanchard, 2009; Scott & Walsh, 2014; Waisbrod & Reicher, 2014). Adolescents begin to demonstrate an interest in sexual activities and may more frequently talk and ask questions about sexual parts and acts, using more sexually explicit language (South Australian Government, Department for Education and Child Development et al., 2013). Youth of this age are also likely to look at nude pictures of people and draw sexual parts, view erotica, and use the internet to chat online with same-age peers (Hornor, 2004; South Australian Government, Department for Education and Child Development et al., 2013).

Just like there are age differences in sexual behaviors exhibited by children and youth, there are also gender differences. Females tend to be more discriminate in where and when they exhibit sexualized behaviors and talk about sexuality than males. Males are more likely to talk about sex and display sexual behaviors not only in private but also in more public locations, such as school and day care (Miragoli et al., 2017).

Sexualized behaviors that are less common, but are not necessarily problematic, in children with typical emotional, cognitive, and physical development include attempts to touch the genitals of adults or to use a tongue while kissing, rubbing body parts against others, and exhibiting behaviors that naively imitate adult sexual acts (American Academy of Pediatrics, 2014; Hornor, 2004). Sexual behavior that causes stress or discomfort in others, and behaviors that are markedly different or have changed for a particular child, however, may be cause for concern (South Australian Government, Department for Education and Child Development, Catholic Education SA, & Association of Independent Schools of SA, 2013). Children up to 5 years of age may display additional troubling behaviors such as explicit sexual knowledge or talk and a developmentally inappropriate interest in adult sexual behaviors (Kenny et al., 2015; South Australian Government, Department for Education and Child Development et al., 2013). Violating the privacy of others through attempts to watch them use the restroom or pulling pants down or skirts up without permission may also be cause for concern (South Australian Government, Department for Education and Child Development et al., 2013). Children ages 5–9 years who repeatedly ask about sexual activity or who utilize crude language when talking about sex beyond their developmental level, and those who masturbate with another peer, are demonstrating concerning behaviors (South Australian Government, Department for Education and Child Development et al., 2013).

In the years leading up to adolescence, concerning behaviors may include changes in behavior, attire, or friend groups, particularly if the changes are sudden and are beyond normative developmental stages (South Australian Government, Department for Education and Child Development et al., 2013). Preteens, ages 9–12, may also exhibit concerning behaviors such as bullying that includes sexual aggression, developmentally inappropriate sexual knowledge and conversations, and fearful preoccupation of sexually transmitted infections or pregnancy (South Australian Government, Department for Education and Child Development et al., 2013). Youth of this age may also inappropriately engage with adults on the internet, share personally identifiable information about themselves online, and spend inordinate amounts of time online or using social media (South Australian Government, Department for Education and Child Development et al., 2013).

Concerning behaviors in teens also include their use of technology, specifically, spending extensive amounts of time online or with social media, to the exclusion of other activities or live contact with friends; providing strangers online with personally identifiable information; and presenting themselves as a different age, gender, or sexuality to others online (South Australian Government, Department for Education and Child Development et al., 2013). Sexually concerning behaviors for teens ages 13–18 may also include practicing unprotected sex with same-age peers, having multiple sexual partners, and alcohol and substance use coupled with sexual activities (South Australian Government, Department for Education and Child Development et al., 2013). Adolescents with concerning behaviors may also engage in viewing of pornography, violating the personal space of others, bullying or aggressive sexual acts toward others, and using sexually obscene language and drawing sexually graphic images that negatively impact others (South Australian Government, Department for Education and Child Development et al., 2013).

Caregivers should be encouraged to intervene and redirect children demonstrating these concerning behaviors, without embarrassing or shaming the children, and to watch and document their observations if the behaviors persist after redirection. When these types of behaviors are present, and persist after intervention, an assessment of the child who demonstrates them and his or her family and environment may be warranted but may not necessarily require a report to the authorities (Chaffin et al., 2008).

Recognizing problematic sexual behaviors

Several decades ago, professionals were taught to look for "the big three" to identify children who may have been sexually abused. Children who set fires, wet their beds, and engaged in cruelty to animals were often labeled victims of sexual contact; children who exhibited sexualized, "adult-like" behaviors were often regarded as youth who were reenacting their own sexual victimization (Vosmer et al., 2009). While sexual victimization is one hypothesis to consider, children who display such problematic behaviors should be immediately assessed not only for possible sexual victimization or exposure, but also for medical and mental health issues, exposure to domestic or community violence, extensive alcohol and drug use by caregivers, chronic neglect, and inadvertent exposure to developmentally inappropriate sexual materials (Cale & Lussier, 2017; Chaffin et al., 2008; South Australian Government, Department for Education and Child Development et al., 2013). Cultural norms, family practices, and the context of the behaviors should also be considered and evaluated (Friedrich et al., 1998; Vosmer et al., 2009).

Just as caregivers and professionals need to understand what sexual behaviors are natural and healthy for children and youth, they similarly need to understand behaviors that are generally considered to be inappropriate or problematic, depending on the individual child's developmental level. While curiosity about sexuality develops as youth mature, even young children are curious about their bodies (Friedrich et al., 1998; Sexuality Information and Education Council of the United States,

2004; Vosmer et al., 2009). Self-exploration and interest in their own body parts and those of others need not be red flags of maltreatment. However, problematic sexual behaviors in children may be indicative of medical or mental health issues for children, and these behaviors should be identified, reported to child welfare professionals, and immediately assessed.

Some of the most concerning behaviors youth may exhibit include threats, violence, bribery, secrecy, power differentials, dehumanization, and degradation, or coercion to engage another into sexual acts (Chaffin et al., 2008; Kenny et al., 2015; Miragoli et al., 2017; South Australian Government, Department for Education and Child Development et al., 2013; Vosmer et al., 2009). In a study conducted with experts on children who displayed sexually inappropriate behaviors, the following behaviors were of particular concern when exhibited by children under 10 years of age: children who engage in sexual acts beyond their physical or cognitive age, children who insert objects into the privates of other children, children who watch or download pornography, and children who prompt complaints from other children due to their sexualized behaviors (Vosmer et al., 2009).

Additional problematic sexual behaviors that warrant immediate intervention for children include the placement of a child's mouth on the genital area of dolls or others, sexual behaviors between youth with more than 4 years age difference, and children who request sexual stimulation from others (Hornor, 2004). Problematic sexual behaviors preoccupy these children for inappropriate amounts of time and often are not abandoned even after multiple attempts to redirect them (Hornor, 2004; Kenny et al., 2015; South Australian Government, Department for Education and Child Development et al., 2013).

Friedrich et al. (2005) identified "intrusive" behaviors for male and female youth in the child welfare system, ages 10–12, including touching sex parts of other children, adults, and animals; attempts to undress other children or adults against their will; attempts to engage in sexual acts with others, including oral–genital contact; attempts to look at people when nude or undressing; and displays of their genitals to others.

Problematic sexual behaviors also identified and tracked for these youth included boundary issues with adults and children, including kissing and hugging unknown individuals or rubbing against people; flirtatious comments; talking about sex and making sexual sounds; desire to watch nudity on television; drawing sex parts; more knowledge about sex than other same-age youth; and for males, touching their own genitalia while in public (Friedrich et al., 2005). The presence of these problematic sexual behaviors were assessed for these youth over the course of a year, and the vast majority of youth who displayed these behaviors at the first assessment continued to have them at the end of the 12-month period, even though many of these youth were receiving mental health treatment of some kind (Friedrich et al., 2005).

Preteens and adolescents with problematic sexual behaviors may engage in frequent masturbation in front of others or to the point of self-injury; electronically sending sexually provocative images of themselves to strangers; seeking out sexually aggressive or violent pornography; arranging to personally meet with online acquaintances; interacting sexually with substantially younger or more vulnerable individuals; or sexual contact with animals (South Australian Government, Department for Education and Child Development et al., 2013). Sexually themed bullying, humiliation, and degradation of others, or other planned sexual contacts with others that include force or manipulation are also problematic behaviors in adolescents that warrant immediate intervention and reports to child protection and law enforcement professionals (South Australian Government, Department for Education and Child Development et al., 2013).

While caregivers and professionals need to recognize sexual behaviors that may be problematic, there is consensus in the field that children under the age of 10 who exhibit inappropriate sexual behaviors should not be pathologized, or labeled "sex offenders," "sexual abusers," or "predators" (Chaffin et al., 2008; Vosmer et al., 2009). Language such as this should be rejected because

> [it] implies that children are similar to adult sex offenders and engage in sexual activities for gratification of their own sexual needs. Most young children who display [sexually inappropriate behaviors] do not follow these patterns, do not normally engage in such behaviours for own sexual gratification or grow up to become juvenile or adult sex offenders. By using terminology derived from adults, the potential threat such children pose to society may be overemphasized, increasing demands for protection from such children. Hence, these children could become stigmatized and any interest they show in sexuality be seen as a form of pathology.
> ***(Vosmer et al., 2009, p. 283).***

Educating caregivers about sexual behaviors and body safety

It is not uncommon for caregivers to seek out advice from professionals, such as teachers, counselors, or medical providers, when they are experiencing stress about their parenting role or concerned about the behaviors or exhibited emotions of the children for whom they provide care (Golden, 2006; Rooke, Thompson, & Day, 2004; Simoni, 1993; Telleen, 1990). However, sexual education in schools is often limited to bare facts, such as "the sperm and the egg chase," without addressing personal beliefs, attitudes, or values (Cappello, 2001, p. 4). Sexual education that only addresses corporal aspects, as opposed to sexuality within the context of relationships, may result in negative outcomes, such as more sexual experiences for youth, more adolescent pregnancies, and less overall knowledge about sex (McNeely & Blanchard, 2009; Scott & Walsh, 2014).

Body safety and child abuse prevention programing also often occurs in the school setting; however, program participation may be more likely to elicit a disclosure of victimization that has already occurred rather than prevent abuse from happening in the first place (Marriage et al., 2017). Some professionals assert that school-based body safety and child abuse prevention programs on their own are insufficient, as the onus for prevention and protection lies with the children themselves (Hawkins, 2013; Rudolph, Zimmer-Gembeck, Shanley, & Hawkins, 2017). Children are developmentally incapable of fully comprehending the grooming techniques, manipulation, and intentions of individuals who seek to sexually abuse them (Rudolph et al., 2017). Furthermore, their victimization may be presented as a positive experience and physiologically feel good to them, leaving them unsure or unwilling to disclose these activities to caregivers or other adults (Rudolph et al., 2017). Consequently, a public health perspective that allows for a more proactive and comprehensive approach may be more effective in protecting children and youth, by educating caregivers and the broader community about sexual development and sexual violence (Tabachnick, McCartan, & Panaro, 2016).

Children and youth with disabilities, who may have more frequent contact with health and mental health-care providers as a result of their diagnoses, similarly should be provided with information and education regarding their bodies and their sexual development (McNeely & Blanchard, 2009; Scott & Walsh, 2014). Sexual education for youth with disabilities is frequently overlooked, as this population may be considered developmentally or cognitively unable to comprehend the information presented or may be considered "asexual," and not in need of this type of information (Kok & Akyuz, 2015). However, the risk of victimization is higher for children and youth with disabilities for a variety of reasons, such as inabilities to physically defend themselves or escape an offender, language deficits that impede their ability to report victimization or make adults believe their outcries, or a desire for attention and affection from inappropriate or unsafe sources when alienated due to their disabilities (Bennett & Baladerian, 2005). Research demonstrates that children with speech and language disabilities are three times more likely to be sexually abused than children without these disabilities; children with disorders such as affective, anxiety, or conduct disorders; autism; or schizophrenia are five and a half times more likely to be sexually abused than children without such behavioral disorders (Sullivan & Knutson, 2000).

Sexual minority and marginalized youth, or those who are identified as lesbian, gay, bisexual, transsexual, queer or questioning, may also be in need of more deliberate and specialized education regarding sexual health and body safety (McNeely & Blanchard, 2009; Scott & Walsh, 2014). Sexual minority youth experience increased risks for sexual and physical victimization and harassment (Alvy, Hughes, Kristjanson, & Wilsnack, 2013; Mitchell, Ybarra, & Korchmaros, 2014; Sterzing, Ratliff, Gartner, McGeough, & Johnson, 2017), and youth who feel marginalized or stigmatized due to their sexual identity are more likely to experience complex trauma if sexually victimized, due to the stigmatizing and traumatic nature of sexual abuse (Robinson, 2018; Scott & Walsh, 2014). This population can also benefit from additional education on overcoming sexual obstacles and difficulties they experience during their sexual development (Mitchell et al., 2014; Robinson, 2018; Scott & Walsh, 2014).

Health and mental health-care providers are in a unique position to offer caregivers education and support, and referrals to other services as needed, regarding healthy sexual development of their children (Breuner et al., 2016; Kok & Akyuz, 2015). In order to serve in the role of sexuality educators for caregivers, health and mental health-care providers need to not only understand normative sexual development but also be comfortable themselves when talking about body parts and sexual development of children (South Australian Government, Department for Education and Child Development et al., 2013). In one study of doctors and nurses, Kurtuncu et al. (2015) found that a variety of factors impacted the medical provider's ability to identify correct statements regarding children's sexual development and sex education, including the "age-group, marital status, the status of having children, educational status, and occupation" of the professionals (p. 219). More than 84% of these medical professionals agreed that parents should be providing children with sexual education, as opposed to schools, leading Kurtuncu et al. (2015) to conclude that medical professionals should receive sexual education to better support caregivers in rearing their children, particular regarding children up to 6 years of age.

Caregivers with an understanding of appropriate, healthy sexual development in their children are better able to present education and information to their children on a developmentally appropriate level and provide them with an understanding of why and how their bodies are changing. Open conversations with children about their bodies at early ages help reduce embarrassment during discussions about sexuality and normalize children's experiences; these conversations may also help positively influence children's development of their sexual identity and provide a foundation for healthy, stable relationships with partners later in their lives (Kurtuncu et al., 2015; Scott & Walsh, 2014).

Caregivers should be encouraged to start talking to their children about their bodies in a developmentally appropriate manner as early as other conversations about safety and other forms of development (Kurtuncu et al., 2015). For example, caregivers should be encouraged to teach their children as young as 2 or 3 years of age medically accurate names for their genitalia along with names for other body parts. The simple act of giving names to all body parts, and making it permissible for children to use these medically accurate names, helps children talk about their bodies and what is happening to them, including any abuse and victimization they may experience.

A colleague of this author had an experience with a child who, at approximately 4 years of age, did not know the medically accurate name for her genitalia. Her brother had been fondling her vaginal area, and the child made repeated statements to her teacher that her brother was "messing with [her] pocketbook." The teacher, misunderstanding the child's repeated attempts at disclosing sexual contact, finally responded with exasperation, and told the child to put her "pocketbook" away where her brother could no longer touch it. The child cried out, "But it's right here!" pointing to her vaginal area. Had the child known the medically accurate terminology for her genitalia, her teacher would have been able to understand her outcry the first time and could have reported the child's disclosure to the proper authorities. This would have resulted in a much earlier intervention and treatment for the disclosing child, as well as for her brother regarding his problematic sexual behaviors.

Along with teaching children medically appropriate terminology for all of their body parts, including their genitalia, caregivers should also be encouraged to talk to their children about body safety. Utilizing developmentally appropriate language, caregivers should be encouraged to teach their children that touches to their bodies should only be done to ensure their health and safety, and that they should tell one of five trusted adults when someone touches their body parts, or when something happens that makes them feel uncomfortable, embarrassed, scared, unsure, or confused. Caregivers should help the child name five trusted adults, both within and outside of the family, and help the child tell these individuals that they are the child's trusted adults.

Caregivers should also be encouraged to empower the child to say "no" to individuals—children and adults alike—who may try to coerce, manipulate, or groom a child into sexual contact; and to understand the dynamics of victimization that may keep children from telling if they do experience abusive contact. Health and mental health-care providers can encourage caregivers to have safety meetings with their children twice a year and talk about all types of safety, such as body safety, bullying and hazing, bike safety, water safety, and fire safety. When conversations about body safety are as common as other types of safety, children are less likely to be compelled to maintain a secret about touches and sexual victimization should they experience such contact. The National Center for Missing and Exploited Children (www.missingkids.org) is one of several nationally recognized youth-serving organizations that has developed child abuse prevention and education materials for children, caregivers, and professionals and can be utilized to help support caregivers in having difficult conversations with their children. Caregivers are encouraged to learn not just about signs and symptoms of sexual victimization, but of other forms of child maltreatment, as well. It is not uncommon for children to experience multiple forms of maltreatment (Finkelhor, Turner, Hamby, & Ormrod, 2011). Emotional maltreatment and physical abuse may accompany sexual abuse or be utilized by an offender to control his or her victims through manipulation and fear.

Body safety and sex education should also include conversations about sexually explicit material and information to which children may have access via digital media. Children as young as 4 months of age have interactions with various forms of digital media today, as opposed to access to television at 4 years of age in 1970 (Chassiakos et al., 2016). Digital media, such as cell phones and apps, online gaming, and open computer access, now afford youth much more direct interactions with individuals whom they do not know personally, leaving them vulnerable to manipulation, sexually explicit conversations, and exposure to inappropriate sexual material. Cases involving commercial sexual exploitation of children and child sexual abuse images frequently begin with and are facilitated by digital technology. Chassiakos et al. (2016) recommend that caregivers provide online safety education for their children from an early age and regularly monitor their children's digital media usage. Health and mental health-care providers should also explore the use of digital media with children and youth and offer information on preventing online exploitation (Chassiakos et al., 2016). For more information on monitoring and responding to problematic use of digital media, please see Domoff (2020).

Another concerning aspect of digital media is sexting, defined by Chassiakos et al. (2016) as "the electronic transmission of nude or semi-nude images as well as sexually explicit text messages" (p. e10). While Ybarra and Mitchell (2014) concluded that sexting is relatively uncommon, with less than 10% of youth aged 13–18 years surveyed engaging in sexting behaviors (contrasted with Strassberg, McKinnon, Sustaíta, & Rullo, 2013, who found 20% of youth sent sexually explicit images), they did find that youth who sexted were more likely to have multiple and concurrent sex partners. Similarly, Ševčíková (2016) found that vaginal sex was associated with sexting in males ages 11–16 years, and older adolescent females. Youth who engaged in sexting behaviors also experienced more alcohol use and more emotional issues than youth who did not (Ševčíková, 2016). Choi, Van Ouytsel, and Temple (2016) found that adolescent females who share sexually explicit images via digital media also experienced sexual coercion both online and offline. These youth are in particular need of education to promote healthy sexual relationships and should be assessed for other form of victimization (Choi et al., 2016).

Sex education provided and developmentally appropriate discussions that caregivers have with their children about their bodies can also be very helpful to child protection professionals should a child experience or disclose sexual victimization. It is not uncommon for children who are reported victims of sexual abuse to not know specifically what parts of their genitalia were touched. One study was conducted with female children, ages 5–17 years, who were suspected victims of sexual abuse (Milam & Nugent, 2017). Medical providers, as part of a forensic medical examination of the children, attempted to ascertain whether the females were able to appropriately use the word "inside" when describing the contact they experienced. As part of the history-gathering phase of the examination, the females were asked about whether anyone had talked to them about their body parts, whether they had names for those parts, and how many openings or holes they had in their genitalia. Youth who were menstruating were also asked whether the blood during their menses came out of the same hole or a different hole from where they urinated (Milam & Nugent, 2017, p. 29). More than 83% of the females were unable to "demonstrate accurate knowledge of genital anatomy" (Milam & Nugent, 2017, p. 30). Milam and Nugent (2017) found that the older females were more likely to report their contact as "outside" when contact was penetration was of the labia, but not of the vaginal cavity. Younger girls tended to report that they were touched "inside" when the contact penetrated either the labia or genital opening. Female ethnic minority children as a whole were even less accurate than other children in their knowledge their genital anatomy (Milam & Nugent, 2017). While penetration of the vagina, however slight, fits the legal criteria for sexual penetration in all states, this lack of understanding of genitalia in female youth may result in failure to identify legal sexual penetration, a more serious criminal offense than sexual contact or touch.

In another study, conducted by Burrows, Bearman, Dion, and Powell (2017), youth ages 4–17 years had difficulty in identifying body parts that were involved in their suspected sexual victimization.

During field interviews with suspected child victims, nearly half of the children interviewed did not initially utilize accurate anatomical—or even clear colloquial—names for body parts. Interviewers typically needed to ask an additional two to three questions to achieve the highest level of understanding regarding body parts involved, with the apparent most effective question seeking the location of the body part on the child's body (Burrows et al., 2017, p. 230). While children were able to clarify their statements with location with statements such as "between my legs" (Burrows et al., 2017), this may not provide full clarity when results of this study are combined with that of Milam and Nugent (2017), and female children are uneducated about their genital anatomy.

Interventions for children and youth with sexual behavior problems

Problematic sexual behaviors exhibited by children should be reported to law enforcement and child protective services, as mandated by state and federal laws. Appropriate and effective interventions for children and youth with sexual behavior problems will vary depending on the age of the child and the severity of the behaviors exhibited. After concerns have been reported, caregivers are encouraged to continue to monitor and document the behaviors of their children who exhibit sexually problematic behaviors, regardless of whether law enforcement investigators or child protection workers remain involved with the family.

Education, counseling, and support are critical to help the child who engaged in harmful sexual behaviors learn more appropriate interactions, to enable the caregivers to appropriately develop and maintain appropriate boundaries, and to ensure other children in the family remain safe. Safety plans are needed for youth who have continued access to other children outside the home, such as the school or day-care setting (South Australian Government, Department for Education and Child Development et al., 2013). This may include increasing supervision or modifying school or activity schedules of the child who displayed problematic behaviors to ensure that any victims of the harmful sexual behaviors feel safe (South Australian Government, Department for Education and Child Development et al., 2013). Of particular importance here, is that the child victim(s) and the families be accommodated regarding what feels "safe" to them. If removal from the school setting is required to ensure education is not interrupted and access to social support systems is maintained, the rights of the victim child should take priority over those of the youth engaging in harmful behaviors, and the victim should be allowed to remain in his or her home school setting

(South Australian Government, Department for Education and Child Development et al., 2013). Access to certain areas, participation in some activities, or contact with vulnerable individuals may also need to be modified for youth displaying problematic sexual behaviors (South Australian Government, Department for Education and Child Development et al., 2013).

When caregivers become aware of sexualized behaviors of children, there are a variety of responses that may be appropriate, depending on what the behaviors are. When the exhibited behaviors are normative, developmentally appropriate sexual behaviors, no intervention may be needed, or, depending on where the behavior took place or what the child said, caregivers may need to simply support the child, talk to the child, and/or explain—in a developmentally appropriate way—healthy sexuality (Marriage et al., 2017). Angry, shameful, or punitive responses may result in embarrassment and guilt for the child and may negatively impact the child's later sexual development.

For behaviors that may be slightly outside the sexual developmental norm, or may be concerning to the caregiver or others, caregivers may need to provide the child with more supervision and track the behaviors exhibited (Marriage et al., 2017). Some concerning behaviors may simply require calm redirection of the child to another more appropriate location or activity, or a more appropriate mode of expressing thoughts and feelings (Marriage et al., 2017).

Problematic sexual behaviors in children and youth should be addressed with a professional, such as a medical provider or mental health practitioner, and caregivers should seek out support and education in addressing these behaviors with the youth (Marriage et al., 2017). If the behaviors result in, or may result in harm to the youth or others, protective measures should be enacted immediately, and reports should be made to law enforcement and child protective services, as appropriate (Marriage et al., 2017).

In a recent study, Ensink et al. (2018) sought to assess the longevity and possible correlating factors of internalized and externalized sexual behavioral problems in children ages 2–12 years. Over the course of a 2-year span, nearly half of the youth experienced persistent sexual behavioral problems, and more than 25% of the youth demonstrated transient sexual behavior problems (Ensink et al., 2018). Interestingly, Ensink et al. (2018) found that persistent sexual behavior problems may be more likely to appear in children who have been sexually penetrated or sexually victimized by a parental figure, as opposed to someone with more emotional distance from the child. This study demonstrates the importance of recognizing problematic sexual behaviors in children and providing them with the support and treatment required to mitigate the effects of victimization.

Effective treatment modalities for children and youth who exhibit sexual behavior problems include trauma-focused therapies and cognitive behavioral therapy with psycho-education; family-focused treatment that provides information and education regarding misinformation also holds merit (Ensink et al., 2018; Waisbrod & Reicher, 2014). Group and play therapies may also be effective with children, and involvement of caregivers is critical to effect lasting change on children's maladaptive behaviors (Waisbrod & Reicher, 2014). Of key importance, is that current research supports the position that youth with sexual behavior problems differ from adults who sexually offend in a variety of ways and subsequently should not be subjected to the same punishment or treatment modalities as adult offenders (Chaffin et al., 2008; Hunter & Lexier, 1998).

A multidisciplinary response to youth with sexual behavior problems

Instances of problematic sexual behaviors exhibited by children should be assessed by a multidisciplinary team, with clear delineation of roles and responsibilities for all members (Chaffin et al., 2008; South Australian Government, Department for Education and Child Development et al., 2013). Team members should include law enforcement officers, child protection workers, forensic interviewers, child protection attorneys, prosecutors, victim advocates, and medical and mental health professionals. Law enforcement officers have the responsibility of fully investigating allegations of sexual contact with youth, including the identification of corroborating evidence of victimization. Child protection workers need to be able to assess the risk factors of leaving the child in an environment that may be exposing him or her to inappropriate materials or abusive experiences. Forensic interviewers, familiar with child development, linguistic, cultural, and legal issues, are able to facilitate reports by children who may have experienced abuse or witnessed violence in their homes or communities. Prosecuting and child welfare attorneys need to fully understand and take advantage of their ethical responsibilities and professional discretion when considering charging and petition options to assist child victims, offenders, and sexually reactive youth. Advocates, medical providers, and mental health professionals should be involved in supporting the child and family throughout the investigative processes, educating investigators and attorneys on clinical issues and child abuse dynamics, and completing a full assessment to ascertain the health, welfare, and safety of the child.

Sexual development does not occur in a vacuum. When assessing sexualized behaviors observed in children and youth, professionals must take multiple factors into consideration. The age of the child displaying concerning sexual behaviors must be considered (Chaffin et al., 2008; Thigpen & Fortenberry, 2009). As children age, their sexual knowledge increases, and the sexual behaviors in which they engage may normally increase and become more secret. Family norms and traditions should also be considered, including practices regarding family nudity, siblings to whom the youth has exposure, and whether the child attends day care or is around other children of various ages (Chaffin et al., 2008; Miragoli et al., 2017; Thigpen & Fortenberry, 2009). Environmental characteristics and factors should be considered as well, including educational level of the parents and caretakers, exposure to community and family violence, and victimization from other forms of maltreatment (Chaffin et al., 2008; Thigpen & Fortenberry, 2009). Children and youth may exhibit problematic sexual behaviors due to exposure to child sexual abuse images and adult pornography and should be assessed for what may have been accidental exposure, or intentional victimization by others. Greenfield (2004) explains that exposure to inappropriate sexual media can result in various emotional responses, such as disgust, shock, embarrassment, and fear. Exposure to inappropriate sexual material can also result in aggression against women, in both sexual and nonsexual exchanges (Greenfield, 2004), as well as earlier sexual experiences and riskier sexual behaviors (Collins et al., 2017). While a clinical assessment may provide helpful information for diagnosing and treating children and youth who display problematic sexual behaviors, this assessment should not be in lieu of a complete child protection or criminal investigation, but instead, complement it (Chaffin et al., 2008).

Criminal issues

The age at which youth can be criminally charged for sex offenses varies by state. Some states automatically charge juveniles ages 16 and older as an adult if the offense committed is of a "serious" nature as delineated in their statutes, including but not limited to sex offenses such as first-degree rape, sexual abuse of a child, lewd or lascivious acts upon the person of a child under 14, or sodomy. In some states, this mandatory transfer to adult criminal court for these sex offenses occurs at ages as young as 14. These mandatory transfers of juveniles who sexually offend to adult criminal court do not take into consideration any prior status offenses or background of the youth. In the alternative, some states permit waiver to adult court for youth who commit sex offenses—some as young as twelve years of age—for offenses such as "gross sexual imposition" or crimes of violence, or if the youth has previously been adjudicated as delinquent. Some states employ concurrent jurisdiction for sex offenses committed by youth, and transfer from juvenile court to adult criminal court is by prosecutorial discretion. Vermont permits waiver from juvenile court to adult criminal court in cases of sexual assault and aggravated sexual assault for youth as young as 10 years of age, and more than five states decree that a youth of any age can be tried as an adult if the sex offense is serious enough and the child is competent to stand trial.

Once convicted of a sex crime—or other violent acts—juveniles are often required to register in compliance with the Sex Offender Registration and Notification Act (SORNA) (2006). Some states require registration only if the youth is convicted of sexual acts in adult criminal court. Other states require registration for juveniles only if they have attained the age of fourteen years. In two states—Maryland and Virginia—youth as young as 13 years of age must register for certain sex offenses; North Carolina permits registration of youth as young as 11 years of age.

Prosecuting attorneys may use their discretion in charging out sex offenses against juveniles. Such discretion can be used to ensure appropriate treatment for youth while still holding them accountable for their actions and addressing the needs of their victims and their families. One such discretionary tactic is a diversion program. In diverting a case a prosecutor can have the youth evaluated for his or her offenses and move forward with prosecution only if the youth does not comply with recommendations for offender treatment (Ratnayake, 2013; Vieth, 2001).

Due to the multiple and varied origins of inappropriate sexual behaviors demonstrated by youth, as well as the amenability to treatment and low frequency of identified sexual recidivism of these offenders, distinguishing sex crimes committed by youth from other types of criminal offenses may not be the most appropriate policy (Chaffin et al., 2008). A careful assessment of the child's developmental level, personal and family history, motives behind the acts, and risk for recidivism should be conducted in each case. Mandatory, draconian policies that group adolescents, who are still engaged in moral and cognitive development, with serious adult offenders are not in the best interests of youth.

Juvenile court issues

Juvenile court, sometimes called youth or family court, has original jurisdiction in most proceedings concerning a delinquent child, a child in need of supervision, a neglected child, an abused child, or a dependent child. Exceptions and waivers to adult criminal court are outlined previously. Youth who commit certain less serious sex crimes may be more effectively served by the filing of juvenile delinquency charges, as opposed to prosecution in adult criminal court. With a juvenile court conviction, a history of offenses is tracked, but the information is often not available to the public, thus reducing stigma and shame for youth (see, e.g., Minnesota Statute § 260B.171, subdiv. 4, 2018; Ratnayake, 2013; Vieth, 2001).

Civil child protection issues

A holistic assessment should be completed when allegations of sexual behaviors between youth arise. This is particularly important when the child alleged to have initiated the sexual contact is under 10 years of age. Both the target child and the initiating child should be assessed as possible victims. While not diagnostic, youth with sexual behavior problems may themselves have been victimized or exposed to violence or inappropriate sexualized materials (Chaffin et al., 2008). Forensic interviews should be conducted with the target child to identify the extent of the sexual victimization, and whether the contact was mutual or if any force, coercion, or secrecy was involved. The initiating child should be assessed as well, to identify the source of the sexualized behaviors. The family environment impacts the sexual development of a child (Chaffin et al., 2008; Thigpen & Fortenberry, 2009); therefore a careful assessment of the initiating child's family should also be conducted.

It is not uncommon to hear of instances where the caregivers of the initiating child will not allow child protective services or law enforcement officers access to interview the child. In these instances, it may be appropriate to initiate an investigation of the uncooperative parents for neglect. The sexual health of a child is also an important mental health consideration, and when parents ignore the mental health needs of their children, it may be considered neglect. In cases where youth who display problematic sexual behaviors that are not eligible for criminal or juvenile sanctions, or such sanctions that are not appropriate, alternative services should be provided. Youth who display problematic sexualized behaviors are themselves at future risk for sexual victimization (Chaffin et al., 2008). Youth should receive appropriate sexual education, counseling, and support services to mediate these behaviors, and caregivers should receive support and parenting education to more effectively respond to such behaviors (Chaffin et al., 2008). When addressed through a child protection petition, states or counties can provide services not only to the youth displaying problematic sexual behaviors, but also to the family, who have the best capacity to monitor the youth's treatment and provide adequate supervision (Ratnayake, 2013; Vieth, 2001).

Conclusion

Information regarding sexual development of children and youth, as well as information regarding normative and problematic sexual behaviors, continues to be produced. Professionals working with children and families need to be committed to continuing to expand their knowledge about sexual development and problematic sexual behaviors to better educate and support children and families. Youth who are provided information about their bodies and healthy sexuality are more likely to engage in healthy sexual behaviors, to value their own bodies and personal health, and to make informed, positive decisions about their reproductive health (Breuner et al., 2016).

Educational settings may provide youth with sexual education about their bodies, and caregivers may impart upon their children information about values and beliefs. Medical providers can dispense information that complements what children and youth receive in other settings by providing reliable information on sexual health and development. Health and mental health-care providers can also model difficult conversations with children and youth for their caregivers. Their access and proximity to children and families, and the role health and mental health-care providers play in ensuring all aspects of children's safety and health—including sexual health—leave them in a prime position to support children and families and make referrals to other professionals as needed. Finally, when health and mental health-care professionals become aware of problematic sexual behaviors in children, they should follow statute and report these harmful behaviors to the authorities. "Safe environments rely on people believing they *can and should* report the harmful behaviors of others" (South Australian Government, Department for Education and Child Development et al., 2013, p. 22).

Important points to remember

- Some examples of normative sexual behaviors in children ages 2–6 years include masturbation or self-touching, showing their genitals to and looking at the genitals of their peers, as well as attempts to view adults in the nude.
- Nonaggressive kissing between similar-aged children and self-stimulation that occurs in private are generally typical and natural sexual behaviors for children between 6 and 9 years of age. During this time of development, children may masturbate to self-sooth, and begin to demonstrate an increased sense of privacy about their bodies.

- Youth ages 10–12 years begin to formulate their associations with sex and girlfriends and/or boyfriends. When children are approaching early adolescence, masturbation becomes more common, as does a youth's interest in sex.
- Adolescents begin to demonstrate an interest in sexual activities and may more frequently talk and ask questions about sexual parts and acts, using more sexually explicit language. Youth of this age are also likely to look at nude pictures of people and draw sexual parts, view erotica, and use the internet to chat online with same-age peers.
- Children ages 5–9 years who repeatedly ask about sexual activity or who utilize crude language when talking about sex beyond their developmental level, and those who masturbate with another peer, are demonstrating concerning behaviors.
- In a study conducted with experts on children who displayed sexually inappropriate behaviors, the following behaviors were of particular concern when exhibited by children under 10 years of age: children who engage in sexual acts beyond their physical or cognitive age, children who insert objects into the privates of other children, children who watch or download pornography, and children who prompt complaints from other children due to their sexualized behaviors (Vosmer et al., 2009).
- Friedrich et al. (2005) identified "intrusive" behaviors for male and female youth in the child welfare system, ages 10–12, including touching sex parts of other children, adults, and animals; attempts to undress other children or adults against their will; attempts to engage in sexual acts with others, including oral–genital contact; attempts to look at people when nude or undressing; and displays of their genitals to others.
- While caregivers and professionals need to recognize sexual behaviors that may be problematic, there is consensus in the field that children under the age of 10 who exhibit inappropriate behaviors should not be pathologized, or labeled "sex offenders," "sexual abusers," or predators.
- Caregivers should be encouraged to teach their children as young as 2 or 3 years of age medically accurate names for their genitalia along with names for other body parts. The simple act of giving names to all body parts, and making it permissible for children to use these medically accurate names, helps children talk about their bodies and what is happening to them, including any abuse and victimization they may experience.
- Utilizing developmentally appropriate language, caregivers should be encouraged to teach their children that touches to their bodies should only be done to ensure their health and safety, and that they should tell one of five trusted adults when someone touches their

body parts, or when something happens that makes them feel uncomfortable, embarrassed, scared, unsure, or confused. Caregivers should help the child name five trusted adults, both within and outside of the family, and help the child tell these individuals that they are the child's trusted adults.
- Digital media, such as cell phones and apps, online gaming, and open computer access, now affords youth much more direct interactions with individuals whom they do not know personally, leaving them vulnerable to manipulation, sexually explicit conversations, and exposure to inappropriate sexual material. Cases involving commercial sexual exploitation of children and child sexual abuse images frequently begin with and are facilitated by digital technology.
- Advocates, medical providers, and mental health professionals should be involved in supporting the child and family throughout the investigative processes, educating investigators and attorneys on clinical issues and child abuse dynamics, and completing a full assessment to ascertain the health, welfare, and safety of the child.

References

Adichie, C. N. (2017). *Dear Ijeawele, or a feminist manifesto in fifteen suggestions.* New York: Anchor Books.

Alvy, L. M., Hughes, T. L., Kristjanson, A. F., & Wilsnack, S. C. (2013). Sexual identity group differences in child abuse and neglect. *Journal of Interpersonal Violence, 28*(10), 2088–2111.

American Academy of Pediatrics. (2014). *Preventing sexual violence: An educational toolkit for health care professionals: Sexual behaviors in children.*

Bennett, S., & Baladerian, N. J. (2005). Children with disabilities and child maltreatment. *ISPCAN's The Link, 14*(2), 1–8.

Breuner, C. C., Mattson, G., AAP Committee on Adolescence., & AAP Committee on Psychosocial Aspects of Child and Family Health. (2016). Sexuality education for children and adolescents. *Pediatrics, 138*(2), e1–e11. Available from <https://pediatrics.aappublications.org/content/pediatrics/138/2/e20161348.full.pdf>.

Burrows, K. S., Bearman, M., Dion, J., & Powell, M. B. (2017). Children's use of sexual body part terms in witness interviews about sexual abuse. *Child Abuse & Neglect, 65,* 226–235.

Cale, J., & Lussier, P. (2017). Sexual behaviour in preschool children in the context of intra-parental violence and sexual coercion. *Criminal Behaviour and Mental Health, 27,* 176–190.

Cappello, D. (2001). When sex ed meets parented: Supporting parents as sexuality educators. *SIECUS Report, 29*(2), 4–6.

Chaffin, M., Berliner, L., Block, R., Johnson, T. C., Friedrich, W. N., Louis, D. G., ... Silovsky, J. F. (2008). Report of the ATSA task force on children with sexual behavior problems. *Child Maltreatment, 13,* 199–218.

Chaffin, M., & Bonner, B. (1998). "Don't shoot, we're your children": Have we gone too far in our response to adolescent sexual abusers and children with sexual behavior problems? *Child Maltreatment, 3,* 314–316.

Chassiakos, Y. R., Radesky, J., Christakis, D., Moreno, M. A., Cross, C., & Council on Communications and Media. (2016). Children and adolescents and digital media. *Pediatrics, 138*(5), e1–e18. Available from <https://pediatrics.aappublications.org/content/pediatrics/138/5/e20162593.full.pdf>.

Choi, H., Van Ouytsel, J., & Temple, J. R. (2016). Association between sexting and sexual coercion among female adolescents. *Journal of Adolescence, 53*, 164–168.

Collins, R. L., Strasburger, V. C., Brown, J. D., Donnerstein, E., Lenhart, A., & Ward, M. (2017). Sexual media and childhood well-being and health. *Pediatrics, 140*(s2), S162–S166.

Domoff, S. E. (2020). Problematic use of screen media and mobile devices. In M. Knox (Ed.), *Clinician's toolkit for children's behavioral health*. Elsevier Inc, 175–198.

Ensink, K., Godbout, N., Bigras, N., Lampron, J., Sabouri, S., & Normandin, L. (2018). Persistent and transitory sexualized behavior problems in children. *Child Psychiatry & Human Development, 49*(4), 621–631.

Finkelhor, D., Turner, H., Hamby, S. L., & Ormrod, R. (2011). *Polyvictimization: Children's exposure to multiple types of violence, crime, and abuse*. Washington, DC: Office of Juvenile Justice and Delinquency Prevention, U.S. Department of Justice.

Friedrich, W. N., Bakery, A. J. L., Parker, R., Schneiderman, M., Gries, L., & Archer, M. (2005). Youth with problematic sexualized behaviors in the child welfare system: A one-year longitudinal study. *Sexual Abuse: A Journal of Research and Treatment, 17*(4), 391–406.

Friedrich, W. N., Fisher, J., Broughton, D., Houston, M., & Shafran, C. R. (1998). Normative sexual behavior in children: A contemporary sample. *Pediatrics, 101*(4), 1–8.

Golden, C. (2006). *Mothers' parenting stress and its relationship to their help-seeking behavior*. Kent State University dissertation.

Greenfield, P. M. (2004). Inadvertent exposure to pornography on the Internet: Implications of peer-to-peer file-sharing networks for child development and families. *Applied Developmental Psychology, 25*, 741–750.

Hawkins, R. (2013). Protecting children from sexual abuse. *InPsych, 35*(5), 16–17.

Hornor, G. (2004). Sexual behavior in children: Normal or not? *Journal of Pediatric Health Care, 18*, 57–64.

Hunter, J. A., Jr., & Lexier, L. J. (1998). Ethical and legal issues in the assessment and treatment of juvenile sex offenders. *Child Maltreatment, 3*(4), 339–348.

Johnson, T. C. (1996). *Understanding children's sexual behaviors: What's natural and healthy*. Available from www.tcavjohn.com.

Johnson, T. C. (2002). Some considerations about sexual abuse and children with sexual behavior problems. In J. A. Chu & E. S. Bowman (eds.), *Trauma and sexuality: The effects of childhood sexual, physical, and emotional abuse on sexuality identity and behavior* (pp. 92–114).

Kenny, M. C., Dinehart, L. H., & Wurtele, S. K. (2015). Recognizing and responding to young children's sexual behaviors in the classroom. *Young Exceptional Children, 18*(1), 1–13.

Kok, G., & Akyuz, A. (2015). Evaluation of effectiveness of parent health education about the sexual developments of adolescents with intellectual disabilities. *Sexuality & Disability, 33*, 157–174.

Kurtuncu, M., Akhan, L. U., Tanir, I. M., & Yildiz, H. (2015). The sexual development and education of preschool children: Knowledge and opinions from doctors and nurses. *Sexuality and Disability, 33*, 207–221.

Marriage, N. D., Blackley, A. S., Panagiotaros, K., Seklaoui, S. A., van den Bergh, J., & Hawkins, R. (2017). Assessing parental understanding of sexualized behavior in children and adolescents. *Child Abuse & Neglect, 72*, 196–205.

McNeely, C., & Blanchard, J. (2009). *The teen years explained: A guide to healthy adolescent development*. Baltimore, MD: Center for Adolescent Health at the Johns Hopkins Bloomberg School of Public Health.

Milam, L. J., & Nugent, W. R. (2017). Children's knowledge of genital anatomy and its relationship with children's use of the work "inside" during questioning about possible sexual abuse. *Journal of Child Sexual Abuse, 26*(1), 23–39.

Miragoli, S., Camisasca, E., & Di Blasio, P. (2017). Child sexual behaviors in school context: Age and gender differences. *Journal of Child Sexual Abuse, 26*(2), 213–231.

Mitchell, K. J., Ybarra, M. L., & Korchmaros, J. D. (2014). Sexual harassment among adolescents of different sexual orientations and gender identities. *Child Abuse & Neglect, 38*, 280–295.

Public Welfare and Related Activities, Minn. Stat. § 260B.171, subdiv. 4 (2018).

Ratnayake, A. (2013). Juvenile sex offenses: Finding justice. *Prosecutor, Journal of the National District Attorneys Association, 23*(9). Available from <http://www.ndaa.org/pdf/Update%20Vol23_No9.pdf>.

Robinson, B. A. (2018). Child welfare systems and LGBTQ youth homelessness: Gender segregation, instability, and intersectionality. *Child Welfare, 96*(2), 29–45.

Rooke, O., Thompson, M., & Day, C. (2004). School-based open access parenting programmes: Factors relating to uptake. *Child and Adolescent Mental Health, 9*(3), 130–138.

Rudolph, J., Zimmer-Gembeck, M. J., Shanley, D. C., & Hawkins, R. (2017). Child sexual abuse prevention opportunities: Parenting, programs, and the reduction of risk. *Child Maltreatment, 23*(1), 96–106.

Scott, S. M., & Walsh, A. M. (2014). Adolescent sexual development: An overview of recent research. *Canadian Journal of Community Mental Health, 22*(1), 21–30.

Ševčíková, A. (2016). Girls' and boys' experience with teen sexting in early and late adolescence. *Journal of Adolescence, 51*, 156–162.

Sex Offender Registration and Notification Act (SORNA). (2006). *Title I, Adam Walsh Child Protection and Safety Act of 2006 (Public Law 109–248).*

Sexuality Information and Education Council of the United States. (2004). *Guidelines for comprehensive sexuality education* (3rd ed.). Available from <http://www.siecus.org/_data/global/images/guidelines.pdf>.

Simoni, J. M. (1993). Latina mothers' help seeking at a school-based mutual support group. *Journal of Community Psychology, 21*(3), 188–199.

South Australian Government, Department for Education and Child Development, Catholic Education SA, & Association of Independent Schools of SA. (2013). *Responding to problem sexual behaviour in children and young people*. Adelaide: Department for Education and Child Development.

Sterzing, P. R., Ratliff, G. A., Gartner, R. E., McGeough, B. L., & Johnson, K. C. (2017). Social ecological correlates of polyvictimization among a national sample of transgender, genderqueer, and cisgender sexual minority adolescents. *Child Abuse & Neglect, 67*, 1–12.

Strassberg, D. S., McKinnon, R. K., Sustaíta, M. A., & Rullo, J. (2013). Sexting by high school students: An exploratory and descriptive study. *Archives of Sexual Behavior, 42*(1), 15–21.

Sullivan, P. M., & Knutson, J. F. (2000). Maltreatment and disabilities: A population-based epidemiological study. *Child Abuse & Neglect, 24*, 1257–1274.

Tabachnick, J., McCartan, K., & Panaro, R. (2016). Changing course: From a victim/offender duality to a public health perspective. In D. R. Laws, & W. O'Donohue (Eds.), *Treatment of sex offenders: Strengths and weaknesses in assessment and intervention* (pp. 323–342). eBook: Springer. Available from <http://dennyjaworld.com/jbcontents/14584203270863908_treatment_of_sex_offenders_strengths_and_weaknesses.pdf#page = 327>.

Telleen, S. (1990). Parental beliefs and help seeking in mothers' use of a community-based family support program. *Journal of Community Psychology, 18*(3), 264–276.

Thigpen, J. W., & Fortenberry, J. D. (2009). Understanding variation in normative childhood sexual behavior: The significance of family context. *Social Services Review, 83*, 611–631.

Vieth, V. I. (2001). When the child abuser is a child: Investigating, prosecuting and treating juvenile sex offenders in the new millennium. *Hamline Law Review, 25*, 47–78.

Vosmer, S., Hackett, S., & Callanan, M. (2009). "Normal" and "Inappropriate" childhood sexual behaviours: Findings from a Delphi study of professionals in the United Kingdom. *Journal of Sexual Aggression, 15*(3), 275–288.

Waisbrod, N., & Reicher, B. (2014). What happened to Eric? The derailment of sexual development. *Journal of Child Sexual Abuse, 23*, 94–113.

Ybarra, M. L., & Mitchell, K. J. (2014). "Sexting" and its relation to sexual activity and sexual risk behavior in a national survey of adolescents. *Journal of Adolescent Health, 55*, 757–764.

Index

Note: Page numbers followed by "*t*" refer to tables.

D

Kolibri 360 GmbH
Ferdinand-Jühlke-Straße 7
99095 Erfurt, Deutschland
produktsicherheit@kolibri360.de